QuickBooks Pro 2013:
Level 2 of 2

D1283380

TRISHA CONLON
Chemeketa Community College

LABYRINTH
LEARNING™

Berkeley, CA

QuickBooks Pro 2013: Level 2
by Trisha Conlon

Copyright © 2014 by Labyrinth Learning

Labyrinth Learning
2560 9th Street, Suite 320
Berkeley, California 94710
800.522.9746
On the web at lablearning.com

President:
Brian Favro

Product Development Manager:
Jason Favro

Managing Editor:
Laura Popelka

Production Editor:
Margaret Young

Production Manager:
Rad Proctor

eLearning Production Manager:
Arl S. Nadel

Editorial/Production Team:
Donna Bacidore, Everett Mike Cowan,
Sandy Jones

Indexing: Joanne Sprott

Interior Design:
Mark Ong, Side-by-Side Studios

Cover Design:
Words At Work

ITEM: 1-59136-479-5
ISBN-13: 978-1-59136-479-5

Manufactured in the United States of America.

10 9 8 7 6 5 4 3 2 1

Table of Contents

LESSON 5: CORRECTING AND CUSTOMIZING IN QUICKBOOKS 191

Quick Reference Tables

Preface

QuickBooks® Pro 2013: Level 2 provides essential coverage of QuickBooks 2013 software. Topics covered include physical inventory, payroll, estimates and time tracking, balance sheet accounts, budgets, correcting, customizing, and more.

For almost two decades, Labyrinth Learning has been publishing easy-to-use textbooks that empower educators to teach complex subjects quickly and effectively, while enabling students to gain confidence, develop practical skills, and compete in a demanding job market. We add comprehensive support materials, assessment and learning management tools, and eLearning components to create true learning solutions for a wide variety of instructor-led, self-paced, and online courses.

Our textbooks follow the *Labyrinth Instruction Design,* our unique and proven approach that makes learning easy and effective for every learner. Our books begin with fundamental concepts and build through a systematic progression of exercises. Quick Reference Tables, precise callouts on screen captures, carefully selected illustrations, and minimal distraction combine to create a learning solution that is highly efficient and effective for both students and instructors.

This course is supported with *comprehensive instructor support* materials that include printable solution guides for side-by-side comparisons, test banks, customizable assessments, customizable PowerPoint presentations, detailed lesson plans, preformatted files for integration to leading learning management system, and more.

Visual Conventions

This book uses many visual and typographic cues to guide students through the lessons. This page provides examples and describes the function of each cue.

`Type this text`	Anything you should type at the keyboard is printed in this typeface.
	Tips, Notes, and Warnings are used to draw attention to certain topics.
Command→ Command→ Command, etc.	This convention indicates a Ribbon path. The commands are written: Ribbon Tab→Command Group→Command→Subcommand.
	These margin notes indicate shortcut keys for executing a task described in the text.
	Features new to this edition of the software are indicated with this icon.
	If there is an Intuit video related to the QuickBooks topic being discussed, this convention will point you to it.

Exercise Progression

The exercises in this book build in complexity as students work through a lesson toward mastery of the skills taught.

- **Develop Your Skills** exercises are introduced immediately after concept discussions. They provide detailed, step-by-step tutorials.
- **Reinforce Your Skills** exercises provide additional hands-on practice with moderate assistance.
- **Apply Your Skills** exercises test students' skills by describing the correct results without providing specific instructions on how to achieve them.
- **Critical Thinking** exercises are the most challenging. They provide generic instructions, allowing students to use their skills and creativity to achieve the results they envision.

Acknowledgements

We are grateful to the instructors who have used Labyrinth titles and suggested improvements to us over the many years we have been writing and publishing books. This book has benefited greatly from the reviews and suggestions of the following instructors.

Teresa Allen, *Tyler Junior College*

Kim Anderson, *Elgin Community College*

Marcia Bercot, *SkillSource*

Ed Bonner, *National Career Skills Institute*

David Campbell, *Northern Virginia Community College*

Lori Chambers, *Manhattan Area Technical College*

Nancy Dugan, *Eastern Iowa Community Colleges*

Valorie Duvall, *South Plains College*

Nancy Escudero, *Small Business Development Center (SBDC)*

Saria Fox, *Asher College*

Evangelina Gallegos-Garner, *South Texas Vocational Institute*

Theresa Hagelbarger, *Villa Park High School*

Diane Hageman, *San Mateo Adult School*

Penny Hahn, *Henderson Community College*

Amanda Hayman, *Technical College of the Lowcountry*

Scott Hibbs, *Madison Area Technical College*

Lorene Hintz, *Great Northern Development Corp.*

Stacy Jemmott-Hunt, *Midlands Technical College*

Connie Keim, *Upper Valley Career Center (JVS) and Troy High School*

Tynia Kessler, *Lake Land College*

Dave Kiley, *Muskegon Community College*

Lee Kirk, *Utah Valley University*

Dawn Krause, *Macomb Community College*

Kathryn Langston, *Ozarka College*

Gayle Larson, *Highline Community College*

Kathy Lavieri, *Great Oaks Institute of Technology and Career Development*

Gabriele Lenga, *Truckee Meadows Community College*

Pieri Levandofsky, *Medina County Career Center*

Sue Lobner, *Nicolet Area Technical College*

Teresa Loftis, *San Bernardino Adult School*

Claire Moore, *Placer Adult Education*

Leah Morrison, *Hawkeye Community College*

LoAnn Nelson, *Lake Region State College*

Patti Norris, *Central Oregon Community College*

Allan O'Bryan, *Rochester Community and Technical College*

Monika Olsen, *Acalanes Adult Education*

John Oppenheim, *OneOC*

Larry Overstreet, *College Of DuPage*

Beth Quimby, *River Valley Community College*

Floydette Rector, *Mt. Tabor High School*

David Reilly, *Forest Hill Community High School*

Delvan Roehling, *Ivy Tech Community College*

Charles Rovner, *Ulster County Community College*

Crystalynn Shelton, *UCLA Extension*

Stanley Snyder, *Colorado Mountain College*

Rita Thayer, *Sandusky City Schools*

Charles Thompson, *Edison State College*

Norma Tyler, *Central Tech*

Keith Wallace, *Billings Public School District 2*

Randy Watkins, *Contra Costa College*

Sonora White, *Caddo Kiowa Technology Center*

Mary Ann Whitehurst, *Southern Crescent Technical College*

John D. Williams, *University of New Mexico – Taos*

Peter Young, *San Jose State University*

Dealing with Physical Inventory

LESSON OBJECTIVES

After studying this lesson, you will be able to:

- Create and use items to track inventory
- Create purchase orders and receive items
- Adjust quantity/value on hand
- Sell items and process sales discounts
- Collect, track, and pay sales tax
- Work with reports to manage your inventory, sales, and receivables

In this lesson, you will examine the inventory features available in QuickBooks. When you turn on the inventory features, QuickBooks allows you to create inventory items and purchase orders, receive items into inventory, sell inventory items, and run inventory-related reports. QuickBooks also creates accounts that you did not need until you began tracking inventory—Inventory Assets and Cost of Goods Sold. You can also create subaccounts for each of these new accounts to track your assets and costs for individual products or product types, if you choose. In addition, you will learn how to set up, track, and pay sales tax in QuickBooks. This lesson will conclude with a look at common inventory, sales, and collection reports.

Rock Castle Construction

In this lesson, you will work with a company file for a construction company called Rock Castle Construction. It is the sample company that comes with the QuickBooks software. Rock Castle Construction is an S corporation and the chief financial officer of the company is Alan Sun. You will begin by helping employee Zoe work with inventory items in QuickBooks. This will include the creation of inventory items, as well as their sales to customers. You will also learn how to set up and receive payments when sales discounts are involved. Finally, you and Zoe will explore reports in QuickBooks that will help Rock Castle manage inventory, report on sales, and make collection calls.

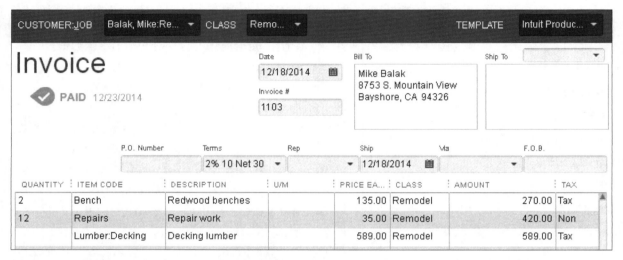

The product invoice template provides fields that are useful when you are dealing with the sale of physical inventory. You can sell inventory and service items on both the product and service invoice templates.

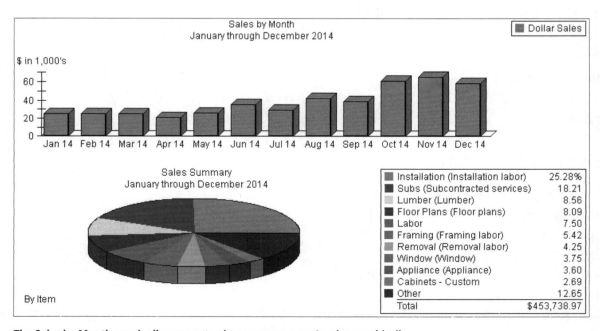

The Sales by Month graph allows you to view your company's sales graphically.

Tracking Inventory in QuickBooks

A useful feature in QuickBooks is inventory tracking. It must be turned on in the Preferences window. Once activated, it will add links to the Home page and options to the menu bar.

Should I Use QuickBooks to Track My Company's Inventory?

Not all companies are perfectly aligned to use QuickBooks to track their inventory. There are several factors that you should consider before deciding to use QuickBooks to track your company's inventory items:

- **How many types of products do I sell?** QuickBooks Pro and Premier work well for companies that have up to a few hundred items. If you have more items, you may want to consider using QuickBooks' Point-of-Sale edition.

- **Does my inventory include perishable items?** The bookkeeping for perishable items can be a bit tedious due to differences between your on-hand quantities and what you have recorded in QuickBooks.

- **Do I sell unique, one-of-a-kind products?** If you sell items such as antiques, you will have to create a new QuickBooks item for each product you sell.

- **Do I manufacture the products that I sell?** If you purchase raw materials and assemble them into products, QuickBooks Pro is not the most compatible software for your company. You may want to look at purchasing QuickBooks: Premier Manufacturing & Wholesale Edition or QuickBooks Enterprise Solutions: Manufacturing & Wholesale Edition, which address the unique needs of manufacturing businesses.

- **How fast do my inventory items become obsolete?** If this time frame is quite short, you may find that updating your inventory in QuickBooks is tedious.

- **How do I value my inventory?** QuickBooks uses the average cost method of inventory valuation. If you are using LIFO, FIFO, or another method, you may want to look at using a different tool to track your inventory.

Beginning with the Enterprise edition of QuickBooks 2012, users are now able to use the FIFO method of inventory valuation.

Inventory Center

In some Premier versions of QuickBooks, there is a new feature called the Inventory Center. This center looks similar to the Customer and Vendor centers. It provides a convenient place for you to manage your inventory items.

Setting Up the Item List

If you want to see anything on a sales form or a purchase order, it must be set up as an item first. Before you can create an inventory item, you must turn on QuickBooks' inventory features in the Preferences window.

Inventory vs. Non-Inventory Parts

In *QuickBooks Pro 2013: Level 1*, you learned about non-inventory parts. Once you turn on the QuickBooks inventory feature, you'll see both inventory and non-inventory parts. Inventory parts are tracked and sold by quantity. Examples of inventory parts might be vitamins that a doctor purchases and sells to her patients or lamps that an interior decorating company buys and resells.

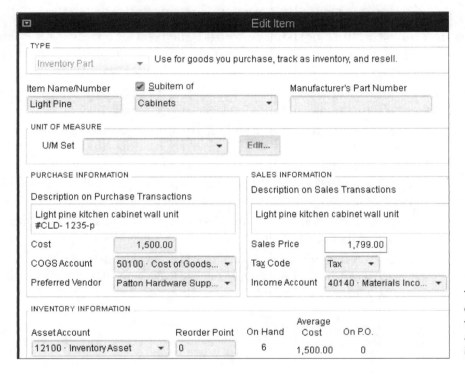

The Inventory Parts window consists of two "sides," one for the purchase information and one for the sales information.

QuickBooks allows you to classify non-inventory parts as well as inventory parts. Examples of items that should be created as non-inventory parts include:

- Items you don't track as inventory, such as nails used by a contractor or thread used by a seamstress
- Items you purchase for a particular customer
- Items you sell but don't first purchase, such as livestock that you breed and sell

Add/Edit Multiple List Entries

As you learned in *QuickBooks Pro 2013: Level 1*, there is a feature in QuickBooks that allows you to easily record multiple entries in your lists.

You can quickly update several entries in your lists by right-clicking and choosing either the Clear Column or Copy Down command.

Using Units of Measure

In the Premier and higher versions of QuickBooks, there is a feature that allows you to convert units of measure. With this feature, QuickBooks users can either work with single units of measure (e.g., buy a pound, sell a pound) or multiple units of measure (e.g., buy a yard, sell a foot).

The unit of measure feature is especially useful to companies that distribute or manufacture items. However, all companies that track inventory could find it handy if they purchase and sell in different units of measure or need to indicate units on purchase or sales forms.

Cost of Goods Sold

When you purchase items at wholesale to resell to your customers, the purchase price you pay is the cost of goods sold (COGS). Your profit is the difference between your sales and COGS.

Inventory Valuation

There are three inventory valuation methods allowed by GAAP:

- **Last-In, First-Out (LIFO):** With this method, the value of the last inventory brought in is used to determine the COGS, whereas the value of the inventory is based on the inventory purchased earlier in the year.

- **First-In, First-Out (FIFO):** With this method, the value of the first inventory brought in is used to determine the COGS, whereas the value of the inventory is based on the inventory purchased last (which more closely resembles the actual replacement cost).

- **Average Cost (or Weighted Average):** With this method, the value of the inventory is determined by dividing the total value of the inventory by the total number of inventory items.

QuickBooks Pro and Premier use the average cost method of inventory valuation; the Enterprise edition uses the FIFO method as well.

Throughout this book you will see reminders of how generally accepted accounting principles (GAAP) apply to tasks that you are completing in QuickBooks via the "Flashback to GAAP" feature.

FLASHBACK TO GAAP: CONSISTENCY

Remember that the company should use the same accounting principles and methods from year to year.

Show Lowest Subaccount Preference

It is often difficult to see the name and number of the subaccount you use in a transaction while working with the narrow account fields in the QuickBooks windows. QuickBooks has a way to help you overcome this problem by allowing you to choose to see only the lowest subaccount in these fields. For example, if you need to choose the Materials Income subaccount, it would normally be displayed as:

40100•Construction Income:40140•Materials Income

By choosing the show lowest subaccount preference, it will simply be displayed as:

40140•Materials Income

QUICK REFERENCE	PREPARING TO TRACK AND SELL INVENTORY
Task	**Procedure**
Turn on QuickBooks' inventory features	▪ Choose Edit→Preferences. ▪ Choose the Items & Inventory category, and the Company Preferences tab. ▪ Click in the box to the left of Inventory and purchase orders are active; click OK.
Turn on the Show Lowest Subaccount preference	▪ Choose Edit→Preferences. ▪ Choose the Accounting category, and then the Company Preferences tab. ▪ Click in the box to the left of the Show Lowest Subaccount Only option; click OK.
Create an inventory part item	▪ Open the Item List; choose to create a new item. ▪ Choose Inventory Part as the type of item. ▪ Enter all required information in both the purchase and sales sides of the window; click OK to record the new item.

How to Use This Book and the Student Files

You may be curious about the large number of student exercise files that come with this book and how using this book as a learning tool compares to working with your own company file. The following questions and answers should help to set you in the right direction!

Why is there a different company file for each exercise?

When you are learning QuickBooks, it is much easier to follow the instructions if your screen matches the illustrations in the book (or your instructor's screen). Having a fresh file at the beginning of each lesson helps ensure that mistakes naturally made by students learning new material do not compound and cause a disconnect between student files and the example illustrations.

A fresh company file for each lesson also means that the lessons in this book can be completed in any order.

What if I want to use one file that continues from lesson to lesson?

You also have the option to use a file that continues from lesson to lesson. You can use most of the end-of-lesson exercise files this way. This means that once you complete the Reinforce Your Skills exercise in Lesson 1, you can then use the file for Lessons 2–4 in order (but not Lesson 5). The same is true for the Apply Your Skills exercises. To use the same company file for the Develop Your Skill exercises from Lesson 1-4 (Lesson 5 uses a different company altogether), you must also complete the "Tackle the Tasks" Critical Thinking exercise at the end of each lesson before continuing to the next lesson. That is, you must complete the Lesson 1 Develop Your Skills exercises and Critical Thinking 1.2 before moving on to the Lesson 2 Develop Your Skills exercises. You may *not* use the Lesson 4 files in Lesson 5.

Is this how I will work in QuickBooks in "real life"?

No, using a separate file for each type of task (e.g., working with vendors, customers, inventory, etc.) is *not* how you will operate in "real life." In the real world, you will have *one* company file only. The multiple company files are for training purposes only.

Do I have to complete the lessons in the order presented in the book?

No, this book is entirely modular, and you can approach the lessons in any order you choose. Lessons may be worked through in any order. Fresh company files provided for each lesson make this possible.

Why do portable company files take so long to restore? What can I do while waiting for a file to restore?

Portable company files are compressed files that QuickBooks must "inflate" before you can use them. Think of the "space bags" you may have seen on an infomercial. Using a vacuum to remove all of the air from a space bag, you can fit some thirty sweaters into a shoebox. (Okay, this is a stretch, but hopefully you get the idea!) This is akin to QuickBooks creating a portable company file. Opening the seal and letting the air back in is like what happens when you restore a portable company file. It takes time for QuickBooks to prepare the portable company files just as it takes time for air to seep back into a space bag so the sweaters can return to their normal volume. If you are using an old computer system or a USB drive, the process will take longer than it will if you have a newer system.

Many users are not happy about waiting for the restore process to occur, but it is a necessity. You may want to begin a lesson by restoring the portable company file first so you can read the concepts discussions while it restores.

What if I want to work with "real" company files rather than portable company files?

You can download either company files or portable company files for this course. Remember that company files will take longer to download and will use more space on your storage drive. On the plus side, you need not restore them in order to use them.

 Follow the exercise directions based on the file type you are using.

How do I "print to PDF"?

Many instructors request students to print reports as PDF files. This makes it easier to submit your work and it saves paper. To print to PDF, first create and display the report. Next, issue the print command and choose to print to a *.pdf file. What you choose in the Printer field may not exactly match this figure. The key is to print to a *.pdf file type.

DEVELOP YOUR SKILLS 1.1

Prepare to Track and Sell Inventory

In this exercise, you will first confirm that inventory features are turned on. Then you will set the show lowest subaccount preference and create inventory items. The first step is to open QuickBooks, and then either open a company file or restore a portable company file.

Before You Begin: *Navigate to the student resource center at http://labyrinthelab.com/qb13-level02 to download the student exercise files for this book. Two versions of the files are available—portable company files and company files.*

1. Start **QuickBooks 2013**.
   If you downloaded the student exercise files in the portable company file *format, follow Option 1 below. If you downloaded the files in the* company file *format, follow Option 2 below.*

Option 1: Restore a Portable Company File

2. Choose **File→Open or Restore Company**.

3. Restore the **Rock Castle Construction** portable file for this lesson from your file storage location, placing your name as the first word in the filename (e.g., Zoe's Rock Castle Construction, Lesson 1).
   It may take a few moments for the portable company file to open. Once it does, continue with step 4.

Option 2: Open a Company File

2. Choose **File→Open or Restore Company**, ensure that **Open a regular company file** is selected, and then open the **Rock Castle Construction** company file for this lesson from your file storage location.
   The QuickBooks company file will open.

3. Click **OK** to close the QuickBooks Information windows. If necessary, click **No** in the Set Up External Accountant User window.

Set Inventory and Show Lowest Subaccount Preferences

Zoe believes that the QuickBooks file has been set up to track inventory, but she will open the Preferences window in order to confirm this, and while she is at it, she will set the show lowest subaccount preference.

4. Choose **Edit→Preferences**.

5. Follow these steps to determine the status of the inventory feature:

A Click the **Items & Inventory** category.　　**B** Click the **Company Preferences** tab.

C Ensure that the **Inventory and purchase orders are active** box is checked.

D Click **OK**.

Before you can set the show lowest subaccount option, you must ensure that all accounts have a number assigned.

6. Choose **Lists→Chart of Accounts**.

7. Scroll through the **Chart of Accounts** to see if there are any that do not have an account number assigned.
   You will find that Subcontracted Federal WH does not have an account number assigned.

8. Right-click **Subcontracted Federal WH**, and then choose **Edit Account**.

9. Type **22000**, and then click **Save & Close**.

10. Close the **Chart of Accounts** window.

11. Choose **Edit→Preferences**, and then follow these steps to turn on the show lowest subaccount option:

A Click the **Accounting** category.　　**B** Click the **Company Preferences** tab.

C Click the **Show lowest subaccount only** checkbox.　　**D** Click **OK**.

Create Multiple Inventory Items

Now you will help Zoe create additional inventory items for the company by utilizing the Add/Edit Multiple List Entries feature.

12. Choose **Lists→Add/Edit Multiple List Entries**.

13. Follow these steps to begin creating your inventory part items (if the Time Saving Tip window appears, click **OK**):

Ⓐ Click the **drop-down arrow**, and then choose **Inventory Parts**.

Ⓑ Click in the **Item Name** column below the last entry, and then type **Int Lights**.

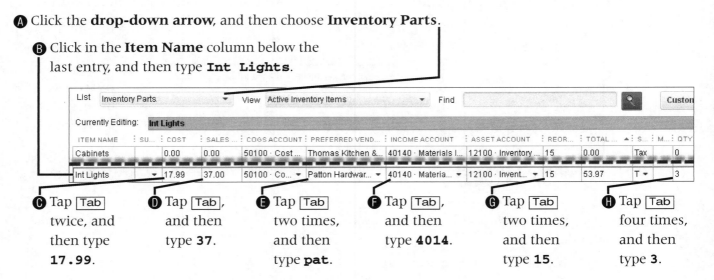

Ⓒ Tap `Tab` twice, and then type **17.99**.

Ⓓ Tap `Tab`, and then type **37**.

Ⓔ Tap `Tab` two times, and then type **pat**.

Ⓕ Tap `Tab`, and then type **4014**.

Ⓖ Tap `Tab` two times, and then type **15**.

Ⓗ Tap `Tab` four times, and then type **3**.

14. Tap `Tab`, and then follow these steps to add a second item:

Ⓐ Type **Bench**.

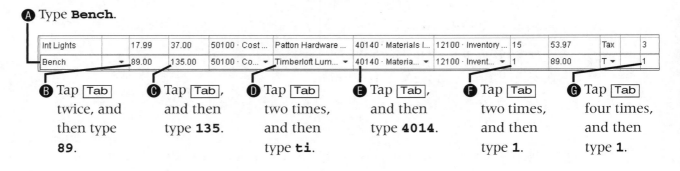

Ⓑ Tap `Tab` twice, and then type **89**.

Ⓒ Tap `Tab`, and then type **135**.

Ⓓ Tap `Tab` two times, and then type **ti**.

Ⓔ Tap `Tab`, and then type **4014**.

Ⓕ Tap `Tab` two times, and then type **1**.

Ⓖ Tap `Tab` four times, and then type **1**.

15. Click the **Save Changes** button at the bottom of the window and click **OK** in the Record(s) Saved window.

16. Close the **Add/Edit Multiple Entries List** window.

In this exercise you entered the basic, required information for your physical inventory items. You can add more information by customizing the columns and adding that information in the Add/Edit Multiple Entries List window or individually in the form where you select the item or in the Edit Item window available through the Item List.

Dealing with Sales Tax in QuickBooks

QuickBooks makes it easy to charge and collect sales tax for items. You can also choose whether to charge tax for individual customers who resell merchandise to their customers and charge sales tax on the final sale rather than pay the tax to you. How you set up sales tax in QuickBooks depends entirely on which state(s) you conduct business in. There are some states that do not collect sales tax at all (yay, Oregon!), and there is variation among the others regarding what is taxed. Some states tax service that is performed, while others do not (charging sales tax on services is the exception rather than the rule). Some tax grocery food items; others do not. You must know the sales tax laws in your state before you set up sales tax for your company.

When dealing with sales tax, take some time to learn about how the sales tax laws are set up in your jurisdiction. How you display items on invoices, in both structure and whether items are stated separately or grouped together, can affect the amount of tax due on a transaction. Taking time up front can save you and your customers money in the long run.

Behind the scenes, the sales tax collected will be directed to a Sales Tax Liability account that QuickBooks automatically creates for you. The funds will be held there until you pay them to the appropriate governing authority.

Sales Tax Items and Groups

To include sales tax on a sales form, you must set up the tax as an item. An interesting situation arises, though, when you have to pay the tax collected to multiple tax agencies. QuickBooks helps you deal with this situation by allowing you to combine multiple sales tax items into a sales tax group. This is necessary, as you can apply only one sales tax item or group to a sales form. Before you can collect sales tax, you must turn on the preference and create a sales tax item or group.

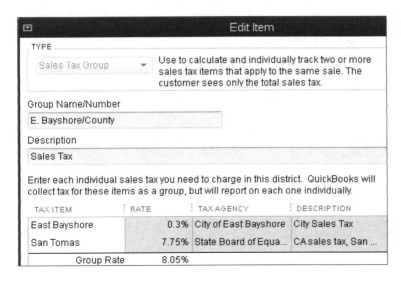

Notice that the sales tax group in this example comprises two sales tax items payable to two separate tax agencies.

Default Tax Rate

Once you have created your sales tax item(s) and group(s), you should set up a default tax rate in your preferences. This rate will appear when you create a sales form for a customer for whom a tax rate is not specified. You should choose the tax rate that you use most of the time as the default; you can change it on a sale-by-sale basis.

Dealing with Multiple Sales Tax Rates

Some companies conduct business in multiple areas. As such, the company must set up different sales tax items and/or groups with the different rates and taxing agencies. You can set one default tax rate for the company or default tax rates for each customer. Do this on the Additional Info tab of the New Customer and Edit Customer windows.

QUICK REFERENCE	SETTING UP SALES TAX IN QUICKBOOKS
Task	**Procedure**
Turn on the QuickBooks sales tax feature	■ Choose Edit→Preferences. ■ Click the Sales Tax category; click the Company Preferences tab. ■ Click in the circle to the left of Yes in the "Do you charge sales tax?" section. ■ Select your most common sales tax item. If necessary, create the item. ■ Click OK to record the new preference.
Create a sales tax item	■ Open the Item List; choose to create a new item. ■ Choose Sales Tax Item as the type of item (the sales tax preference must be set up first). ■ Type the name and description for the item. ■ Set the tax rate agency to which you pay the tax; click OK.
Create a sales tax group	■ You must first set up the items for the group following the above steps. ■ Open the item list, and then choose to create a new item. ■ Choose Sales Tax Group as the type. ■ Type the group name and description. ■ Choose each sales tax item that is to be included in the group; click OK.
Set your company's default tax rate	■ Choose Edit→Preferences. ■ Click the Sales Tax category, and then click the Company Preferences tab. ■ Choose your default tax rate from the "Your most common sales tax item" field drop-down button; click OK.
Set a customer's default tax rate	■ Open the Customer Center, and then double-click the customer whose default tax rate you wish to set. ■ Choose the Additional Info tab. ■ Choose the correct tax rate from the Tax Item field drop-down arrow; click OK.

INTRODUCING "BEHIND THE SCENES"

Throughout this book you will see a special section called "Behind the Scenes" whenever you are learning about an activity performed within QuickBooks. This section will go over the accounting that QuickBooks performs for you when you record a transaction. Please note that the account names used in this feature use QuickBooks, rather than traditional accounting, nomenclature.

Set Up Sales Tax for a New Area

In this exercise, you will help Zoe create a new sales tax item, since the company is doing business with Tea Shoppe at the Lake in San Diego County, which has a different tax rate. Before you can create any sales tax items or groups, you must have the preference turned on. Your first step is to help Zoe verify that the preference is on.

1. Choose **Edit→Preferences**.

2. Follow these steps to view the sales tax preference status:

Ⓐ Click the **Sales Tax** category.

Ⓑ Click the **Company Preferences** tab.

Ⓒ Verify that **Yes** is selected.

Ⓓ Click **OK**.

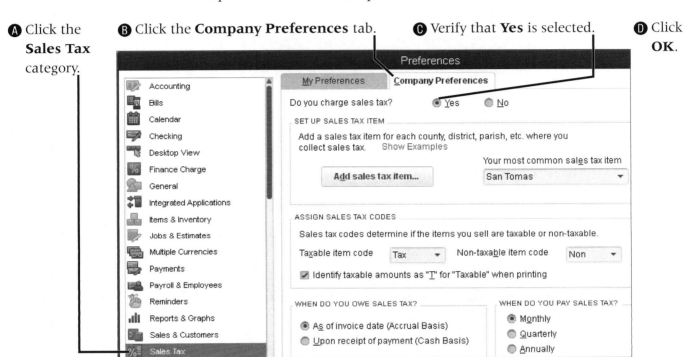

Create a New Sales Tax Item

Now that you have verified that the sales tax preference is correct, you can set up the new item to track sales tax from San Diego County.

3. Click the **Items & Services** task icon in the Company area of the Home page.

4. Click the **Item** menu button, and then choose **New** from the menu.

Items & Services

5. Follow these steps to create the new sales tax item:

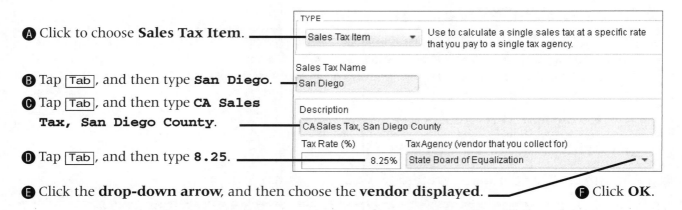

Ⓐ Click to choose **Sales Tax Item**.

Ⓑ Tap ⌧Tab⌧, and then type **San Diego**.

Ⓒ Tap ⌧Tab⌧, and then type **CA Sales Tax, San Diego County**.

Ⓓ Tap ⌧Tab⌧, and then type **8.25**.

Ⓔ Click the **drop-down arrow**, and then choose the **vendor displayed**.

Ⓕ Click **OK**.

6. Close the **Item List**.

Use the New Sales Tax Item in a Transaction

Since you have only one customer in San Diego County, you will not set that as the default sales tax item. Instead, you will choose it only when selling to that customer.

7. Choose **Customers→Enter Sales Receipts**.

8. Follow these steps to record a sales transaction for a customer in San Diego County:

Ⓐ Type **The Tea Shoppe at the Lake**, and Quick Add it as a vendor.

Ⓑ Choose **Remodel** as the Class.

Ⓒ Tap ⌧Tab⌧ twice, and then tap ⌧+⌧ to set the date to **12/17/2014**.

Ⓓ Tap ⌧Tab⌧ three times, and then type **826**.

Ⓔ Choose **Check** as the Payment Method.

Ⓕ Tap ⌧Tab⌧, and then type **i**.

Ⓖ Tap ⌧Tab⌧ twice, and then type **16**.

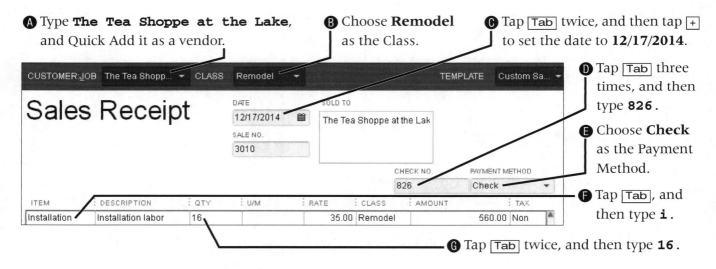

 Tea Shoppe at the Lake already exists on the Vendor list, and we cannot duplicate the entry. Therefore, in sub-step A above, you added the word "The" to the business name for the Customers & Jobs List entry.

Ⓗ Click below Installation, and then type **cou**.

Ⓘ Click the **drop-down arrow**, and then choose **San Diego**.

Ⓙ Click **Save & Close**.

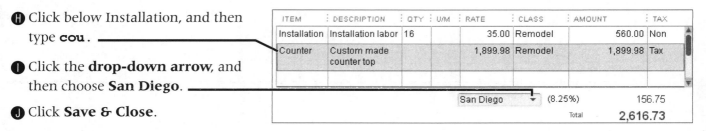

9. Click **Yes** in the Name Information Changed window.

This will change the default sales tax item for Tea Shoppe at the Lake, if necessary.

> **BTS BRIEF**
>
> **12000•Undeposited Funds DR 2,616.73; 40130•Labor Income CR <560.00>; 40140•Materials Income CR <1,899.98>; Sales Tax Payable CR <156.75>**

Creating Purchase Orders

Many businesses use purchase orders for ordering items into inventory. When a purchase order is created, nothing occurs "behind the scenes," as you have done nothing yet to debit or credit an account.

Non-Posting Accounts

When you create your first purchase order, QuickBooks creates a non-posting account (an account that *does not* affect your P&L report or your balance sheet report), called Purchase Orders. Non-posting accounts appear at the end of your Chart of Accounts. By creating these accounts for you, QuickBooks allows you to create reports based on them.

QUICK REFERENCE	WORKING WITH PURCHASE ORDERS
Task	**Procedure**
Create a purchase order	■ Choose Vendors→Create Purchase Orders; choose the desired vendor.
	■ Enter the items you are ordering; click Save & Close.
Produce an open purchase orders report	■ Choose Lists→Chart of Accounts; scroll to the bottom of the list.
	■ Double-click the Purchase Orders account; set the correct date range for the report (if necessary).

DEVELOP YOUR SKILLS 1.3
Work with Purchase Orders

In this exercise, you will help Zoe create purchase orders for Rock Castle Construction and view the purchase orders report.

1. Click the **Purchase Orders** task icon in the Vendors area of the Home page.

2. Follow these steps to create a purchase order:

Ⓐ Type **ti**, and then tap `Tab` to choose the vendor.   **Ⓑ** Tap `Tab` four more times, and then type **121914**.

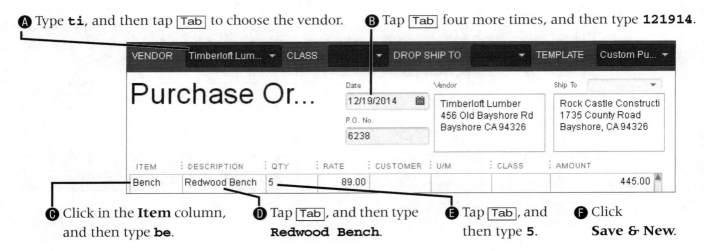

Ⓒ Click in the **Item** column, and then type **be**.

Ⓓ Tap `Tab`, and then type **Redwood Bench**.

Ⓔ Tap `Tab`, and then type **5**.

Ⓕ Click **Save & New**.

3. Click **Save Anyway** in the Items not assigned classes window.

In this case, a class was not assigned. It will be assigned later when you know if it is for a new construction or remodel job. Remember that purchase orders do not affect what occurs behind the scenes.

4. Follow these steps to create the second purchase order:

Ⓐ Type **pat**, and then tap `Tab` to choose the vendor.

Ⓑ Tap `Tab` three more times, and then type **121914**.

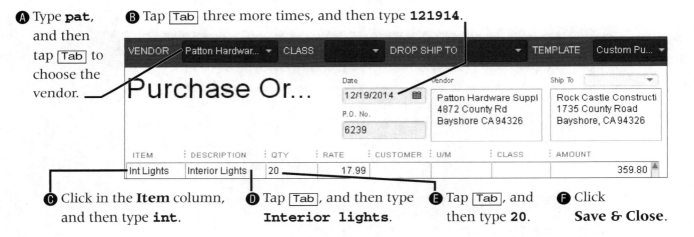

Ⓒ Click in the **Item** column, and then type **int**.

Ⓓ Tap `Tab`, and then type **Interior lights**.

Ⓔ Tap `Tab`, and then type **20**.

Ⓕ Click **Save & Close**.

5. Click **Save Anyway** in the Items not assigned classes window.

View the Open Purchase Orders Report

Next you will take a look at the Purchase Orders account QuickBooks created for Rock Castle Construction when the first purchase order was created.

6. Click the **Chart of Accounts** task icon in the Company area of the Home page.

7. Scroll to the bottom of the list and notice the non-posting **90100•Purchase Orders** account.

Chart of Accounts

8. Double-click the **Purchase Orders** account.

QuickBooks creates a QuickReport showing open purchase orders.

9. Type **a** to set the date range to all; then, scroll to the bottom of the report to view the purchase orders you just created.

10. Choose **Window→Close All**.

Receiving Items

When you receive the items on a purchase order, you need to enter them into inventory. You can carry this transaction out in either one or two steps, depending on how your vendor delivers the accompanying bill.

The Two Methods of Receiving Items

If a vendor sends the inventory items and the bill together, you can record them as one transaction. On the other hand, if you receive the items first and the bill later, you will enter them in two separate steps.

By clicking the drop-down arrow next to the Receive Inventory link on the Home page, you can choose how to enter the receipt of your items, either with or without the bill.

If you received the inventory items and later received the bill, click the Enter Bills Against Inventory link on the Home page to enter the bill for the items at a later date.

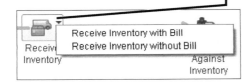

If you are going to pay a bill that is attached to a purchase order with a credit card, use the Enter Credit Card Charges window so QuickBooks will prompt you to receive against open purchase orders.

When you receive the items, QuickBooks will use the Items tab rather than the Expenses tab in the Enter Bills window. If you recall from *QuickBooks Pro 2013: Level 1*, the Items tab is used to enter items into an inventory asset account rather than record an expense.

Including Expenses on a Bill for Items

You may incur additional shipping and handling charges when you order inventory items. These charges should not be entered on the Items tab but rather as an expense on the Expenses tab. Once QuickBooks enters the information on the Items tab, you can click on the Expenses tab to enter any additional expenses due with the bill.

Notice how the delivery charges are displayed on the Expenses tab of the Enter Bills window while the inventory items are displayed on the Items tab.

Discount Payment Terms

Your vendors may offer you discount payment terms in an attempt to get you to pay your bills earlier, which in turn improves their cash flow. Payment terms are created in the Terms List, which is one of the Customer & Vendor Profile Lists. You can change the terms on an individual invoice as needed without permanently changing them for the customer.

You will use the payment terms of 1% 10 Net 30 when entering a bill in this section. This means that if you pay the bill within 10 days of receipt, you will receive a 1 percent discount. But, if you don't pay within the first 10 days, the full bill is due in 30 days.

FLASHBACK TO GAAP: COST

Remember that when a company purchases assets, it should record them at cost, not fair market value. For example, if you bought an item worth $750 for $100, it should be recorded at $100.

BEHIND THE SCENES

Regardless the path you take, the behind the scenes action is the same: An Inventory Asset will be debited, and Accounts Payable will be credited.

12100-Inventory Asset		20000-Accounts Payable	
445			445

QUICK REFERENCE	RECEIVING INVENTORY
Task	**Procedure**
Receive the inventory and the bill together	■ Choose Vendors→Receive Items and Enter Bill; choose the desired vendor. ■ Click Yes in the Open PO's Exist window. ■ Click in the checkmark column to the left of the PO against which you are receiving items; click OK. ■ Make any necessary changes to the Enter Bills window; click Save & Close or Save & New.
Receive the inventory and the bill separately	Task 1: Update inventory when you receive the items: ■ Choose Vendors→Receive Items; choose the desired vendor. ■ Click Yes in the Open PO's Exist window. ■ Click in the checkmark column to the left of the PO against which you are receiving items; click OK. ■ Make any necessary changes to the Item Receipt window; click Save & Close. Task 2: Enter the bill after you receive it: ■ Choose Vendors→Enter Bill for Received Items; choose the desired vendor. ■ Click within the line of the proper item receipt; click OK. ■ Make any changes to the Enter Bills window; click Save & Close.

Task	Procedure
Include an expense on a bill for items	■ After the Item information is entered in the Enter Bills window, click the Expenses tab. ■ Choose the correct expense account in the Expense column; tap $\boxed{\text{Tab}}$. ■ Type the amount of the expense and correct the total amount due for the bill; click Save & Close.

DEVELOP YOUR SKILLS 1.4
Receive Inventory

In this exercise, you will receive the benches and later receive the bill for them. Following the receipt of the bill for the benches, you will receive the light fixtures and the bill for them together.

1. Choose **Company→Home Page**.

2. Click the **Receive Inventory drop-down arrow** in the Vendors area of the Home page, and then choose **Receive Inventory without Bill**.

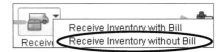

3. Type **ti**, and then tap $\boxed{\text{Tab}}$.
   QuickBooks fills in Timberloft Lumber, and the Open PO's Exist window appears.

4. Click **Yes** in the Open PO's Exist window.

5. Click to place a checkmark in the first column for PO number **6238** dated 12/19/14, and then click **OK**.
   QuickBooks displays the Create Item Receipts window with the information from the purchase order filled in. Notice that the items appear on the Items tab at the bottom of the window, not on the Expense tab!

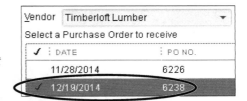

6. Tap $\boxed{+}$ on the keyboard to change the date to **12/22/2014**.

7. Click **Save & Close** to record the item receipt; then, click **Save Anyway** in the Items not assigned classes window.
   The class will be assigned to the items when they are sold to a customer for either new construction or a remodel.

Receive the Bill

The benches were entered into inventory when you received them. Now the bill for the items has arrived and you need to enter it.

Enter Bills Against Inventory

8. Click the **Enter Bills Against Inventory** task icon in the Vendors area of the Home page.

9. Follow these steps to choose the correct Item Receipt:

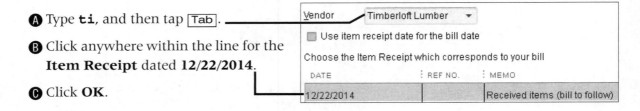

Ⓐ Type **ti**, and then tap Tab.

Ⓑ Click anywhere within the line for the **Item Receipt** dated **12/22/2014**.

Ⓒ Click **OK**.

Vendor	Timberloft Lumber ▼

☐ Use item receipt date for the bill date

Choose the Item Receipt which corresponds to your bill

DATE	REF NO.	MEMO
12/22/2014		Received items (bill to follow)

QuickBooks will display the Enter Bills window.

10. Tap Tab, type **122314** as the date, and then tap Tab again.

> **BTS BRIEF**
>
> 12100•Inventory Asset DR 445.00; 20000•Accounts Payable CR <445.00>

11. Click **Save & Close** to record the new bill; click **Yes** to record your changes.

12. Click **Save Anyway** in the Items not assigned classes window.

Receive Inventory Items with a Bill and Add an Expense to the Bill

The interior light fixtures and the bill for them arrived at the same time. The bill also included a shipping fee of $35 that must be accounted for on the bill.

13. Click the **Receive Inventory drop-down arrow** in the Vendor area of the Home page, and then choose **Receive Inventory with Bill**.

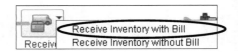

Receive Inventory with Bill
Receive Inventory without Bill

14. Type **pat**, and then tap Tab.
QuickBooks fills in Patton Hardware Supplies as the vendor and the Open PO's Exist window appears.

15. Click **Yes** in the Open PO's Exist window.

16. Click to place a checkmark in the first column for PO number **6239**.

17. Click **OK** to move to the Enter Bills window; click **OK** in the Warning window.
Patton Hardware Supplies was short by three lights for your order, so you need to record a receipt of only 17 interior light fixtures.

Vendor	Patton Hardware Supplies ▼

Select a Purchase Order to receive

✓	DATE	PO NO.
✓	12/19/2014	6239

18. Follow these steps to complete the bill:

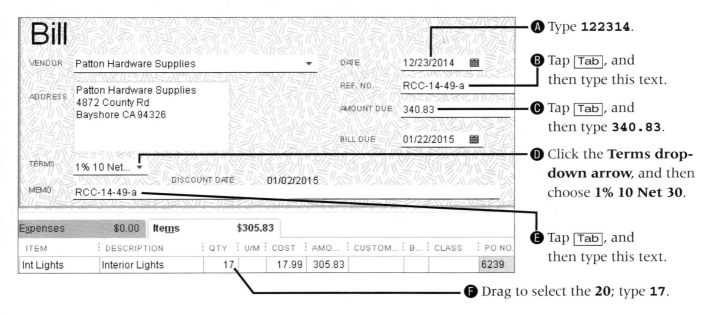

Ⓐ Type **122314**.

Ⓑ Tap Tab, and then type this text.

Ⓒ Tap Tab, and then type **340.83**.

Ⓓ Click the **Terms drop-down arrow**, and then choose **1% 10 Net 30**.

Ⓔ Tap Tab, and then type this text.

Ⓕ Drag to select the **20**; type **17**.

You will receive a 1% discount if you pay the bill by the discount date (01/02/2015).

Enter an Expense on the Bill for Inventory Items

When you received the bill for the interior lights, there was also a shipping charge of $35. You will now enter that as an expense on the bill.

19. Follow these steps to enter the shipping expense:

Ⓐ Click to display the **Expenses** tab.   Ⓑ Type **po** to choose 63100•Postage.

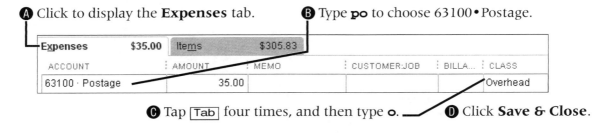

Ⓒ Tap Tab four times, and then type **o**.   Ⓓ Click **Save & Close**.

BTS BRIEF

12100•Inventory Asset DR 305.83; 63100•Postage DR 35.00; 20000•Accounts Payable CR <340.83>

20. Click **No** to reject changing the current terms for Patton Hardware Supplies; click **Save Anyway** in the Items not assigned classes window.

Selling Inventory Items

Once you have created, ordered, and received your items, it is time to start selling them! You will use the same Create Invoices window you used in *QuickBooks Pro 2013: Level 1*. In the last section, you learned about discount payment terms as they relate to your payables. In this section, you will apply them to a receivable transaction.

Emailing Invoices

For the majority of companies, email is one of the primary ways they do business nowadays. QuickBooks allows you to easily email invoices to customers, rather than having to send them via "snail mail" or fax. To indicate that you wish to send invoices and other forms to your customers via email, use the Additional Info tab of either the New or Edit Customer window. If you choose to email an invoice to a customer, that customer will receive it as a PDF file attached to the email along with a message that you set in the Preferences window.

Customer Send Method

The customer send method is the way that you primarily send invoices and other forms to a customer. You can change this on each transaction for the customer if it is not always the same method. In the Preferences window, you can customize both personal and company preferences for this feature.

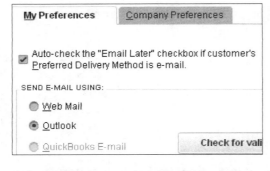

In the Send Forms category of the Preferences window, you can set preferences for both yourself and the company (if you are the administrator). The administrator controls how the email message sent with the invoice (or other type of form) to customers will appear.

Batch Invoicing

The batch invoicing feature allows you to fill out the invoice just once for the customers in the "batch" and then create invoices for all of them. In order to complete this task, you should first create a billing group of the customers for whom you wish to create a batch invoice (although you can add customers one at a time as well).

Make sure that the terms, sales tax code, and preferred delivery method are set for any customer you wish to include in the batch.

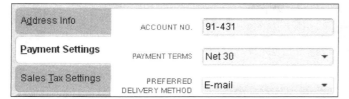 

On each customer record, the payment terms and preferred delivery method are on the Payment Settings tab, and the sales tax code is on the Sales Tax Settings tab. To make changes, go to edit the customer from the Customer Center.

Batch Invoices Summary

Once you have created a batch of invoices for customers, you will see the Batch Invoices Summary window. Here you can choose to either print or email the invoices (based on the preferred send method for each customer).

Send a Batch of Forms

You can send more than just invoices from QuickBooks. In the Preferences window, you have the ability to set the default message for eleven different types of forms and reports.

When you are ready to send all of the forms and reports that you have indicated you wish to send, issue a command from the File menu that displays the Select Forms to Send window. From this window, you can choose to send any form listed in the queue.

Note the types of forms and reports that you can choose to send from QuickBooks.

Producing Sales Orders

If you have the Premier or Enterprise edition of QuickBooks, there is a sales order feature available that allows you to manage customer orders for both products and services. You can track items that have been ordered by a customer but are currently out of stock, schedule work to be done, plan costs for labor, and estimate future revenue based on the work that has been scheduled.

Benefits of Sales Orders

There are certain benefits to using the sales order feature in QuickBooks:

- You can create one invoice for multiple sales orders.
- You can create multiple invoices for one sales order if you can only partially fulfill an order.
- You can track items that are on backorder.
- You can print a Sales Order Fulfillment Worksheet, which gives you a "big picture" and allows you to determine which orders to fill with the current inventory.

Once a sales order has been created, you can print a pick list that will assist you in fulfilling the order from inventory. If the order is for a service, you can schedule the service.

Tracking Sales Orders

Sales orders will not affect what goes on behind the scenes because no money has changed hands. You can track open sales orders the same way you track open purchase orders, by creating a QuickReport from the non-posting account called 90200•Sales Orders, which is located at the bottom of the Chart of Accounts. Remember that, in order for you to complete the sale and for things to happen correctly behind the scenes, you must invoice the customer from the sales order.

BEHIND THE SCENES

The accounting that occurs for product sales is different from what occurs when you sell services. Take a look behind the scenes.

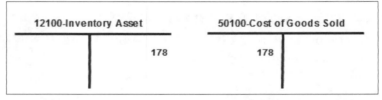

When an inventory item is sold, it "moves" the value of the item from the Inventory Asset account to the Cost of Goods Sold account.

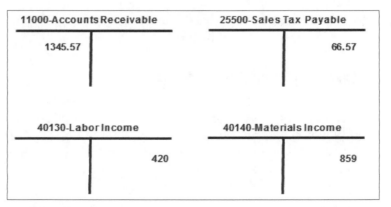

Don't forget our friend sales tax... The rest of what happens behind the scenes looks similar to what happens when service items are sold. Notice that the credits (Materials Income + Labor Income + Sales Tax Payable) equal the debits (Accounts Receivable).

Task	Procedure
Create a batch of invoices and a new billing group	■ Choose Customers→Create Batch Invoices. ■ Click the Billing Group drop-down arrow; choose Add New. ■ Type the name of the new group; click Save. ■ Click to select a customer; click Add. Continue as necessary. ■ Click Save Group; click Next. ■ Enter the item information for the invoice and a customer message; click Next. ■ Review the list of invoices that you will create; click Create Invoices. ■ Choose to print or email invoices from the Batch Invoices Summary window.
Email an invoice from the Create Invoices window	■ Open the Create Invoices window and display the desired invoice. ■ Click the Send button drop-down arrow; choose E-mail Invoice. ■ Review the email message in your email program and make any changes. ■ Choose to send the email from your email program.
Send a batch of forms	■ Choose File→Send Forms. ■ Click to deselect any forms you do not wish to send. ■ Edit any emails you wish; click Send Now.
Create a sales order	■ Choose Customers→Create Sales Orders. ■ Fill in all relevant information; click Save & Close. ■ If the order is for a product, you can print a pick list to assist in fulfilling it. ■ If the order is for a service, you should schedule the service at this time.
Create an invoice from a sales order	■ Choose Customers→Create Invoices. ■ Choose the customer for whom you wish to create the invoice. ■ Mark the appropriate order in the Available Sales Orders window; click OK. ■ Choose whether the invoice is for all sales orders or only selected items. ■ Verify all of the information that has been filled in, adding any additional items if desired; click Save & Close.

DEVELOP YOUR SKILLS 1.5

Sell Inventory Items

In this exercise, you will first help Zoe create an invoice for a customer with discount payment terms. Then you will assist her in creating a batch of invoices for maintenance services.

Mike Balak has asked Rock Castle Construction to repair the deck at the back of his house and install two redwood benches. You will need to create a new job for the customer.

1. Click the **Customers** button on the Icon Bar.

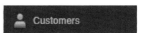

2. Single-click **Balak, Mike** on the Customers & Jobs List.

3. Click the **New Customer & Job** button, and then choose **Add Job**.

4. Type **Repair Deck**, and then click **OK**.

Create an Invoice with Discount Payment Terms

Now that the job has been created, you will create an invoice with discount payment terms that will be emailed for it. The job you just created should still be selected in the Customers & Jobs List.

5. Click the **New Transactions** button, and then choose **Invoices**. *The Create Invoices window will appear with the Customer:Job entered.*

6. Follow these steps to complete the invoice for Mike Balak's deck repair job:

Ⓐ Tap Tab, and then type **r**.　　Ⓑ Tap Tab twice, and then type **121814**.　　Ⓒ Click the **Terms drop-down arrow** and choose **2% 10 Net 30**.

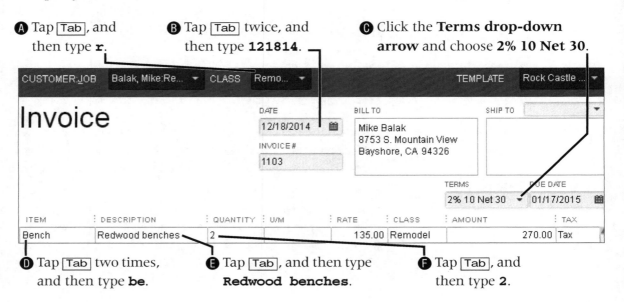

Ⓓ Tap Tab two times, and then type **be**.　　Ⓔ Tap Tab, and then type **Redwood benches**.　　Ⓕ Tap Tab, and then type **2**.

Ⓖ Click below *Bench* here, and then type **rep**.　　Ⓗ Tap Tab two times, and then type **12**.

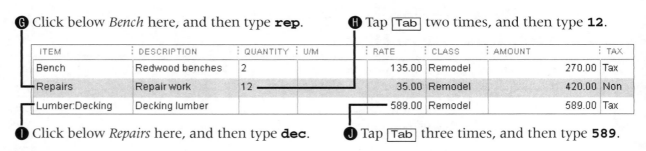

Ⓘ Click below *Repairs* here, and then type **dec**.　　Ⓙ Tap Tab three times, and then type **589**.

Ⓚ On the Ribbon, click to choose to **Email Later**.

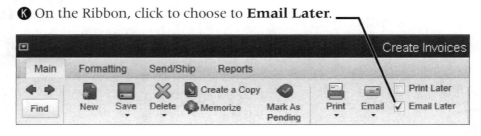

Notice that this is when you apply a class to the benches.

> **BTS BRIEF**
>
> **11000•Accounts Receivable DR 1,345.57; 40140•Materials Income CR <859.00>; 40130•Labor Income CR <420.00>; Sales Tax Payable CR <66.57>; 50100•Cost of Goods Sold DR 178.00; 12100•Inventory Asset CR <178.00>**

7. Click **Save & Close**; click **No** in the Name Information Changed window.

8. Close the **Customer Center**.

Create a Batch of Invoices and a New Billing Group

Now it is time to create a batch of invoices for several customers who subscribe to a monthly repair service fee. These customers pay a flat fee for repairs for the month.

9. Choose **Customers→Create Batch Invoices**; then, click **OK** in the "Is your customer info set up correctly?" window.
   The Batch Invoice window will appear.

10. Follow these steps to create a new billing group:

Ⓐ Click the **Billing Group drop-down arrow**.

Ⓑ Click **Add New**.

The Group Name window appears.

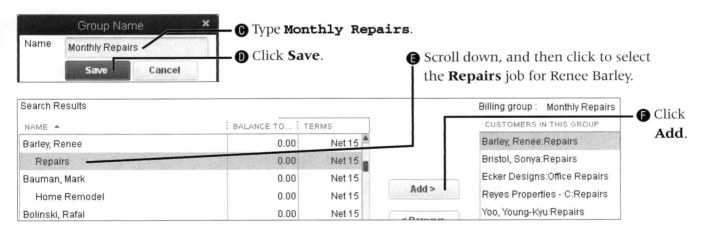

Ⓒ Type **Monthly Repairs**.

Ⓓ Click **Save**.

Ⓔ Scroll down, and then click to select the **Repairs** job for Renee Barley.

Ⓕ Click **Add**.

11. Scrolling down as you go, repeat **steps E and F** above until your list looks like the Customers in This Group list displayed to the right in the illustration above.
    You can also double-click on an item in the list on the left to add it to the group on the right.

12. Click the **Save Group** button located below the Customers in This Group list, and then click **Next**.

13. Follow these steps to set the item information for the invoice:

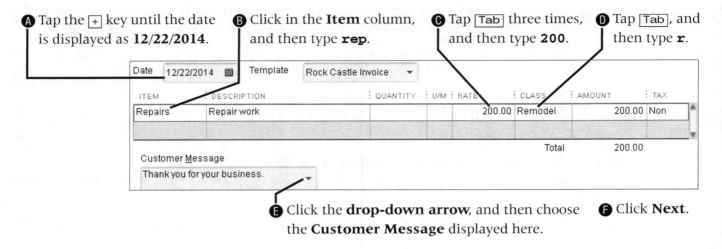

A Tap the + key until the date is displayed as **12/22/2014**.

B Click in the **Item** column, and then type **rep**.

C Tap Tab three times, and then type **200**.

D Tap Tab, and then type **r**.

E Click the **drop-down arrow**, and then choose the **Customer Message** displayed here.

F Click **Next**.

14. Review the list of invoices that you are preparing to create.

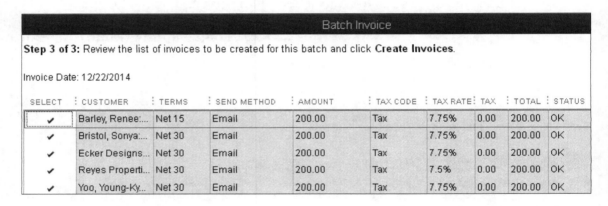

You will see a screen that shows all of the invoices to be created. If you were to choose to not create an invoice for a member of the group, you could deselect it at this step.

15. Click **Create Invoices**.
The Batch Invoice Summary window displays.

BTS BRIEF

11000•Accounts Receivable DR 1,000.00; 40130•Labor Income CR <1,000.00>

16. Close the **Batch Invoice Summary** window because you will choose to send all six of the invoices you have created in this exercise in the next few steps.

Choose to Send Forms from QuickBooks

In the final section of this exercise, you will send the invoice for Mike Balak that you marked to be sent by email as well as the five invoices you created as a batch.

17. Choose **File→Send Forms**.
   The Select Forms to Send window will be displayed.

18. Follow these steps to email the six invoices you just created:

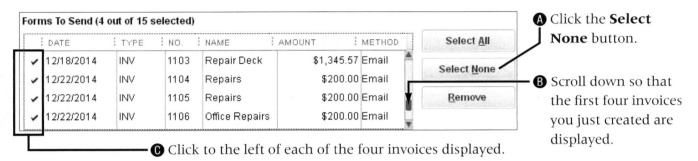

Ⓐ Click the **Select None** button.

Ⓒ Click to the left of each of the four invoices displayed.

Ⓑ Scroll down so that the first four invoices you just created are displayed.

QuickBooks displays only four forms at a time in the Select Forms To Send window, so you will have to continue scrolling to view the other two invoices you just created.

Ⓓ Scroll down to display the last two invoices you just created.

Ⓔ Click to the left of the two additional invoices.

19. Click **Send Now**, and then click **OK** in the Warning window.
   You cannot send invoices from a sample file. This exercise took you through all of the steps so that you will be able to do it in your own company file in the future.

20. Close the **Select Forms To Send** and **Customer Service** windows.

Processing Sales Discounts and Electronic Payments

In *QuickBooks Pro 2013: Level 1*, you learned how to receive customer payments for the entire invoice amount. Now you will deal with a discounted customer payment. The procedure for receiving a discounted payment is almost identical to receiving a "regular" payment, except that you must identify the account to be debited for the discount amount.

You can easily apply the discount in the QuickBooks Discount and Credits window. QuickBooks calculates the discount based on the payment terms.

Working with Electronic Customer Payments/Wire Transfers

In some instances, you may receive payments from your customers electronically. One method of dealing with this situation is to use a new payment type called Electronic Payment. When the bank notifies you that you have received an electronic payment, you enter the receipt in the Receive Payments window, noting Electronic Payment as the payment type. You will then be able to run reports, filtering by payment type, if you need to track electronic customer payments.

Online Invoice Payments

With QuickBooks 2013, you can now accept invoice payments through an online service. You can even choose to have these payments automatically recorded in your QuickBooks file. This feature is free for your customers, and costs businesses a small fee per transaction.

Invoice payments can be collected online by QuickBooks users with the 2013 version of the software.

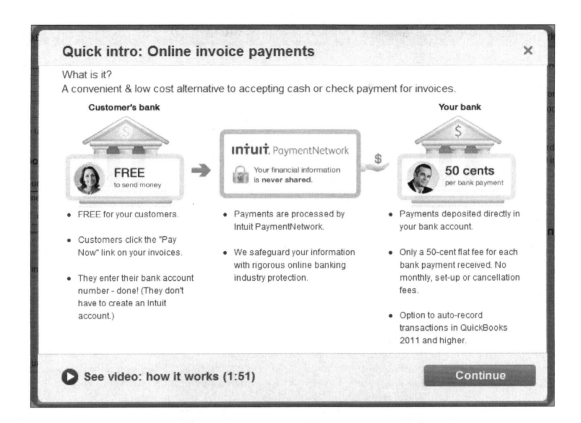

Quick intro: Online invoice payments   ✕

What is it?
A convenient & low cost alternative to accepting cash or check payment for invoices.

Customer's bank   **Your bank**

FREE
to send money

INTUIT. PaymentNetwork
Your financial information is **never shared.**

50 cents
per bank payment

- FREE for your customers.

- Customers click the "Pay Now" link on your invoices.

- They enter their bank account number - done! (They don't have to create an Intuit account.)

- Payments are processed by Intuit PaymentNetwork.

- We safeguard your information with rigorous online banking industry protection.

- Payments deposited directly in your bank account.

- Only a 50-cent flat fee for each bank payment received. No monthly, set-up or cancellation fees.

- Option to auto-record transactions in QuickBooks 2011 and higher.

▶ See video: how it works (1:51)   Continue

To learn more, Choose Customers→Create Invoices, click the Online Pay button on the Ribbon, and then click the "See video: how it works" link at the bottom of the Quick Intro window.

The Shipping Manager

You can ship a package right from QuickBooks from both the Create Invoices and Enter Sales Receipt windows using FedEx, UPS, and now the United States Postal Service (through Stamps.com). You can use either your existing account(s) for any of these services, or you can sign up right from QuickBooks. QuickBooks will process the shipment and create a shipping label for you with the customer information that you have stored in QuickBooks. In addition, you can track your shipments from within QuickBooks.

The Customer Snapshot

You learned about the Company Snapshot in *QuickBooks Pro 2013: Level 1*. In this lesson, you will have a chance to take a tour of the Customer Snapshot.

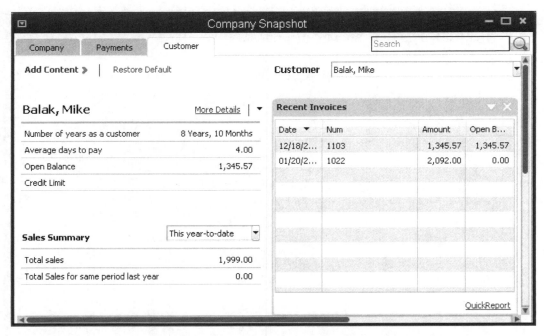

On the Customer tab of the Company Snapshot window, you can select a customer at the top and then view information about that customer in the rest of the window. Adding, moving, and removing content from this window is easy, as is restoring it to how it first appeared by restoring the default view.

Task	Procedure
Receive an electronic payment	■ Choose Lists→Customer & Vendor Profile Lists→Payment Method List; create a new payment method called **Electronic Payment**.
	■ Choose Customers→Receive Payments; choose the desired customer/job.
	■ Enter the payment information; enter **Electronic Payment** as the payment type.
	■ Click Save & Close to record the payment.
	■ Choose Banking→Make Deposits; click to choose the electronic payment.
	■ Click OK to move to the Make Deposits window; enter the desired account.
	■ Enter the date of the deposit; click Save & Close.
Display the Customer Snapshot	■ Choose Company→Company Snapshot.
	■ Click the Customer tab.

DEVELOP YOUR SKILLS 1.6

Receive a Discounted Payment Electronically

In this exercise, you will help Zoe record a discounted payment and process an electronic payment for Rock Castle Construction.

1. Choose **Lists→Customer & Vendor Profile Lists→Payment Method List**.

2. Click the **Payment Method** menu button, and then choose **New**.

3. Follow these steps to set up the new payment method:

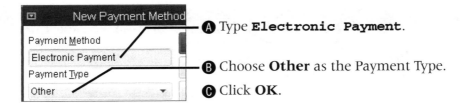

Ⓐ Type **Electronic Payment**.

Ⓑ Choose **Other** as the Payment Type.

Ⓒ Click **OK**.

4. Close the **Payment Method List** window.

Process a Discounted Electronic Payment

Mike Balak has decided to take advantage of the early payment option, and he is paying electronically. You will help Zoe to record this transaction.

5. Click the **Receive Payments** task icon in the Customers area of the Home page.

6. Follow these steps to record the discounted payment:

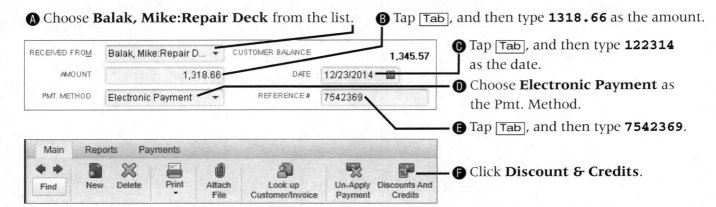

A Choose **Balak, Mike:Repair Deck** from the list.

B Tap Tab, and then type **1318.66** as the amount.

C Tap Tab, and then type **122314** as the date.

D Choose **Electronic Payment** as the Pmt. Method.

E Tap Tab, and then type **7542369**.

F Click **Discount & Credits**.

Notice the Underpayment section of this window. Whenever you enter a payment amount that is less than the total amount due, you will see this section. You can then choose how to handle the underpayment. You will apply a discount to the invoice to take care of the underpayment in this case.

7. Click the **drop-down arrow** to choose **Remodel** as the Discount Class.

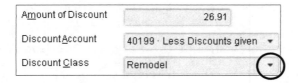

8. Click **Done** to return to the Receive Payments window.

BTS BRIEF

12000•Undeposited Funds DR 1,318.66; 40199•Less Discounts Given DR 26.91; 11000•Accounts Receivable CR <1,345.57>

9. Click **Save & Close** to complete the payment receipt.

Deposit an Electronic Payment

The last step is to record the deposit of the electronic payment into your bank account.

10. Click the **Record Deposits** task icon in the Banking area of the Home page. *The Payments to Deposit window will appear.*

Record Deposits

11. Click the **Electronic Payment** you just entered to select it, and then click **OK**.

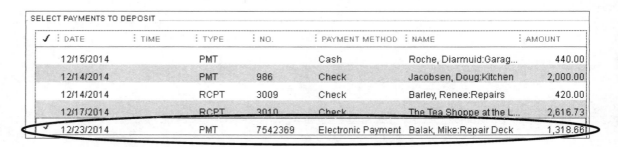

12. Tap ⌞Tab⌟, and then type **122314** as the date.

> **BTS BRIEF**
>
> 10100•Checking DR 1,318.66; 12000•Undeposited Funds CR <1,318.66>

13. Click **Save & Close** to record the deposit to 10100•Checking.

Adjusting Quantity/Value on Hand

There may be times when you have inventory that is no longer in sellable condition. You should remove these items from inventory and expense the amount. Other times you may need to adjust the value of your inventory due to obsolescence or some other reason. Or, you may need to adjust both the quantity and the value of your inventory.

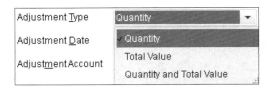

In the Adjust Quantity/Value on Hand window, you can choose the type of the adjustment via a drop-down list.

Adjusting the Quantity of Your Inventory

You can either enter the new quantity on hand (if you have just conducted an annual inventory, this may be the best choice) or the quantity difference (this option works well if you know how many items you have to remove). If you choose to enter the quantity difference, make sure to enter a minus sign in front of the number to show a decrease in the number of items.

Adjusting the Value of Your Inventory

If you don't need to adjust the quantity of your inventory but rather need to adjust the value of your inventory, you can use the same window. As was discussed earlier in this lesson, Quick-Books Pro and Premier use the average cost method of inventory valuation. You can adjust the average cost per inventory item by adjusting the total value of the inventory. Obsolescence or an incorrect beginning cost for inventory may require you to take this step.

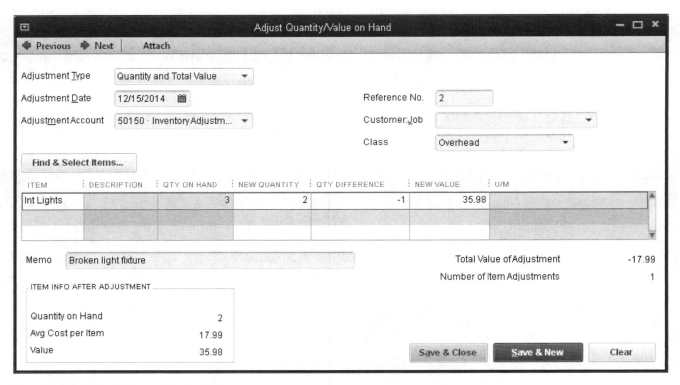

The Adjust Quantity/Value on Hand window

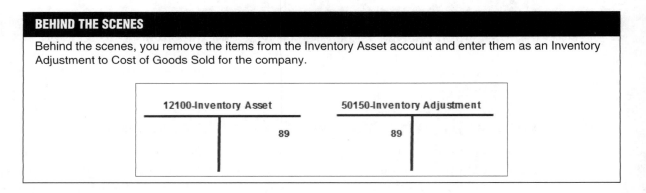

BEHIND THE SCENES

Behind the scenes, you remove the items from the Inventory Asset account and enter them as an Inventory Adjustment to Cost of Goods Sold for the company.

12100-Inventory Asset	50150-Inventory Adjustment
89	89

QUICK REFERENCE	ADJUSTING QUANTITY/VALUE ON HAND
Task	**Procedure**
Adjust quantity or value of inventory items	■ Choose Vendors→Inventory Activities→Adjust Quantity/Value on Hand.
	■ Choose the adjustment type and date.
	■ Choose Inventory Adjustment as the Adjustment Account; choose an adjustment class.
	■ Choose the desired items, indicate the new quantities and/or values, and type any memos.
	■ Click Save & Close or Save & New.

Make an Inventory Adjustment

When delivering one of the benches to a job site, the bench fell off of the truck and was damaged beyond repair. You will help Zoe to mark this inventory item out of inventory.

1. Click the **Inventory Activities drop-down arrow** in the Company area of the Home page, and then choose **Adjust Quantity/Value On Hand**.

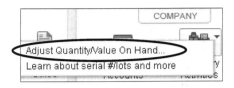

2. Follow these steps to make an inventory adjustment:

Ⓐ Ensure **Quantity** is the Adjustment Type.

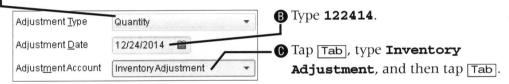

Ⓑ Type **122414**.

Ⓒ Tap `Tab`, type **Inventory Adjustment**, and then tap `Tab`.

Inventory Adjustment is a new account, so QuickBooks will prompt you to set it up.

Ⓓ Click **Set Up**.

Ⓔ Type **50150** as the Number.

Ⓕ Click **Save & Close** to create the new account.

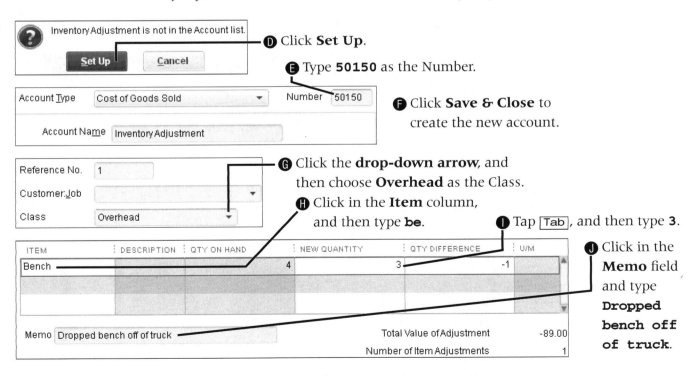

Ⓖ Click the **drop-down arrow**, and then choose **Overhead** as the Class.

Ⓗ Click in the **Item** column, and then type **be**.

Ⓘ Tap `Tab`, and then type **3**.

Ⓙ Click in the **Memo** field and type **Dropped bench off of truck**.

BTS BRIEF

50150•Inventory Adjustment DR 89.00; 12100•Inventory Asset CR <89.00>

---

3. Click **Save & Close** to record the inventory adjustment.

Paying Sales Tax

You have been collecting sales tax for your inventory sales. Now it is time to learn how to pay the collected tax to the appropriate tax agencies.

Sales Tax Payable

As you have seen, when you bill a customer and collect sales tax, QuickBooks holds the funds in a current liability account. These taxes are never actually the property of your business (an asset), so you have been using a liabilities payable account as a place to "store" the taxes until it is time to remit them.

When you are ready to pay your sales tax, it is *imperative* that you do so through the Pay Sales Tax window. This is to ensure that the proper liability account is affected behind the scenes when the payment is processed.

When you are ready to pay sales tax, you must use the proper procedure, or you will not "empty" the Sales Tax Payable account behind the scenes.

The Sales Tax Liability Report

You can choose to run a sales tax liability report to see what funds you are holding in your sales tax payable account. This report will give you the values you need to file your sales tax return: total sales, taxable sales, nontaxable sales, and the amount of tax collected.

The Manage Sales Tax Window

The Manage Sales Tax window helps you manage all of your sales tax activities and reports easily by providing links to all of the tasks you will be performing when working with sales tax, from setting it up to paying it.

Dealing with Adjustments in Sales Tax

There are many situations that could result in an incorrect amount in the Pay Sales Tax window or on the sales tax liability report. You may have charged a customer a tax rate for the wrong jurisdiction or tax may have been charged for a nontaxable item. There could also be rounding errors, penalties, or credits/discounts that you need to take into account.

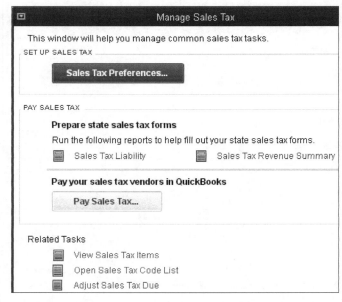

The Manage Sales Tax window helps you deal with all QuickBooks preferences, activities, and reports related to sales tax.

You can make an adjustment to the tax owed through the Pay Sales Tax window or by choosing Adjust Sales Tax Due from the Vendors menu. Make sure that you don't use Sales Tax Payable as the "pay from account." Instead, you should use the following types of accounts:

- **For a rounding error:** You can set up a special account or use the Miscellaneous Expense. Some businesses opt to create a special income account for a negative error or a special expense account for a positive error.

- **For a credit or to apply a discount:** Use an income account such as Other Income.

- **For interest due, fines, or penalties:** Use an expense account such as Interest Expense or Non-deductible Penalties.

If you make an adjustment to the sales tax liability account, you will need to choose the adjustment the next time you pay sales tax in order to get the correct amount to pay.

Changing a Tax Jurisdiction

If a customer is charged sales tax for the wrong jurisdiction, you need to go back to the original transaction and choose the correct sales tax item or group. If you charged tax on a nontaxable item (or vice versa), you need to adjust the invoice or sales receipt where the sale was made. This may require you to issue a credit to the customer if they overpaid or reissue the invoice/receipt (or a statement) if they underpaid.

BEHIND THE SCENES

When you pay sales tax, behind the scenes you will see the funds leave the Sales Tax Payable account as a debit.

25500-Sales Tax Payable		10000-Checking	
1,180.95			1,180.95

QUICK REFERENCE — PAYING SALES TAX

Task	Procedure
Pay sales tax	■ Choose Vendors→Sales Tax→Pay Sales Tax. ■ Choose the bank account from which you will be paying the taxes. ■ Enter the date of the check and the date through which to show sales taxes. ■ Choose which taxes to pay by clicking in the Pay column; click OK.
Run a sales tax liability report	■ Choose Reports→Vendors & Payables→Sales Tax Liability. ■ Set the correct date range for the report.
Adjust the amount of sales tax owed	■ Choose Vendors→Sales Tax→Adjust Sales Tax Due. ■ Enter the date, vendor, account, amount, and memo; click OK.

Pay Sales Tax

In this exercise, you will help Zoe pay to the appropriate tax agencies all the tax collected that is due December 31, 2014. The first step is to run a report to determine how much sales tax is owed and to whom.

1. Click the **Manage Sales Tax** task icon in the Vendors area of the Home page. *QuickBooks displays the Manage Sales Tax window.*

2. Click the **Sales Tax Liability** link in the Manage Sales Tax window.

3. Click the **Dates drop-down arrow**, and then choose **This Month**.

Take a look at the information this report contains. The information you need to pay and file your taxes is in the last column, Sales Tax Payable as of Dec 31, 2014, which is $1,180.95.

4. Close the **Sales Tax Liability** report.

Pay the Sales Tax

From the report you just ran, you know that Rock Castle owes $1,180.95 as of 12/31/14 to the State Board of Equalization and $0.29 to City of East Bayshore.

5. Click the **Pay Sales Tax** button in the Manage Sales Tax window.

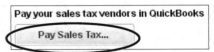

6. Ensure that **10000•Checking** is the Pay From Account.

7. Follow these steps to pay the taxes due:

Ⓐ Tap Tab, and then type **123114**.

Ⓑ Tap Tab, and then type **123114** again.

Ⓒ Click the **Pay All Tax** button (note that the button name changes after it has been clicked).

Ⓓ Ensure that the **To be printed** checkbox is checked.

Ⓔ Click **OK**.

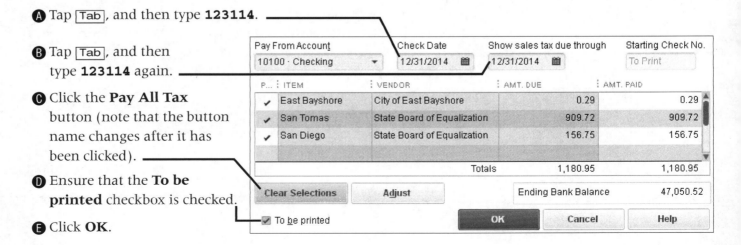

The liability check has now been entered into the queue of checks to be printed.

8. Close the **Manage Sales Tax** window.

Producing Inventory, Sales, and Receivables Reports and Graphs

QuickBooks features many preset reports to help you efficiently manage inventory, sales, and receivables. You will produce these reports in much the same way as you have created reports for other aspects of your business.

Physical Inventory Worksheet

Periodically, it is important to physically count your inventory items and to make sure that what is "on the books" is actually what you have in stock. Many businesses do this type of procedure annually and adjust their books accordingly. QuickBooks provides a great report that can aid in this process—the Physical Inventory Worksheet. It shows the name, description, preferred vendor, and on-hand quantity of each item you have in inventory. It also provides a column with blank lines, where you can record what you actually have during a physical inventory count.

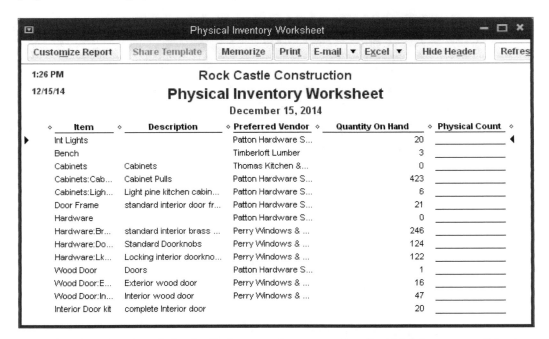

Notice that there is no Description for the inventory items entered earlier. This is because we did not enter that information in the Add/Edit Multiple List Entries window, but you can do so by going back there and adding columns or by editing in the Edit Item window.

The following table lists many reports useful when you work with inventory items.

Inventory Report Name	What it will tell you...
Inventory Valuation Summary	The value of your inventory by item
Inventory Valuation Detail	The details of the transactions that affect the value of inventory
Inventory Stock Status by Item	The inventory items you need to reorder and the current number in stock of each item
Inventory Stock Status by Vendor	Similar to the Inventory Stock Status by Item but arranged by vendor
Physical Inventory Worksheet	A printable worksheet used to count physical inventory or to compare physical quantity to the number QuickBooks has recorded

Receivables Reports

In the Customers & Receivables category of the Report Center, you can see all of the reports designed to help you track and collect the money owed to your company. In addition, you will be able to view a brief description of each of these reports.

The Collections Center

QuickBooks provides you with a tool that helps you manage your receivables—the Collections Center. You can access this tool through the Customer Center and, from it, you can send a batch email to customers with either overdue or almost due invoices. QuickBooks also makes it easy for you to contact customers with overdue invoices by providing the phone number as a part of the Collections Center.

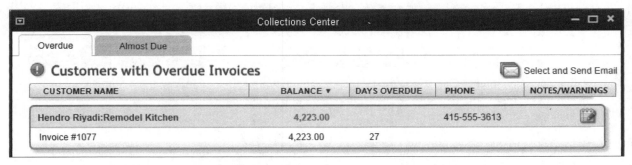

The Collections Center window. Notice the tabs at the top that allow you to switch between Overdue and Almost Due invoices.

Tracking Sales

The Sales area of the Report Center features reports and graphs that help you stay on top of your company's sales. You can choose from reports grouped by Sales by Customer, Sales by Item, and Sales by Rep (if sales reps have been set up). You can also view sales information by job if you have jobs set up for your company. The Sales Graph can graphically display your sales by item, customer, and rep.

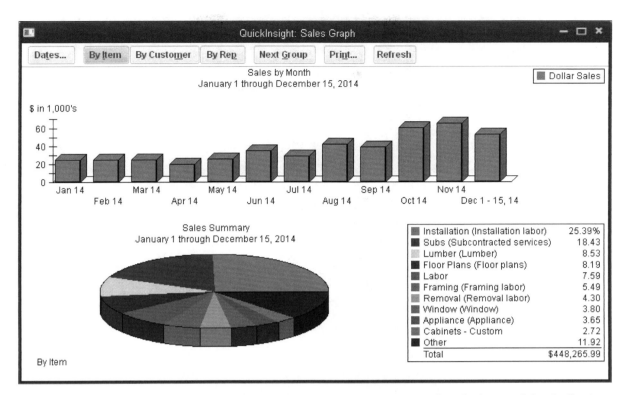

Graphs are a great way to illustrate your company's information. Here, you can see the sales by month for the fiscal year to date as well as the sales by item. Remember that if QuickBooks doesn't provide a preset graph that works for you, you can export your data to Excel and create your graphs there.

QUICK REFERENCE	PRODUCING INVENTORY, RECEIVABLES, AND SALES REPORTS AND GRAPHS
Task	**Procedure**
Display an inventory, receivable or sales report or graph	■ Open the Report Center. ■ Choose the category of the report you wish to run. ■ Click the report; click the Display button.
Display the Collections Center	■ Open the Customer Center. ■ Click the Collections Center button on the toolbar.

Display the Collections Center and Create Inventory and Sales Reports

In this exercise, you will help Zoe run a variety of reports and graphs and take a look at the Collections Center. You will begin by taking a look at the Collections Center to see what is owed to the company.

1. Click the **Customers** button on the Icon Bar.

2. Click the **Collections Center** button on the toolbar.

The Collections Center opens with the Overdue tab selected.

3. Click the **Almost Due** tab.
You can now see the invoice that is close to being due.

4. Close the **Collections Center**, and then the **Customer Center**.

Determine the Inventory Value

This report will show Zoe the dollar value (based on purchase price) of the company's inventory.

5. Choose **Reports→Inventory→Inventory Valuation Summary**.

6. Tap a to set All as the date range for the report.
The report will show the number of items you have in inventory as well as their asset value (cost) and retail value.

7. Close the report.

Determine Which Items to Reorder

This report will help Zoe determine when she needs to order additional items.

8. Choose **Reports→Inventory→Inventory Stock Status by Item**.

9. Tap a to set the date range to All.

Rock Castle Construction
Inventory Stock Status by Item
All Transactions

	◇ Item Description	◇ Pref Vendor	◇ Reorder Pt	◇ On Hand	◇ U/M	◇ Order	◇ On PO	◇ Next Deliv	◇ Sales/Week ◇
Inventory									
Int Lights	▶	Patton Hard...	15	20			3	12/19/2014	0 ◀
Bench		Timberloft L...	1	3			0		1.4
Cabinets									
Cabinet Pulls	Cabinet Pulls	Patton Hard...	15	423	ea		0		0.6
Light Pine	Light pine kitchen c...	Patton Hard...	0	6			0		0.1
Cabinets - Other	Cabinets	Thomas Kitc...	15	0		✓	0		0
Total Cabinets				429	ea		0		0.7

Notice that a checkmark appears in the Order column when it is time to place an order.

10. Close the **Inventory Stock Status by Item** window.

Create a Sales Graph

Finally, you will create a graph that will show you all of the sales by month and the sales by customer for the fiscal year to date.

11. Choose **Reports→Sales→Sales Graph**.

12. Click the **By Customer** button on the toolbar.

Notice the sales graph in the lower area of the window by customer. There are so many customers for the company that you will have to use QuickZoom to drill down to those classified as "Other."

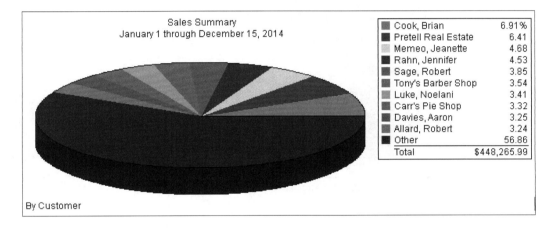

13. Close the **Sales Graph** window.

14. Choose the appropriate option for your situation:

■ If you are continuing on to the next lesson or to the end-of-lesson exercises, leave QuickBooks open.

■ If you are finished working in QuickBooks for now, choose **File→Exit**.

Concepts Review

Concepts Review   http://labyrinthelab.com/qb13-level02

To check your knowledge of the key concepts introduced in this lesson, complete the Concepts Review quiz by going to the URL listed above.

Reinforce Your Skills

Before you begin the Reinforce Your Skills exercises:

■ *Restore* **Tea Shoppe at the Lake, Lesson 1 (Portable)** *from your file storage location. Make sure to place your name as the first word in the company filename (e.g., Susie's Tea Shoppe at the Lake, Lesson 1).*

REINFORCE YOUR SKILLS 1.1

Set Up Inventory and Sales Tax Items

In this exercise, you will set up sales tax and inventory items for Susie. The first step is to turn on the sales tax preference and set up a sales tax item.

1. Choose **Edit→Preferences**.

2. Display the **Company Preferences** tab of the Sales Tax category.

3. Turn on the **sales tax preference**.

4. Set up a new sales tax item using the following information.

Sales Tax Name	**SD County**
Description	**San Diego County Sales Tax**
Tax Rate	**8.25%**
Tax Agency	**San Diego County Treasurer** (Quick Add as a vendor)

5. Click **OK** to add the new sales tax item.

6. Choose **SD County** as the most common sales tax item.

7. Click **OK** to close the Preferences window and accept the new preference.

8. Click **OK** in the Updating Sales Tax window; then, click **OK** to acknowledge the closing of all open windows.

Turn On Inventory Preferences

Susie has decided to start offering custom-built woodworking items for sale to her customers. You will now help her set up her QuickBooks file to deal with her inventory along with the new income and expenses involved.

9. Choose **Edit→Preferences**.

10. Click the **Items & Inventory** category, and then click the **Company Preferences** tab.

11. Click in the box to the left of **Inventory and purchase orders are active**.

12. Click **OK** to close the Preferences window; click **OK** to close the Warning window, if necessary.

Create a New Income Account

The next step for Susie to take is to set up a separate income account for her product sales.

13. Choose **Lists→Chart of Accounts**.

14. Click the **Account** menu button, and then choose **New**.

15. Choose **Income** as the account type, and then click **Continue**.

16. Type **Craft Sales**, and then click **Save & Close**.

17. Close the **Chart of Accounts**.

Create a New Inventory Item

Now Susie needs to set up an inventory item to be able to sell her product using the sales forms.

18. Choose **Lists→Item List**, click the **Item** menu button, and then choose **New**.

19. Choose **Inventory Part** as the item type.

20. Use the following illustration to create the new item; click **OK** when you are finished.

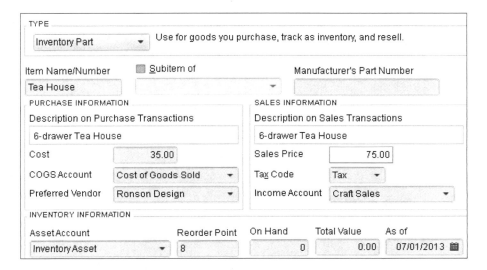

21. Close the **Item List**.

Create Purchase Orders and Receive Items

In this exercise, you will help Susie order and receive inventory items. You will begin by creating a purchase order for the tea houses.

1. Choose **Vendors→Create Purchase Orders**.

2. Use the following illustration to enter the information into the purchase order.

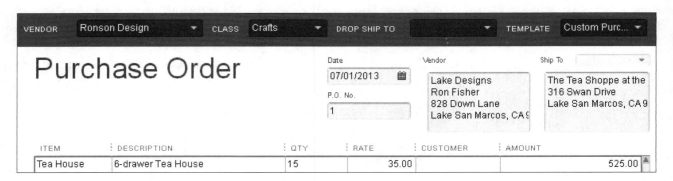

3. Click **Save & Close**.

Receive the Items

The items have arrived without the bill, so Susie needs to receive them into QuickBooks.

4. Choose **Vendors→Receive Items**.

5. Choose **Ronson Design** as the vendor, tap Tab, and then click **Yes** to receive against an open purchase order.

6. Click in the **checkmark** column to the left of the purchase order dated 7/1/2013, and then click **OK**.

7. Change the date of the **Item Receipt** to **7/5/2013**, and then click **Save & Close**.

Receive the Bill

The bill for the houses has just arrived, so it is time to enter it into QuickBooks.

8. Choose **Vendors→Enter Bill for Received Items**, and then choose **Ronson Design** as the vendor.

9. Click on the Item Receipt dated **7/5/13** to select it, and then click **OK**.

10. Tap Tab, and then tap + until the date reads **7/8/2013**.

11. Enter **Inv. #TSL-1** as the Ref. No. and Memo, and then enter **Net 15** as the terms.

12. Click **Save & Close**, clicking **Yes** to agree to change the transaction.

13. Click **Yes** to permanently change the information for Ronson Designs.

Sell Inventory Items

Once the products have been entered into inventory, it is time to start selling! In this exercise, you will record inventory sales.

1. Choose **Customers→Enter Sales Receipts**.

2. Use the following illustration to enter the information for the sales receipt.

3. Click **Save & New** to record the sale.

Record Sales from a Craft Fair

Susie rented a booth at a local craft fair and sold her tea houses. You will now help her to enter the sales.

4. Choose **Crafts** as the Class.

5. Enter **7/10/2013** as the date of the sale, and then **Cash** as the Payment Method.

6. Choose **Tea House** as the Item, with a quantity of **5**.

7. Enter **Craft Fair Sales** as the memo.

8. Click **Save & Close** to record the sale.

Process Payments and Pay Sales Tax

In this exercise, you will help Susie deposit all of the payments received into the Checking account and then pay the sales tax due.

1. Choose **Banking→Make Deposits**.
   The Payments to Deposit window will appear.

2. Click the **Select All** button, and then click **OK**.

3. Change the date of the deposit to **7/23/2013**, and then click **Save & Close**.
   All of the payments waiting in the Undeposited Funds account have now been deposited into the Checking account.

Pay Sales Tax

4. Choose **Vendors→Sales Tax→Pay Sales Tax**.

5. Ensure **Checking** is the account from which the payment will come.

6. Set the **Check Date** and **Show sales tax due through** to **7/31/13**.

7. Choose for the check to be **printed** and to **pay all tax due**.

8. Click **OK** to send the liability check to the queue to be printed.

REINFORCE YOUR SKILLS 1.5

Adjust Inventory

In this exercise, you will help Susie make an adjustment to her inventory because she provided a tea house to a silent auction in exchange for advertising for her business.

1. Choose **Vendors→Inventory Activities→Adjust Quantity/Value on Hand**.

2. Set the Adjustment Type to **Quantity**, and the date to **7/26/2013**.

3. Choose **Advertising and Promotion** as the Adjustment Account, and then **Other** as the Class.

4. Click in the **Item** column, and then type **t**.

5. Tap ⌈Tab⌋, and then type **8** in the New Quantity column.

6. Click in the **Memo** field, and then type **Donation to Lake San Marcos Elementary silent auction**.

7. Click **Save & Close**.

REINFORCE YOUR SKILLS 1.6

Produce Reports

In this exercise, you will create an inventory report that details the quantity and value of inventory on hand. Then you will change information on a source transaction using QuickZoom.

1. Choose **Reports→Inventory→Inventory Valuation Detail**.

2. Tap ⌈a⌋ to set the date range to All.

3. Using **QuickZoom**, go to the bill for the tea houses.

4. Change the terms of the bill to **Net 30**.

5. **Save the bill** with the changes, choosing to have the new terms appear next time and become a permanent change to the vendor record.

6. Click **Yes** to refresh the report.

7. **Close the report**, choosing not to memorize it.

8. Choose the appropriate option for your situation:
   - If you are continuing on to the next lesson or the rest of the end-of-lesson exercises, leave QuickBooks open.
   - If you are finished working in QuickBooks for now, choose **File→Exit**.

Apply Your Skills

Before you begin the Apply Your Skills exercises:

■ *Restore* **Wet Noses Veterinary Clinic, Lesson 1 (Portable)** *from your file storage location. Make sure to place your name as the first word in the company filename (e.g., Sadie's Wet Noses Veterinary Clinic, Lesson 1).*

APPLY YOUR SKILLS 1.1
Set Up Sales Tax and Inventory Items

In this exercise, you will help Sadie set up sales tax and inventory items that she will begin selling to her customers. You will help Dr. James to set up to collect sales tax on inventory items. Service items will remain not taxable.

1. Open the **Preferences** window and set the preference to collect sales tax.

2. Set up a new sales tax item (**King County Sales Tax** for **10%**, payable to **King County Treasurer**), and then set it as the **most common sales tax item**.

3. Click **OK** to close the Preferences window and accept the new preference.

4. Choose to make **all existing customers taxable** but not all existing non-inventory and inventory parts.

Turn On the Preference and Create a New Income Account

Before you can set up inventory items, you must turn on the preference and have an income account for the item sales to flow into.

5. Open the **Preferences** window, and then turn on the **Inventory and purchase order** feature; click OK in the Preferences window.

6. Choose **Company→Home Page**.

7. Open the **Chart of Accounts**, and then create a new income account called **Sales**. Close the **Chart of Accounts** when finished.

Create New Inventory Items

Now you will set up the new items that will be sold.

8. Using either the **Item List** or the **Add/Edit Multiple List Entries** window, create the following inventory part items.

Item Name	Toothbrush	Chew Toy	Cat Collar
Purchase/Sales Description	Dog toothbrush and paste kit	The great indestructible ball!	Designer cat collar
Cost	6.49	3.71	8.00
Preferred Vendor	Seattle Vet Supply	Bothell Pet Supply Co.	Take a Walk
Sales Price	14.99	8.99	19.99
Income Account	Sales	Sales	Sales
Reorder Point	15	20	10

9. Close the **Item List** or **Add/Edit Multiple List Entries** window.

Purchase and Receive Inventory Items

In this exercise, you will help Dr. James purchase and receive her new inventory items in order to have them in stock.

Create Purchase Orders

First you must create the purchase orders.

1. Open the **Create Purchase Orders** window.

2. Order 25 toothbrushes from Seattle Vet Supply on 7/1/13 using Product Sales as the Class.

3. Click **Save & New**.

4. Order 40 chew toys from Bothell Pet Supply Co. on 7/2/13 using Product Sales as the Class.

5. Click **Save & New**.

6. Order 15 cat collars from Take a Walk on 7/2/13 using Product Sales as the Class.

7. Click **Save & Close**.

Receive the Items

You will now receive the items into inventory.

8. You received all 25 toothbrushes from Seattle Vet Supply on 7/7/2013, along with the bill. Receive the items and enter the bill, making sure to receive against the purchase order you created. Click **Save Anyway** when the Items not assigned classes window appears. (It will appear as you have accounts prefilled on the Expenses tab with no amounts allocated to them.)

9. You received 33 of the chew toys from Bothell Pet Supply Co. The rest are on backorder, so you did not receive the bill yet. Receive these 33 items into inventory on 7/8/2013. Click **Save Anyway** when the Items not assigned classes window appears. (It will appear as you have accounts prefilled on the Expenses tab with no amounts allocated to them.)

10. You received all 15 of the cat collars from Take a Walk on 7/12/2013, along with the bill. Included on the bill was a shipping charge of $12.95. Receive the items into inventory and enter the bill. Create a new Postage and Delivery expense account for the shipping charge, and use **Product Sales** as the class.

11. On 7/14/2013, you received a bill for the chew toys you received on 7/8/2013, along with a shipping charge of $13.50 and a note stating that they would not be charging you a shipping charge for the backordered chew toys.

12. Receive the seven chew toys that were on backorder, along with the bill, on 7/25/2013.

Sell Inventory

In this exercise, you will help Sadie process sales for the new inventory items.

Sell Inventory

Jill Ann Tank came in to pick up two of the new cat collars she heard you talking about.

1. Using an **Enter Sales Receipts** window, sell Jill Ann Tank two of the new designer cat collars on 7/14/2013, choosing Product Sales as the Class. She pays with cash.

Sell Inventory with Discount Payment Terms

One of the dog handlers from King County Sheriff decided to get toothbrushes and chew toys for the dogs. You will create an invoice using the Police Dog price level and discount payment terms.

2. Sell seven toothbrushes and seven chew toys to King County Sheriff K-9 Unit on 7/15/2013. The Terms should be 2% 10 Net 30 and the class Product Sales. Use the Police Dog price level for both line items. Choose to not make the change in Terms permanent.

Sell Inventory with Service and Non-Inventory Items

Inventory items can be sold on invoices with any other type of item. You will create an invoice that includes service, inventory, and non-inventory items.

3. Stacy LiMarzi brought in his cat, Reagan, for a scheduled new-patient exam on 7/19/2013. Create an invoice for him for the New Patient Exam, a FIV/FeLV test, and a dose of Revolution for a cat. Stacy noticed the new cat collars in the lobby and decided to get one for Reagan as well. Only the collar is taxable.

Receive Payments for Inventory Sales

Now you will receive payment on the two invoices you just created.

4. Open the **Receive Payments** window, and then choose King County Sheriff K-9 Unit as the customer. Receive check 7796 for $162.87 to pay for invoice 178 on 7/21/2013, applying the 2 percent discount of $3.32 since the payment was received within 10 days. Create a new income account called Less Discounts Given as the Discount Account, and Product Sales should be the Discount Class, clicking Save & New when you have entered all of the information correctly.

5. Choose Stacy LiMarzi as the customer and 7/22/2013 as the Date. Stacy has paid the entire amount of invoice 179 with check 448. **Save & Close** the transaction.

Pay Sales Tax

You will now help Sadie to pay the sales tax that she collected.

6. Choose **Vendors→Sales Tax→Pay Sales Tax**.

7. Set the **Check Date** and **Show sales tax due through** to **7/31/13**, ensuring that **Checking** is the payment account.

8. Choose for the check to be **printed**, and to **pay all tax due**.

9. Click **OK** to send the liability check to the queue to be printed.

Answer Questions with Reports

In this exercise, you will answer questions for Dr. James by running reports. You may wish to display the Report Center in List View to help you answer the questions. Ask your instructor if you should print the reports, print (save) them as PDF files, export them to Excel, or simply display them on the screen.

1. How many inventory items do we currently have in stock?

2. How much is the inventory that we have in stock worth?

3. What is the sales amount for each customer during the month of July 2013?

4. What item have we "sold" the most of during the month of July 2013?

5. Who should we be making collections calls on as of 6/30/2013? Can the phone number be included on the report?

6. Submit your reports based on the guidelines provided by your instructor.

7. Choose the appropriate option for your situation:

   ■ If you are continuing on to the next lesson or the Critical Thinking exercises, leave QuickBooks open.

   ■ If you are finished working in QuickBooks for now, choose **File→Exit**.

Critical Thinking

In the course of working through the following Critical Thinking exercises, you will be utilizing various skills taught in this and previous lesson(s). Take your time and think carefully about the tasks presented to you. Turn back to the lesson content if you need assistance.

1.1 Sort Through the Stack

Before You Begin: Restore the **Monkey Business, Lesson 1 (Portable)** *file from your storage location. (Remember that you are to leave the password field blank for Mary.) You also have the option of opening Monkey Business, Lesson 1 from your storage location.*

You have been hired by Mary Minard to help her with her organization's books. She is the owner of Monkey Business, a nonprofit organization that provides low-income students with help in preparing for college placement exams and applying for scholarships. You have just sat down at her desk and found a pile of papers. It is your job to sort through the papers and make sense of what you find, entering information into QuickBooks whenever appropriate and answering any other questions in a word-processing document saved as **Critical Thinking 1.1**. Remember, you are digging through papers on a desk, so it is up to you to determine the correct order in which to complete the tasks.

- Sticky note from Mary: We are going to start stocking SAT Prep guides and College 101 texts. I would like to see if we can set them up in QuickBooks. Our accountant told me that we should use the "average cost" method to keep track of our inventory. Will we be able to track this in QuickBooks? (Explain your answer.)

- Packing slip and bill from Woods Publishing: Enter items into inventory and enter the bill for payment on 8/4/2013. Monkey Business received 40 copies of The Ultimate SAT Prep Guide, and a $35 shipping charge was included in the bill.

- Note from Mary: We had a water leak on 8/10/2013 and three copies of College 101 were damaged and cannot be resold. Please figure out a way to take them out of inventory in QuickBooks.

- Scribbled on a scrap of paper: If we can track inventory in QuickBooks, please set up "The Ultimate SAT Prep Guide" as an inventory item, the cost from Woods Publishing is $15.34 and the resale price is $29.95. (There is no sales tax in Oregon.) Also, please set up another inventory item to track "College 101" texts. The cost from Woods Publishing is $18.73 and the resale price is $32.95. As of 8/1/2013, order 40 copies of the SAT Prep text and 50 copies of College 101.

- Handwritten invoice: Four copies of "The Ultimate SAT Prep Guide" for a semiprivate prep session at Achievement, Inc., dated 8/6/2013, due 2% 10 Net 30.

- Packing slip from Woods Publishing: Dated 8/5/2013 for receipt of 23 copies of College 101; the rest are on backorder.

- Photocopy of a check: Check 2007 from Achievement, Inc. dated 8/10/2013 for $117.40 and with a memo stating the company took advantage of the 2 percent discount.

- Scribbled note from Mary: Can you produce a report for me that shows the value of the inventory we currently have in stock? How about the number of each item?

1.2 Tackle the Tasks

Now is your chance to work a little more with Rock Castle Construction and apply the skills that you have learned in this lesson to accomplish additional tasks. Open or restore the **Critical Thinking 1.2** company or portable company file from your file storage location, or open the company file you used in the Develop Your Skills exercises for this lesson. Then, enter the following tasks.

Create Inventory Item	Item Name: Porch Light; Description: Standard Porch Light; Cost: 23.87; Sales Amt.: 40.00; COGS: 50100•Cost of Goods Sold; Pref. Vendor: Patton Hardware Supplies; Income Acct: 40140•Materials Income; Asset Acct.: 12100•Inventory Asset; Reorder: 10; Qty on Hand: 0.
Create Purchase Order	Create a PO to purchase 12 of the porch lights you just entered as an inventory item on 12/19/14.
Receive Items	Receive the porch lights with the bill on 12/23/14. Add a $30 shipping charge to the bill with Overhead as the Class.
Sell Items	Sell two porch lights to Mike Balak for his deck repair job on 12/24/14, terms 2% 10 Net 30. Class is remodel and terms are only for this invoice.
Receive Payment	Receive an electronic payment, 758946, from Mike Balak for the porch lights on 12/28/14. Mike has taken advantage of the early payment discount; use Overhead as the class for the discount amount. Deposit the payment to Checking on the same day.
Adjust Inventory	An interior light was dropped on a job, so you need to mark one interior light out of inventory on 12/27/14, using Overhead as the class.
Run Reports	Create a report that shows a summary of the aging for Rock Castle's receivable (i.e., A/R Aging Summary).

You may use the company file from this exercise for the Develop Your Skills exercises in the next lesson if you wish.

1.3 Use the Web as a Learning Tool

Throughout this book, you will be provided with an opportunity to use the Internet as a learning tool by completing WebQuests. According to the original creators of WebQuests, as described on their website (WebQuest.org), a WebQuest is "an inquiry-oriented activity in which most or all of the information used by learners is drawn from the web." To complete the WebQuest projects in this book, navigate to the student resource center and choose the WebQuest for the lesson on which you are currently working. The subject of each WebQuest will be relevant to the material found in the lesson.

WebQuest Subject: Learning about sales tax where you do business

Using QuickBooks for Payroll

LESSON OBJECTIVES

After studying this lesson, you will be able to:

- Set up QuickBooks to run payroll
- Manage the Employees List
- Create paychecks
- Track and pay payroll liabilities
- Process payroll forms
- Input information from an outside payroll service into QuickBooks

Payroll is a very sensitive subject as it affects people's livelihoods. As an employer, you should be well-informed of all the payroll options and well-equipped to efficiently run payroll for your business. In this lesson, you will examine how QuickBooks deals with payroll, how to manage the Employees List so you can create paychecks and track payroll liabilities, and how to process payroll forms. In addition, you will look at how to deal with payroll if you choose to use an outside service to handle it for you.

Rock Castle Construction

Rock Castle Construction has been doing so well that it needs to hire two more employees to help out. Zoe knows that Alan has been using QuickBooks to run the company's payroll, so she will enter the new employees into the Employees List and create paychecks for them. She will also pay the payroll liabilities and examine payroll options to make sure that the company is using the option that is right for it.

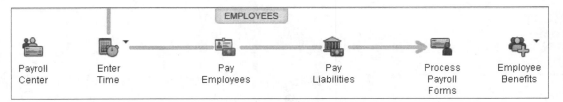

The Employees area of the Home page provides task icons that will help you with payroll and time-tracking tasks.

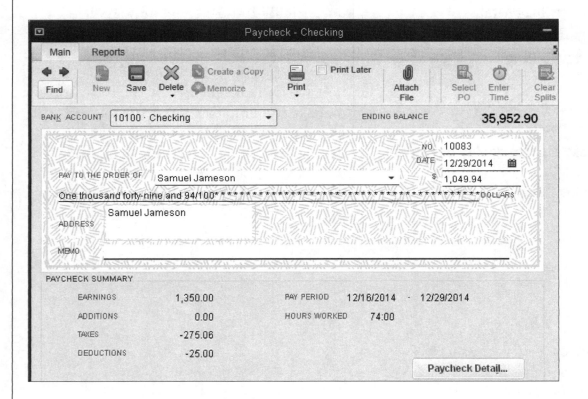

This lesson teaches how to use QuickBooks to run payroll for a company using a basic service. You must contact your local tax agency to determine what tax laws apply to you and to whom you should submit your taxes. Do not use the specific percentages, vendors, or amounts shown, even if it is from your local jurisdiction, because tax laws change all the time! It is your responsibility to stay informed, either on your own or through a paid service (such as those offered by Intuit).

Setting Up QuickBooks to Run Payroll

In this section, you will look at the payroll options in QuickBooks and learn how to properly set up payroll items.

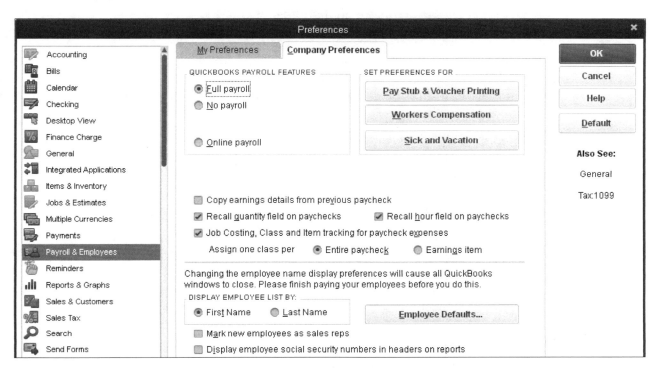

Notice all of the preferences the company administrator has the opportunity to set for payroll.

Payroll Recordkeeping in QuickBooks

In order to produce all of the required federal, state, and local payroll forms and reports, QuickBooks keeps a separate set of records for payroll. This separate set of records tracks payroll liabilities, paychecks (and the items listed on them), and taxes. Due to this method of payroll recordkeeping, only those transactions entered via QuickBooks' payroll features will affect payroll reporting.

Evaluating Payroll Options

QuickBooks payroll offers five options: Manual, Basic, Enhanced, Enhanced for Accountants, and Assisted Payroll. Each option has its pros and cons, and all but the Manual option have an associated fee for the service. Intuit does not recommend the Manual option, as it requires you to stay on top of all tax law changes and there is a higher likelihood of errors and resulting penalties when you have to enter everything yourself. If you choose to use the Assisted Service option, QuickBooks has a "No Penalties" Guarantee in which Intuit will pay any penalties you incur if you provide proper information in a timely manner and have sufficient funds in your bank account.

You may be wondering if it makes sense for you to do your own payroll. The last section in this lesson will provide you with information regarding how you can use QuickBooks for payroll that is run by an outside service and then entered into your QuickBooks company.

If you are using QuickBooks for a Canadian company, Intuit produces a separate line of products for the Canadian market that addresses multiple currencies and Canadian payroll regulations. Find more information at http://quickbooks.ca/.

If you would like to learn more about the payroll options available through QuickBooks, check out the link on the student resource center. QuickBooks can change its payroll options at any time, so it is advised that you check out the website to ensure that you are dealing with the most current information.

QuickBooks is not ideal for all companies' payroll needs. If multiple states require you run payroll for an individual employee, or you withhold a certain percentage of wages on paychecks, using QuickBooks for payroll may not be the best solution for you.

The Payroll Setup Interview

In order to set up payroll in QuickBooks, you are provided with a Payroll Setup Interview that will walk you through all of the steps to make sure you set up taxes, compensation, and benefits correctly. After the interview leads you through the steps to set up your payroll items, it will help you to set up your employees and enter historical amounts so you can begin doing your company's payroll in QuickBooks.

Payroll Items

Anything you wish to include on a paycheck—such as wages, taxes, employee loans, and 401(k) withholdings—must first be set up as a payroll item. The majority of payroll mistakes are made due to payroll items not being set up properly.

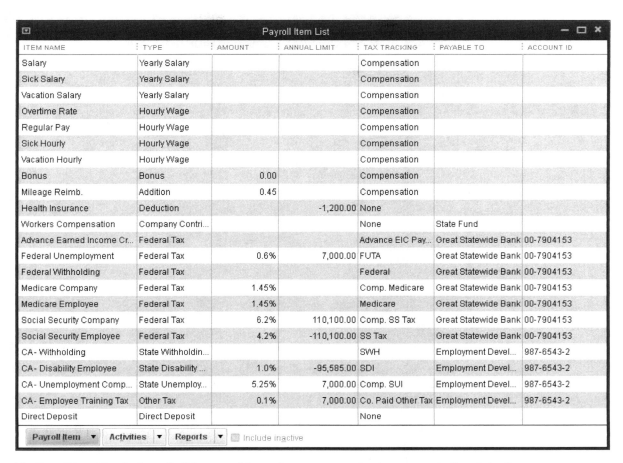

ITEM NAME	TYPE	AMOUNT	ANNUAL LIMIT	TAX TRACKING	PAYABLE TO	ACCOUNT ID
Salary	Yearly Salary			Compensation		
Sick Salary	Yearly Salary			Compensation		
Vacation Salary	Yearly Salary			Compensation		
Overtime Rate	Hourly Wage			Compensation		
Regular Pay	Hourly Wage			Compensation		
Sick Hourly	Hourly Wage			Compensation		
Vacation Hourly	Hourly Wage			Compensation		
Bonus	Bonus	0.00		Compensation		
Mileage Reimb.	Addition	0.45		Compensation		
Health Insurance	Deduction		-1,200.00	None		
Workers Compensation	Company Contri...			None	State Fund	
Advance Earned Income Cr...	Federal Tax			Advance EIC Pay...	Great Statewide Bank	00-7904153
Federal Unemployment	Federal Tax	0.6%	7,000.00	FUTA	Great Statewide Bank	00-7904153
Federal Withholding	Federal Tax			Federal	Great Statewide Bank	00-7904153
Medicare Company	Federal Tax	1.45%		Comp. Medicare	Great Statewide Bank	00-7904153
Medicare Employee	Federal Tax	1.45%		Medicare	Great Statewide Bank	00-7904153
Social Security Company	Federal Tax	6.2%	110,100.00	Comp. SS Tax	Great Statewide Bank	00-7904153
Social Security Employee	Federal Tax	4.2%	-110,100.00	SS Tax	Great Statewide Bank	00-7904153
CA- Withholding	State Withholdin...			SWH	Employment Devel...	987-6543-2
CA- Disability Employee	State Disability ...	1.0%	-95,585.00	SDI	Employment Devel...	987-6543-2
CA- Unemployment Comp...	State Unemploy...	5.25%	7,000.00	Comp. SUI	Employment Devel...	987-6543-2
CA- Employee Training Tax	Other Tax	0.1%	7,000.00	Co. Paid Other Tax	Employment Devel...	987-6543-2
Direct Deposit	Direct Deposit			None		

Payroll Item ▼   Activities ▼   Reports ▼   ☐ Include inactive

The Payroll Item List displays all of the payroll items, from compensation to taxes and other deductions.

If you need to add payroll items at a later date, you can always return to the QuickBooks Payroll Setup Interview or access the Payroll Item List from the menu bar.

Making Payroll Data More Meaningful

When you turn on the payroll preference in QuickBooks, the payroll expense and liability accounts are created for you. QuickBooks then automatically routes payroll items set up through the QuickBooks Payroll Setup to these accounts. If you wish to provide more meaningful information in your reports and make troubleshooting more user-friendly, you may want to consider setting up subaccounts for the payroll accounts QuickBooks creates for you. Once you create these subaccounts, you must remap each payroll item to the correct one through the Payroll Item List.

Verifying Correct Payroll Item Setup

To verify that payroll items are set up correctly and mapped to the correct accounts, you need to run a payroll item listing report. If you see either Payroll Liability-Other or Payroll Expense-Other displayed on a balance sheet or P&L, you know that you have a payroll item mapped to a parent account rather than to a subaccount.

Rock Castle Construction
Payroll Item Listing

Payroll Item	Type	Amount	Limit	Expense Account	Liability Account	Tax Tracking
Salary	Yearly Salary			62710 · Gross Wages		Compensation
Sick Salary	Yearly Salary			62710 · Gross Wages		Compensation
Vacation Salary	Yearly Salary			62710 · Gross Wages		Compensation
Overtime Rate	Hourly Wage			62710 · Gross Wages		Compensation
Regular Pay	Hourly Wage			62710 · Gross Wages		Compensation
Sick Hourly	Hourly Wage			62710 · Gross Wages		Compensation
Vacation Hourly	Hourly Wage			62710 · Gross Wages		Compensation
Bonus	Bonus	0.00		62710 · Gross Wages		Compensation
Mileage Reimb.	Addition	0.45		62710 · Gross Wages		Compensation
Health Insurance	Deduction		1,200.00		24100 · Emp. Health Ins Pa...	None
Workers Compensation	Company Contrib...			62130 · Work Comp	24080 · Worker's Compens...	None
Advance Earned Income C...	Federal Tax				24030 · AEIC Payable	Advance EIC Paym...
Federal Unemployment	Federal Tax	0.8%	7,000.00	62730 · FUTA Expense	24040 · FUTA Payable	FUTA
Federal Withholding	Federal Tax				24010 · Federal Withholding	Federal
Medicare Company	Federal Tax	1.45%		62720 · Payroll Taxes	24020 · FICA Payable	Comp. Medicare
Medicare Employee	Federal Tax	1.45%			24020 · FICA Payable	Medicare
Social Security Company	Federal Tax	6.2%	106,800.00	62720 · Payroll Taxes	24020 · FICA Payable	Comp. SS Tax
Social Security Employee	Federal Tax	6.2%	106,800.00		24020 · FICA Payable	SS Tax
CA - Withholding	State Withholding...				24050 · State Withholding	SWH
CA - Disability Employee	State Disability Tax	1.1%	93,316.00		24070 · State Disability Pay...	SDI
CA - Unemployment Comp...	State Unemploym...	5.25%	7,000.00	62740 · SUTA Expen...	24060 · SUTA Payable	Comp. SUI
CA - Employee Training Tax	Other Tax	0.1%	7,000.00	62740 · SUTA Expen...	24060 · SUTA Payable	Co. Paid Other Tax
Direct Deposit	Direct Deposit				24090 · Direct Deposit Liab...	None

Notice that the Payroll Item Listing report shows you what happens behind the scenes with expense and liability accounts when you use a payroll item.

Common Mistakes When Using QuickBooks for Payroll

Two very common mistakes people make when using QuickBooks for payroll are:

- Making a payroll liabilities adjustment with a journal entry
- Paying the liabilities with a "regular check" rather than a liability check similar to what you used when paying sales tax

In both cases, the Chart of Accounts will be affected but the separate payroll records that QuickBooks keeps will not be. If you have used a regular check for payroll liabilities, you will need to make an adjustment in the Liability Adjustment window, from where you can choose for QuickBooks to not affect the Chart of Accounts.

Another very common error is for people to set up their payroll items incorrectly. If you do choose to use subaccounts and remap your payroll accounts manually, be very careful to map the payroll items correctly!

Entering Historical Amounts

If you are beginning to use the QuickBooks payroll feature for existing employees who have received at least one paycheck from you (and it is not the first day of January), you must enter the payroll history amounts. This will ensure that QuickBooks properly calculates taxes with thresholds. It also ensures that you will be able to produce accurate W-2s at the end of the year.

QuickBooks offers step-by-step help to assist you in entering the required payroll history. Before you begin setting up historical amounts, make sure you have:

- Prior-period paychecks
- Prior liability payments

Step-by-step help for this task is accessible through the QuickBooks Payroll Setup Interview. Once you have entered the information, you will have the opportunity to reconcile and verify your data to ensure it is correct.

QuickBooks Learning Center Tutorials

Sure to be a valuable resource during your study is the QuickBooks Learning Center. It features a large number of instructional QuickBooks videos that are great learning tools for many students. You will find yourself directed to these tutorials through the new "Visualize!" element in this book. Develop Your Skills 1.2 includes steps to show you how to access a video. In this book you will see a special icon and text whenever a QuickBooks Learning Center tutorial is available (see below).

Tab: Thank you for upgrading
Topic: What's New in 2013

In addition, QuickBooks provides help for some topics that are not in video format. When you choose one of these topics in the Learning Center, a web page with more information will open.

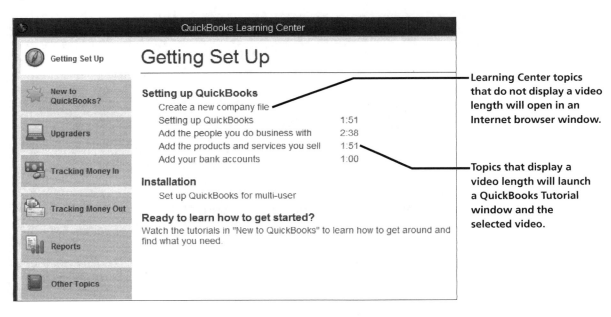

Tab: Other Topics
Topic: Payroll overview

FLASHBACK TO GAAP: TIME PERIOD

Remember that the activities of the business can be divided into time periods.

QUICK REFERENCE	PREPARING TO USE QUICKBOOKS TO RUN PAYROLL
Task	**Procedure**
Turn on QuickBooks payroll preferences	■ Choose Edit→Preferences. ■ Click the Payroll & Employees category; click the Company Preferences tab. ■ Click in the circle to the left of Full Payroll; click OK.
Sign up for a QuickBooks payroll service	■ Choose Employees→Payroll Service Options→Order Payroll Service. ■ Click the Learn More button or dial the indicated phone number.
Access the Payroll Setup Interview	■ Choose Employees→Payroll Setup. ■ Follow the interview to complete the process by answering questions and clicking the Continue button.
Create subaccounts for payroll accounts	■ Choose Lists→Chart of Accounts, right-click the desired item, and then choose New Account. ■ Create Other Current Liability subaccounts for your Payroll Liabilities account. ■ Create Expense subaccounts for your Payroll Expenses account.
Edit payroll items	■ Choose Lists→Payroll Item List; double-click the desired item. ■ Follow the steps on the screen, making any necessary changes. ■ Ensure you have the items mapped to the correct accounts.
Enter payroll year-to-date amounts	■ Complete steps 1–4 of the QuickBooks Payroll Setup Interview. ■ Choose Employees→Payroll Setup (if you are not still viewing the interview). ■ Complete step 5 "Payroll History" of the interview.
Make an adjustment to a payroll liability	■ Choose Employees→Payroll Taxes and Liabilities→Adjust Payroll Liabilities. ■ Enter the adjustment information; click OK.
Run a payroll item listing report	■ Choose Reports→Employees & Payroll→Payroll Item Listing.

Set Up QuickBooks to Run Payroll

In this exercise, you will view how to set the payroll preference for a company. The first step is to open Quick-Books, and then either open a company file or restore a portable company file.

1. Start **QuickBooks 2013**.

   If you downloaded the student exercise files in the portable company file *format, follow Option 1 below. If you downloaded the files in the* company file *format, follow Option 2 below.*

 If you choose, you may use the final company file from Critical Thinking 1.2. In this case, open the Critical Thinking 1.2 company file from your default storage location in Option 2 below.

Option 1: Restore a Portable Company File

2. Choose **File→Open or Restore Company**.

3. Restore the **Rock Castle Construction** portable file for this lesson from your file storage location, placing your name as the first word in the filename (e.g., Zoe's Rock Castle Construction, Lesson 2).

   It may take a few moments for the portable company file to open. Once it does, continue with step 4.

Option 2: Open a Company File

2. Choose **File→Open or Restore Company**, ensure that **Open a regular company file** is selected, and then open the **Rock Castle Construction** company file for this lesson from your file storage location.
The QuickBooks company file will open.

3. Click **OK** to close the QuickBooks Information windows. If necessary, click **No** in the Set Up External Accountant User window.

View the Payroll Preference

If you are setting QuickBooks up to run payroll for the first time in your company file, you will need to set the preference. In this case, you will help Zoe to verify that it is set correctly.

4. Choose **Edit→Preferences**.

5. Click the **Payroll & Employees** category on the left, and then the **Company Preferences** tab.

6. Notice that **Full payroll** is turned on for this company file.

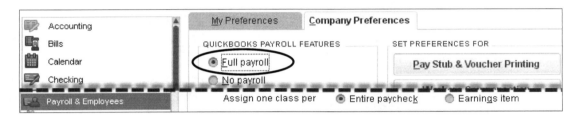

7. Click **Cancel** to close the Preferences window.

Working with Employees in QuickBooks

Just as you used the Vendor Center to track vendors and the Customer Center to track customers and jobs, you will use the Employee Center to track employees. If you recall, Quick-Books defines a customer as someone who pays you money. Well, the QuickBooks definition of an employee is someone to whom you issue a W-2 at the end of the year. Subcontractors are *not* to be entered into the Employees List; remember from *QuickBooks Pro 2013: Level 1* that subcontractors are included in the Vendor List.

Setting Up Employees Through the Payroll Setup Interview

QuickBooks allows you to set up your employees in two ways. You can enter them through the payroll setup interview process, or you can enter them directly into the Employees List accessed via the Employee Center.

Managing the Employees List

Managing the Employees List is similar to managing the Customers & Jobs List and the Vendors List. You will edit, delete, and create new employees the same way you did for customers and vendors. New employees can also be set up as part of the QuickBooks Payroll Setup Interview.

Clicking the Payroll tab displays the Payroll Center, which helps guide you through payroll activities.

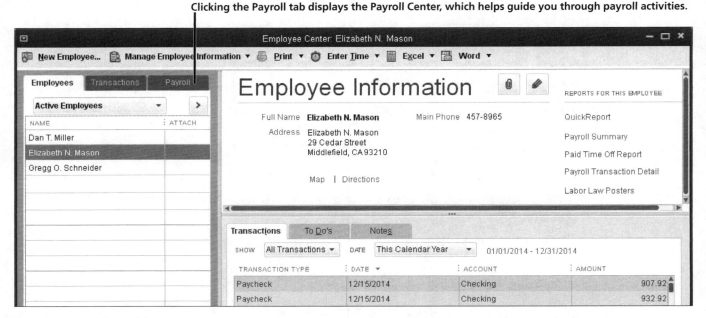

The Employee Center looks very similar to the Vendor and Customer Centers with which you have already worked.

Setting Up a New Employee

To run payroll, you need to enter important tax information for each employee. If you don't have your employees' W-4s handy, you can always add the information later—as long as it is entered before you first run payroll. (This is not optional!)

It is very important to have all of your employees' W-4 and I-9 forms filed neatly with all personnel records. Workman's Compensation companies are very thorough when they review company payroll records. Even though you do not treat independent contractors as employees in QuickBooks, it is important that you have a I-9 form on file for each contractor as well.

Gather Your Employee Information

Before you can set up employees in QuickBooks, regardless of which approach you take, you need to have certain information handy. If you don't have all of the information from the W-4 forms when you set up your employees, you will need to ensure that it is entered before you first run payroll.

Following is a list of necessary employee information required for payroll setup:

- Name
- Address
- Social security number
- Birthday
- Federal and state exemption information

Setting Employee Defaults

Before you set up your employees, you should set the employee defaults. These preferences will be applied to each new employee you create, and you can change them as needed. When setting employee defaults, choose the options that you assume will apply to the majority of employees you will create.

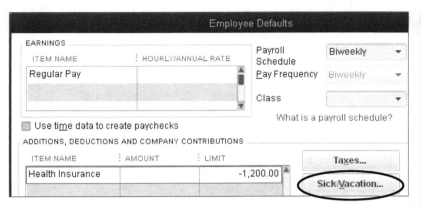

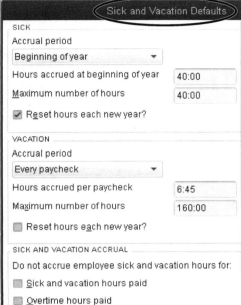

One of the default items you can set deals with how (and if) sick and vacation time is tracked for employees.

Visualize!

Tab: Other Topics
Topic: Paying employees

QUICK REFERENCE	MANAGING THE EMPLOYEES LIST
Task	**Procedure**
Create a new employee	■ Choose Employees→Employee Center; click the New Employee button. ■ Enter all applicable information on each of the tabs; click OK.
Edit an existing employee	■ Choose Employees→Employee Center; double-click the desired employee. ■ Make any necessary changes; click OK.
Set employee defaults outside of the Payroll Setup Interview	■ Choose Employees→Employee Center; click the Manage Employee Information button at the top of the window. ■ Choose Change New Employee Default Settings, enter the new settings, and then click OK.

Set Up and Manage Employees

In this exercise, you will help Zoe set up two new employees for Rock Castle Construction (they began on 12/16/2014) after she has modified the employee defaults for payroll.

1. Click the **Employees** button in the Employees area of the Home page.
   The Employee Center will be displayed.

2. Click the **Manage Employee Information** button, and then choose **Change New Employee Default Settings**.

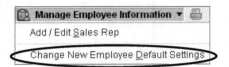

   QuickBooks displays the Employee Defaults window.

3. Follow these steps to edit the new employee default settings (you must click in the Item Name column to see a drop-down arrow displayed that will allow you to choose the items from a list of payroll items):

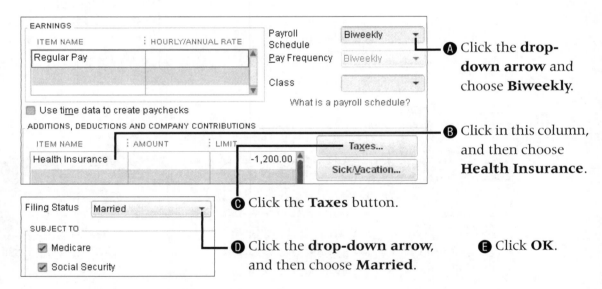

   Ⓐ Click the **drop-down arrow** and choose **Biweekly**.

   Ⓑ Click in this column, and then choose **Health Insurance**.

   Ⓒ Click the **Taxes** button.

   Ⓓ Click the **drop-down arrow**, and then choose **Married**.

   Ⓔ Click **OK**.

   Take a look at any of the other defaults that you have the option of setting, if you wish, making sure to not make any changes to them.

4. Click **OK** in the Employee Defaults window.
   You will once again be viewing the Employee Center window.

Set Up a New Employee Using the Employees List

The next task you will help Zoe with is setting up a new employee.

5. Click the **New Employee** button on the Employee Center toolbar.

6. Follow these steps to set up the personal information for Stephen:

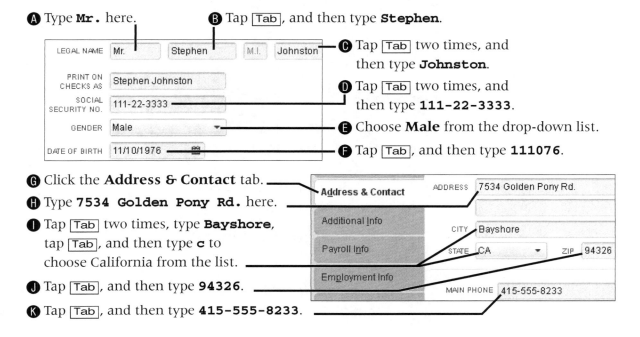

Ⓐ Type **Mr.** here.

Ⓑ Tap `Tab`, and then type **Stephen**.

Ⓒ Tap `Tab` two times, and then type **Johnston**.

Ⓓ Tap `Tab` two times, and then type **111-22-3333**.

Ⓔ Choose **Male** from the drop-down list.

Ⓕ Tap `Tab`, and then type **111076**.

Ⓖ Click the **Address & Contact** tab.

Ⓗ Type **7534 Golden Pony Rd.** here.

Ⓘ Tap `Tab` two times, type **Bayshore**, tap `Tab`, and then type **c** to choose California from the list.

Ⓙ Tap `Tab`, and then type **94326**.

Ⓚ Tap `Tab`, and then type **415-555-8233**.

7. Follow these steps to set up the payroll information for Stephen:

Ⓐ Click **the Payroll Info** tab.　　**Ⓑ** Click here, and then type **18.5**.

Ⓒ Click below **Regular Pay**, and then type **o**.

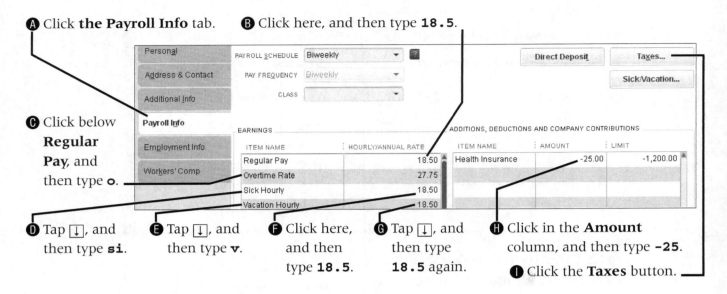

Ⓓ Tap ⬇, and then type **si**.

Ⓔ Tap ⬇, and then type **v**.

Ⓕ Click here, and then type **18.5**.

Ⓖ Tap ⬇, and then type **18.5** again.

Ⓗ Click in the **Amount** column, and then type **−25**.

Ⓘ Click the **Taxes** button.

Don't forget to type the minus sign for the Health Insurance amount!

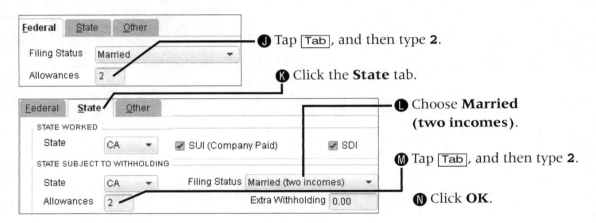

Ⓙ Tap Tab, and then type **2**.

Ⓚ Click the **State** tab.

Ⓛ Choose **Married (two incomes)**.

Ⓜ Tap Tab, and then type **2**.

Ⓝ Click **OK**.

Notice how the various employee defaults that you set were set up filled in for you and that you can change any of them as you set up each individual employee.

8. Click **OK** again to save Stephen's information.

9. Click **Leave As Is**.
By choosing to leave the sick/vacation information "as is," you are applying the employee defaults to Stephen.

Add an Additional Employee

You will now help Zoe to add one more employee, Sam Jameson.

10. Use the following information and the steps outlined in the previous section to add one more employee.

Remember to choose the Payroll Info tab when you are ready to enter the pay rate and exemptions information.

Name	**Mr. Samuel Jameson**
Address	**303 McMurray Place** **Middlefield, CA 93210**
Phone	**415-555-8791**
SS No.	**999-88-7777**
Gender	**Male**
Date of Birth	**013078**
Hourly Rate	**18.00**
Overtime Rate	**27.00**
Sick and Vacation Rate	**18.00**
Filing Status and Allowances	**Single, 1**
Health Insurance	**-25**

11. Click **Leave As Is** to apply the sick/vacation defaults to Sam.

12. Close the **Employee Center**.

Dealing with Payroll Deductions

You have learned about two of the three main tasks associated with setting up QuickBooks to run payroll—setting up payroll items and employees. Now you will need to let QuickBooks know which taxes and deductions to collect and to whom they need to be paid. You can use the QuickBooks Payroll Setup Interview to take a quick whirl through the taxes you have set up to make sure they are correct. In addition, you can view the Payroll Item Listing report to verify that the taxes and deductions are being routed to the right expense and liability accounts as well as the actual Payroll Item List to make sure the vendors to whom you pay them are correct.

You must have your Federal Employer Identification Number listed in your company file in order for payroll to be processed correctly. If you did not enter this correctly or at all when you created your company file, you can make that change at any time.

Workers Compensation Insurance

QuickBooks can process Workman's Comp insurance in much the same way that it processes payroll taxes. To track this payroll expense, the preference must be turned on in QuickBooks.

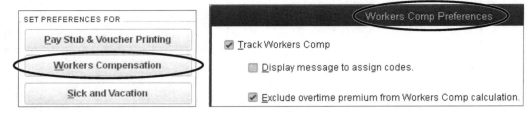

The Workers Compensation button in the Set preferences for area of the Company Preferences tab of the Payroll & Employees category leads to a window that allows you to choose whether to track workers comp in QuickBooks.

QUICK REFERENCE	DEALING WITH PAYROLL TAXES
Task	**Procedure**
Enter your company's FEIN	■ Choose Company→Company Information. ■ Click in the Federal Employer Identification No. field, and then type your FEIN. ♦ If you are a sole proprietor and don't have a FEIN, click in the Social Security Number field, type your SSN, and then click OK.
Choose to track workers comp in QuickBooks	■ Choose Edit→Preferences. ■ Click the Payroll & Employees category; choose the Company Preferences tab. ■ Click the Workers Compensation button; click in the checkbox to the left of Track Workers Comp. ■ Click OK two times to set the new preference.
Create a Payroll Item Listing report	■ Choose Reports→Employees & Payroll→Payroll Item Listing.
View the Payroll Item List	■ Choose Lists→Payroll Item List.

DEVELOP YOUR SKILLS 2.3

Set Up Payroll Taxes

In this exercise, you will make sure that the company's Federal Employer Identification Number is entered properly and that the company is set up correctly to account for payroll taxes.

You will begin by helping Zoe make sure that the company's FEIN is entered correctly in QuickBooks.

1. Choose **Company→Company Information**.

2. Verify that **00-7904153** is the FEIN entered for Rock Castle Construction.

3. Click **OK**.

COMPANY IDENTIFICATION

Federal Employer Identification No.   00-7904153
(EIN is required for Payroll)

Social Security Number
(SSN is used on 1099's if
no EIN is entered)

Verify Correct Payroll Tax Setup

You will now use the QuickBooks Payroll Setup Interview as a tool to make sure the payroll taxes are set up properly. If there is an obvious error, QuickBooks will alert you and ask you to make a change.

4. Choose **Employees→Payroll Setup**.

5. Click in the box to the left of **Taxes**.

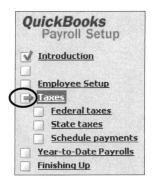

6. Click **Continue**.

You will see a screen that lists all of the federal taxes that have been set up for you. Notice that both Medicare and Social Security have two separate entries; they are paid by both the company and employee.

7. Click **Continue**.

On this next screen, you will see the state taxes that QuickBooks has set up for you. Remember that this book is meant to be a training tool only. You must contact your local tax agency to know how to set up taxes for your jurisdiction!

8. Click **Continue**.

In this next screen, you will see how and when you pay each of your withholding taxes.

9. Click the **Finish Later** button at the bottom left of the QuickBooks Payroll Setup window; click **OK** in the Finish Later window.

Notice that even after your payroll is set up you can use the QuickBooks Payroll Setup feature to examine the information you have entered for it.

Create a Payroll Item Listing Report to Verify Accounts

It is very important for your payroll items to link to the proper accounts in your Chart of Accounts! You will now review a report that shows how the items are linked so you can ensure you are doing payroll properly.

10. Choose **Reports→Employees & Payroll→ Payroll Item Listing**.

The Payroll Item Listing report will be displayed.

11. Note the **Expense Account** and the **Liability Account** columns.

The expense accounts indicate the payroll expenses for your company, from salaries and benefits to employer taxes that you are required to pay. The liability accounts are where you "hold" the funds until you have to pay them to the proper taxing authority. Remember that QuickBooks keeps a separate set of records for payroll behind the scenes, so when you choose to pay your payroll liabilities with a special Liability Check window, it will "empty" these accounts properly.

Expense Account	Liability Account
62710 · Gross Wages	
62710 · Gross Wages	
62710 · Gross Wages	
62710 · Gross Wages	
62710 · Gross Wages	
62710 · Gross Wages	
62710 · Gross Wages	
62710 · Gross Wages	
62710 · Gross Wages	
	24100 · Emp. Health Ins Payable
62130 · Work Comp	24080 · Worker's Compensation
	24030 · AEIC Payable
62730 · FUTA Expense	24040 · FUTA Payable
	24010 · Federal Withholding
62720 · Payroll Taxes	24020 · FICA Payable
	24020 · FICA Payable
62720 · Payroll Taxes	24020 · FICA Payable
	24020 · FICA Payable
	24050 · State Withholding
	24070 · State Disability Payable
62740 · SUTA Expense	24060 · SUTA Payable
62740 · SUTA Expense	24060 · SUTA Payable
	24090 · Direct Deposit Liabilities

12. Close the **Payroll Item Listing** window.

Verify Vendors and Edit a Payroll Item

The final step you will take to verify that your payroll taxes are set up properly is to make sure that you are paying the taxes to the proper vendors.

13. Choose **Lists→Payroll Item List**, resizing the window as necessary so you can see all columns clearly.
    Look in the Payable To column. This shows to whom you must pay each tax that you are holding in your liability accounts. Notice that there is no vendor listed for Health Insurance in the Payable to column. You will help Zoe add this information now.

14. Double-click **Health Insurance** to open it for editing.

An Edit Payroll Item window displays. You will be clicking Next to move through the screens to modify this item.

15. Click **Next** as the name for the item is correct.

16. Follow these steps to set up the vendor to whom you will pay the insurance premiums:

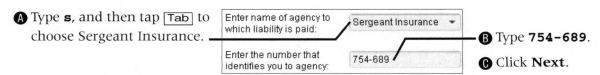

ⓐ Type **s**, and then tap [Tab] to choose Sergeant Insurance.

ⓑ Type **754–689**.

ⓒ Click **Next**.

The Liability account is correct, so you do not need to edit it.

17. Type **o** in the Tax tracking type screen to choose **Other**; click **Next**.

18. Click **Next** in the Taxes screen; click **Next** in the Calculate based on quantity screen.

19. Click **Next** in the Gross vs. net window.

20. Click **Finish** in the Default rate and limit window.
    You will enter the deduction amount when you set up each new employee, rather than entering a default here.

Create a Payroll Item

You will now help Zoe create a new payroll item to track court-mandated child support deductions as well as payments to a charity the company has adopted, Niños del Lago. The Payroll Item List should still be displayed from the previous step, but if not, Choose Lists→Payroll Item List.

21. Click the **Payroll Item menu button**, and then choose **New**.

22. Click **Next** to choose EZ Setup.

23. Click in the circle to the left of **Other Deductions**, and then click **Next**.

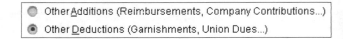

24. Click in the boxes to the left of **Wage garnishment** and **Donation to charity**, and then click **Next**.

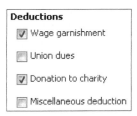

25. Follow these steps to set up the payment schedule for the charity donations:

Ⓐ Type **Ninos del Lago**.

Ⓑ Tap ⎡Tab⎤, and then type **RCC**.

Ⓒ Click in the circle to the left of **Quarterly**.

Ⓓ Click **Next**.

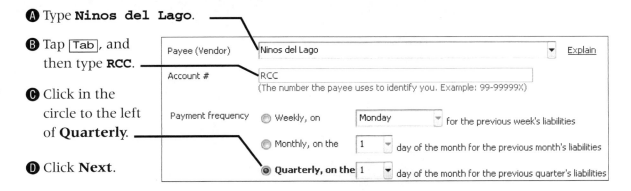

26. Follow these steps to set up the payment schedule for the child support deductions:

Ⓐ Type **County Family Services**.　**Ⓑ** Tap ⎡Tab⎤, and then type **00-7904153**.

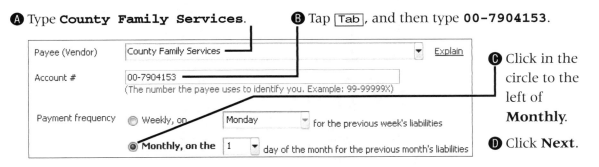

Ⓒ Click in the circle to the left of **Monthly**.

Ⓓ Click **Next**.

27. Click **Finish**.
You will now see the Payroll Item List displayed with your two new payroll items added to it. If you wish, you can rename the items from this list.

28. Close the **Payroll Item List**.

Creating Paychecks

Once you have chosen your payroll method, made sure your payroll items are set up properly, and set up your employees and payroll tax information, you can begin to create paychecks for your employees. When you first choose to pay employees, you will see an Enter Hours window displayed. Once you have entered the paycheck information for each employee, you will see all of the data displayed in the Review and Create Paychecks window.

We are using the QuickBooks sample file. If you use a QuickBooks payroll service, your subscription status will appear here.

The Pay Employees area of the window helps you process payroll for employees. The Related Payroll Activities button gives you the option to edit or void paychecks, add or edit payroll schedules, and create a termination check.

The Pay Scheduled Liabilities area helps you make sure that you pay all of the funds you are holding in your payroll liability accounts on time.

The File Tax Forms area guides you through creation of W-2s and other payroll forms.

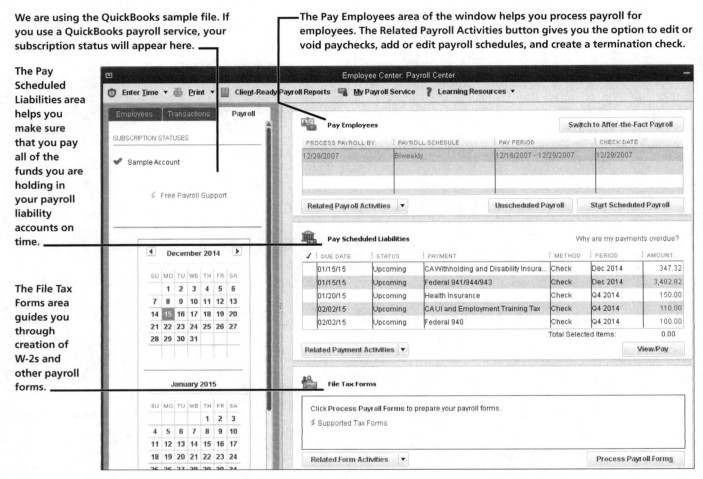

The Payroll Center window. Notice that it helps guide you through all of your payroll tasks.

You will have the opportunity to enter information for each employee in a Review or Change Paycheck window, moving from one employee to another using the Next and Previous buttons.

Working with Payroll Schedules

When you choose to use QuickBooks for payroll, you have the option to set up payroll schedules in order to more efficiently run payroll. Payroll schedules allow you to set how often you pay employees, the date on which the paycheck is due, the date on which you will run payroll, all the while taking into account holidays and weekends to ensure that you pay your employees on time. Another benefit of using scheduled payroll is that you can choose to pay your employees by group or by batch.

Payroll schedules are created from the Payroll Center after the payroll setup is complete. You will have an opportunity to run a scheduled payroll for Rock Castle Construction. In the Reinforce Your Skills exercise, you will run payroll without using a payroll schedule.

Using scheduled payroll does not limit you from creating a paycheck for an employee "off schedule." This can be completed by clicking the Unscheduled Payroll button in the Payroll Center.

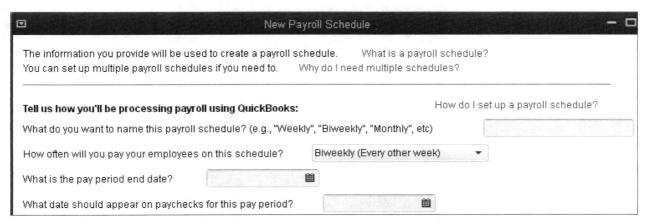

In the New Payroll Schedule window, you can set the vital information that will apply to the payroll schedule being created for a group of employees.

Passing On Billable Time to Customers

In this section, you will learn to pass on billable payroll expenses to customers. When you create a paycheck for an employee who has billable hours, make sure to choose the correct customer or job to which to pass on the expense.

Assigning Sick or Vacation Hours

You learned how to set QuickBooks up to track sick and vacation hours for employees previously in this lesson. To document an employee's use of "banked" paid time off, you will assign the time to payroll items that specifically track the banked time.

Notice the separate Sick Hourly and Vacation Hourly items that you would use to track the sick and vacation hours used by an employee.

QuickBooks makes it easy for you to ensure that an employee has sick and/or vacation hours available to use before you include them on a paycheck.

If you include a Customer:Job in this column, then the payroll expense can be easily passed on to a customer.

Preview Paycheck										✕

Samuel Jameson

PAY PERIOD 12/16/2014 📅 - 12/29/2014 📅

☐ Use Direct Deposit   CLASS Remodel ▾

Earnings

ITEM NAME	RATE	HOURS	W/C CODE	CUSTOMER:JOB
Regular Pay	18.00	72:00	5645	Balak, Mike:Repair Deck
Overtime Rate	27.00	2:00	5645	Balak, Mike:Repair Deck
Sick Hourly	18.00			
Vacation Hourly	18.00			

	SICK AVAILABLE	0:00
	VACATION AVAIL.	6:45
	SICK ACCRUED	
	VAC. ACCRUED	6:45

TOTALS   1,350.00   74:00 hrs

☐ Do not accrue sick/vac

Other Payroll Items

ITEM NAME	RATE	QUANTITY
Health Insurance	-25.00	

Employee Summary   How are these items calculated?

ITEM NAME	AMOUNT	YTD
Regular Pay	1,296.00	1,296.00
Overtime Rate	54.00	54.00
Sick Hourly	0.00	0.00
Vacation Hourly	0.00	0.00
Health Insurance	-25.00	-25.00
Federal Withholding	-151.00	-151.00
Social Security Employee	-56.70	-56.70
Medicare Employee	-19.58	-19.58
CA- Withholding	-34.28	-34.28
CA- Disability Employee	-13.50	-13.50

Company Summary   How are these items calculated?

ITEM NAME	AMOUNT	YTD
CA- Employee Training Tax	0.00	0.00
Social Security Company	83.70	83.70
Medicare Company	19.58	19.58
Federal Unemployment	8.10	8.10

Check Amount: 1,049.94

In the Preview Paycheck window, you will set the number of hours worked for an employee. This information will be used to calculate the payroll taxes for you (providing you subscribe to a QuickBooks payroll service).

BEHIND THE SCENES

When you create paychecks, you will pay employees, pay taxes, and withhold taxes from employee paychecks. In this example, we will look at Samuel Jameson's paycheck, which you will create in the next exercise. You will issue a net paycheck for $1,029.33, with $320.67 of employee deductions going to the Payroll Liability subaccounts (only the parent accounts of Payroll Liabilities and Payroll Expenses are shown in this example) and $184.96 of company-paid taxes going from the Payroll Expenses subaccounts to the Payroll Liability subaccounts. The gross pay is $1,350.

10400-Checking	24000-Payroll Liabilities	62700-Payroll Expenses
1,029.33	184.96	1,350.00
	320.67	184.96

CREATING PAYCHECKS AND PAYROLL SCHEDULES

Task	Procedure
Create employee paychecks	■ Choose Employees→Pay Employees; set the check date and the last day of the pay period. ■ Set the bank account and paycheck options. ■ In the Enter Hours window, click the first employee for whom you wish to enter paycheck information. ■ Enter the hours in the Review or Change Paycheck window; click Next. ■ Repeat the previous step for all of the employees you will be paying, clicking OK after entering the last employee's information. ■ Verify that the information is correct; click Create Paychecks.
Print paychecks	■ Choose File→Print Forms→Paychecks; choose the correct bank account. ■ Select the checks you wish to print; click OK. ■ Select the type of checks you use; click Print.
Print pay stubs	■ Choose File→Print Forms→Pay Stubs; set the correct date range. ■ Select the desired statements, click OK, and then click Print.
Pass billable payroll expenses on to a customer	■ Choose Customers→Create Invoices. ■ Choose the customer to whom you will be passing on the expense. ■ Click the Time/Costs button on the toolbar, and then click the Expenses tab. ■ Choose the hours you wish to pass on; click OK. ■ Finish entering invoice information; click Save & Close.
Create a payroll schedule	■ Choose Employees→Payroll Center. ■ Click the Related Payroll Activities button; choose Add or Edit Payroll Schedules. ■ Click the Payroll Schedule menu button; click New. ■ Enter a name for the schedule, how often the payroll will run, and the pay period end date as well as the paycheck date; click OK. ■ Assign the payroll schedule to all employees with the same pay frequency.
Edit a payroll schedule	■ Choose Employees→Payroll Center. ■ Click the Related Payroll Activities button; choose Add or Edit Payroll Schedules. ■ Click to select the payroll schedule you wish to edit. ■ Click the Payroll Schedule menu button; click Edit. ■ Make any desired changes; click OK.

Create Paychecks for Employees

In this exercise, you will help Zoe run payroll for all employees for the period ending 12/29/2014.

1. Choose **Company→Home Page**.

2. Click the **Pay Employees** task icon in the Employee area of the Home page.
   The Employee Center: Payroll Center window opens. We are using the QuickBooks sample company file for this exercise, and it shows the scheduled payroll as being in the year 2007. We will change the pay period dates as we move through the payroll process. When you do the payroll for your own company, the dates should show up correctly in this window once you have issued the first paycheck—if the payroll schedule is set up properly.

3. Click the **Start Scheduled Payroll** button in the Pay Employees area of the window.

The Enter Payroll Information window displays with the Check Date field selected.

4. Follow these steps to select which employees to pay and when to pay them:

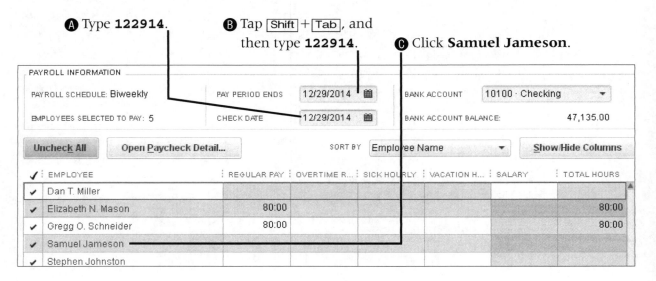

FROM THE KEYBOARD

Shift + Tab to "back tab" or go back one field on a form

The Preview Paycheck window for Samuel Jameson will appear.

You will be creating paychecks for all employees. Since all employees are checked by default, you do not have to make changes in this area. You have already created paychecks in the past for Dan, Elizabeth, and Gregg, so you can choose to use the information that was used the last time a check was created for each of them. If you choose to use previous information, you will have a chance to see what it looks like before you issue the paycheck.

5. Follow these steps to create a paycheck for Samuel:

Ⓐ Type **72**. **Ⓑ** Click the **drop-down arrow**, and then choose **5645** for Carpentry. **Ⓒ** Click the **drop-down arrow**, and then choose **Balak, Mike: Repair Deck**.

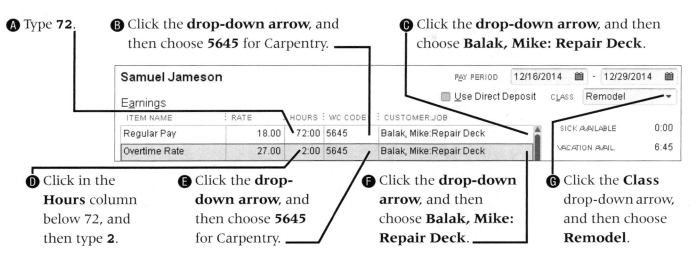

Ⓓ Click in the **Hours** column below 72, and then type **2**. **Ⓔ** Click the **drop-down arrow**, and then choose **5645** for Carpentry. **Ⓕ** Click the **drop-down arrow**, and then choose **Balak, Mike: Repair Deck**. **Ⓖ** Click the **Class** drop-down arrow, and then choose **Remodel**.

Notice that once you filled in the hours worked for Samuel, the tax amounts automatically filled in for you. This will happen for you as well as long as you have subscribed to a QuickBooks payroll service. You can choose to do paychecks manually, but that will require you to enter each amount manually and to stay on top of all tax law changes. It results in a much greater chance for error.

6. Click **Save & Next**.
The Preview Paycheck window for Stephen Johnston displays. Stephen is working on a new home that you are building and has just finished the roofing.

7. Follow these steps to create a paycheck for Stephen:

Ⓐ Type **64**. **Ⓑ** Click the **drop-down arrow**, and then choose **5552** for Roofing. **Ⓒ** Click the **drop-down arrow**, and then choose **New Construction**.

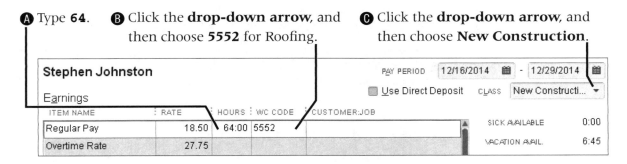

8. Click **Save & Close**.
The Enter Payroll Information window will again be displayed.

9. Click **Continue**; then, click **OK**.
The Review and Create Paychecks window displays, summarizing all of the information for you regarding the paychecks you are choosing to create. If you need to make any changes to a paycheck, simply click on the employee's name. The Preview Paycheck window for that employee will display, from where you can make any changes necessary.

Create Paychecks

In the next step, you will see the Review and Create Paychecks window, which summarizes the payroll infor-mation for this pay period.

10. Ensure that **Print paychecks from QuickBooks** is the Paycheck Option selected.

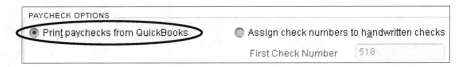

11. Click **Create Paychecks**.

The Confirmation and Next Steps window will be displayed. Notice that this window shows you the "flow" for payroll. It provides buttons for you to make printing paychecks and pay stubs easy.

In the following BTS Brief section, the numbers reflect all five paychecks created in the previous steps, including those that you did not edit for three of the employees. You are also viewing the "parent accounts" in this case, not the various subaccounts.

BTS BRIEF

62700•Payroll Expenses DR 7,350.20; 24000•Payroll Liabilities CR <1,658.23>; 10100•Checking CR <5,691.97>

Print Paychecks and Pay Stubs

Once you have created paychecks, you need to print them. You will help Zoe print the paychecks from the Confirmation and Next Steps window and then help her print the pay stubs using the menu bar command that is always available.

12. Click the **Print Paychecks** button in the Confirmation and Next Steps window.
The Select Paychecks to Print window displays. At this point, you would place preprinted checks into the printer. Of course, for this exercise there are no preprinted checks. You will print them on blank sheets of paper or as a PDF file.

13. Click **OK** to choose to print all five paychecks, using **10080** as the first check number.
The Print Checks dialog box displays. When you are dealing with your own company, look at the checks you place in the printer to verify that the first check number is correct.

14. Follow the desired step, depending on whether you wish to physically print the paychecks:

- Click **Print**. You can also choose this option if you wish to print the checks as an electronic PDF file. Click **OK** to verify that all checks printed correctly.

- Print choosing ***.pdf** as the printer, and then choose where to save the PDF file. Click **OK** to verify that all checks printed correctly.

15. Close the **Confirmation and Next Steps** window.
   Yes, you could have printed the pay stubs from that window, but it is important for you to know how to print paychecks and pay stubs from the menu bar as well!

16. Choose **File→Print Forms→Pay Stubs**.

17. Tap Tab, and then type **122914**.

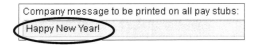

   Now only the pay stubs for the paychecks you just created display. You do not need to worry about changing the "thru" date, as the checks dated 12/29/14 are the latest ones created.

18. Click in the **Company message** field, and then type the following: **Happy New Year!**

19. Click **Preview** to view what the employee pay stubs will look like. Close the **Print Preview** window when you are finished.

20. Close the **Select Pay Stubs** window and the **Employee Center: Payroll Center** window.

Tracking and Paying Payroll Liabilities

In Lesson 1, Dealing with Physical Inventory, you collected sales tax and held it in a current liability account until it was time to pay the tax agencies. When you run payroll, you must collect taxes and other deductions and hold them in a payroll liabilities account until you are required to pay them.

Knowing How Much to Pay

QuickBooks has preset reports that you can run to determine how much you need to pay from what you hold in Payroll Liabilities. Remember that you hold taxes along with other deductions in the payroll liabilities account.

 If you have your bank send in your federal payroll taxes electronically, clear the Print Later checkbox and enter EFTPS (Electronic Federal Tax Payment Service) into the check number field.

The Pay Payroll Liabilities Window

Just as you used the Pay Sales Tax window to pay your sales tax liabilities, you will use a special Pay Liabilities window to pay your payroll taxes and deductions. You should never just "write a check" for your payroll taxes because QuickBooks will not properly debit the liability accounts.

One of the top errors made by new users is to use the Write Checks window for paying payroll liabilities rather than the QuickBooks Pay Liabilities window.

Tab: Other Topics
Topic: Pay taxes and other liabilities

BEHIND THE SCENES

When you pay your payroll liabilities, you decrease the amount in both your checking (by crediting) and payroll liabilities (by debiting) accounts. In the following example, you can see the three liability payments you will make in the next exercise on 12/29/2014. Only the parent account, Payroll Liabilities is used in this example.

10400-Checking		24000-Payroll Liabilities	
	568.71	568.71	
	262.50	262.50	
	5,013.42	5,013.42	
	5,844.63	5,844.63	

QUICK REFERENCE	PAYING PAYROLL LIABILITIES
Task	**Procedure**
Run a payroll liability report	■ Choose Reports→Employees & Payroll→Payroll Liability Balances. ■ Set the proper date range, and then click Refresh.
Pay payroll liabilities	■ Choose Employees→Process Payroll Liabilities→Pay Payroll Liabilities. ■ Set the date range for the liabilities; click OK. ■ Set the bank account and the check date. ■ Select the payroll liabilities you need to pay; click Create.

DEVELOP YOUR SKILLS 2.5

Pay the Payroll Liabilities

In this exercise, you will assist Zoe with the task of paying the payroll liabilities that have been collected.

Zoe first wants to see exactly how much she needs to pay to the various payroll vendors, so she will run a report that shows all of the taxes and deductions being held in the payroll liabilities account. You received a notice that you overpaid the liabilities in November, so you will run a report that shows the balance owed based on the adjustments from November and the total collected in December.

1. Choose **Reports→Employees & Payroll→Payroll Liability Balances**.

2. Follow these steps to set the date range for the report:

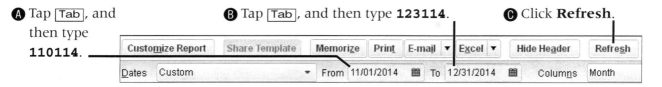

A Tap [Tab], and then type **110114**.

B Tap [Tab], and then type **123114**.

C Click **Refresh**.

| Customize Report | Share Template | Memorize | Print | E-mail ▼ | Excel ▼ | Hide Header | Refresh |

| Dates | Custom | ▼ | From | 11/01/2014 | 📅 | To | 12/31/2014 | 📅 | Columns | Month |

Your report should resemble the illustration below.

Rock Castle Construction
Payroll Liability Balances
November through December 2014

	Nov 14	Dec 14	BALANCE
Payroll Liabilities			
Advance Earned Income Credit ▶	0.00 ◀	0.00	0.00
Federal Withholding	-8.00	1,956.00	1,948.00
Medicare Employee	0.00	297.82	297.82
Social Security Employee	0.00	965.03	965.03
Federal Unemployment	0.00	115.20	115.20
Medicare Company	0.00	297.82	297.82
Social Security Company	0.00	1,273.40	1,273.40
CA - Withholding	-4.00	426.09	422.09
CA - Disability Employee	-17.20	90.67	73.47
CA - Unemployment Company	0.00	233.04	233.04
CA - Employee Training Tax	0.00	10.00	10.00
Health Insurance	0.00	212.50	212.50
Workers Compensation	0.00	1,948.91	1,948.91
Total Payroll Liabilities	**-29.20**	**7,826.48**	**7,797.28**

3. Close the **Payroll Liability Balances** report.

Pay the Payroll Liabilities

Zoe is now ready to pay the payroll liabilities due in January. You will help her pay them by using a liability check. Note that if you are paying liabilities for your own company, you need to pay them based on the schedule that applies to your business.

4. Click the **Pay Liabilities** task icon in the Employees area of the Home page.
   The Employee Center: Payroll Center will be displayed again.

Pay
Liabilities

5. Follow these steps to pay the liabilities due in January:

A Click to the left of the **three payments** due in January.

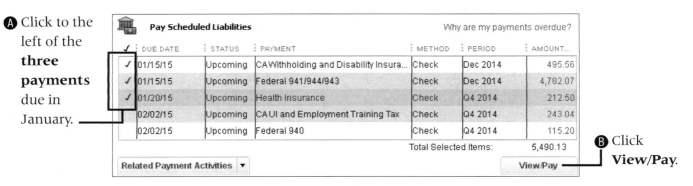

🏛 **Pay Scheduled Liabilities**					Why are my payments overdue?
✓ DUE DATE	STATUS	PAYMENT	METHOD	PERIOD	AMOUNT...
✓ 01/15/15	Upcoming	CAWithholding and Disability Insura...	Check	Dec 2014	495.56
✓ 01/15/15	Upcoming	Federal 941/944/943	Check	Dec 2014	4,782.07
✓ 01/20/15	Upcoming	Health Insurance	Check	Q4 2014	212.50
02/02/15	Upcoming	CAUI and Employment Training Tax	Check	Q4 2014	243.04
02/02/15	Upcoming	Federal 940	Check	Q4 2014	115.20

Total Selected Items: 5,490.13

| Related Payment Activities ▼ | | View/Pay |

B Click **View/Pay**.

The Liability Payment – Checking window will be displayed (notice that it is not *the Write Checks window!), with the check information for the first payroll vendor filled in.*

6. Change the date on the check to **12/29/2014**, and then click **Save & Next**.

   Since this is a sample company file, QuickBooks loads 12/15/2014 as the date each time you go to create a new transaction. In your own company file, the date that would be displayed is the last date you used in another transaction.

   The second liability payment information displays in the window.

7. Change the date on the second payroll liability check to **12/29/2014**, and then click **Save & Next**.

8. Change the date on the third liability check to **12/29/2014**, and then click **Save & Close**.

   A Payment Summary window displays. Notice that you can choose to print the checks right from this window. If you choose to print them at a later date, they will be placed in the queue of checks waiting to be printed. You can access that from the menu bar.

   In the following BTS Brief section, you are viewing the "parent account" for Payroll Liabilities, not the various subaccounts.

BTS BRIEF
24000•Payroll Liabilities DR 5,490.13; 10100•Checking CR <5,490.13>

9. Close the **Payment Summary** and **Employee Center: Payroll Center** windows.

Dealing with Errors in Payroll

When you encounter a situation that needs to be corrected in payroll, you must be very careful and ensure that you handle it in the proper manner. Remember that QuickBooks keeps a separate "set of books" for payroll, so you must make changes via the payroll features in QuickBooks.

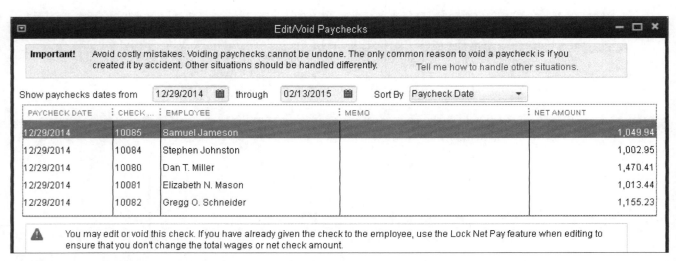

The Edit/Void Paychecks window allows you to choose which paycheck to void or edit and provides guidance. Note the important message at the top of the window regarding voiding paychecks and the message at the bottom of the window that refers to the selected paycheck (Samuel Jameson's).

Fixing a Paycheck

It is only on rare occasions that you should void a paycheck. Two such times that it would be warranted are when you accidentally created a paycheck or when you have to correct a paycheck from a prior year.

Correcting a Paycheck Error from a Prior Year

If you need to change the date of a paycheck from one year to another, you must void the paycheck and reissue it. (In previous versions, you could change a paycheck in a prior year without re-creating it.) Voiding a paycheck is done in basically the same way as voiding any transaction in QuickBooks. Just remember that when you re-create the paycheck, you must do it through the proper method in QuickBooks. In other words, you cannot just create a new check in the Write Checks window.

Lock Net Pay Feature

If you need to make changes to a paycheck and want to make sure that you don't change the amount of the check (which would need to be dealt with in a different way), you can use the QuickBooks Lock Net Pay feature that ensures you don't change the amount of the paycheck or the total wages. When this feature is activated, you will only be able to make changes that do not affect the amount of the check, such as the Class to which it is assigned, vacation or sick time accrual, or select/deselect to use a direct deposit.

Unscheduled Payroll Checks

There may be times when you need to issue a paycheck to an employee, and it is not at the end of a pay period. For instance, you may have underpaid an employee and do not want that employee to have to wait until the next payday to receive the compensation, or you may need to issue a final paycheck. These situations can easily be dealt with in QuickBooks from the Payroll Center window by choosing either to conduct an unscheduled payroll or to create a termination check.

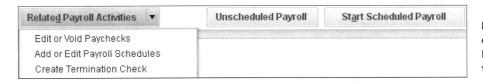

Notice the additional options available in the Pay Employees area of the Payroll Center.

Let's take a look at how to correct some common paycheck errors that may occur.

The Error	The Fix
You have to replace a paycheck that was lost or damaged	Reprint and reissue the check with the next check number; document the event by creating and then voiding a check
You find out that the pay period dates are wrong but still within the same calendar year	Edit the pay period dates in the Review Paycheck window and create a memo in the check register
You discover that an employee was overpaid	Correct the overpayment on the next payroll (rather than reissuing the paycheck)
You discover that an employee was underpaid	Issue an unscheduled payroll check or correct the underpayment on the next payroll
You realize that a paycheck item is incorrect and that the error will not affect the amount of the check	Edit the paycheck information while in Lock Net Pay mode

Depending on the type of payroll service you subscribe to, there may be limitations on how you will be able to correct certain payroll errors.

Making Corrections to a Payroll Liability Payment

Paying a payroll liability with a regular check rather than a liability check will create issues for you behind the scenes, as you learned about in Lesson 5, Correcting and Customizing in QuickBooks. To set things right, you need to void the regular check and then process the payment through the pay payroll liabilities feature in QuickBooks.

QUICK REFERENCE	DEALING WITH PAYROLL ERRORS
Task	**Procedure**
Replace a lost or damaged paycheck	Reissue the check: ■ Choose Banking→Use Register; choose the desired account. ■ Find the applicable check; record the check number and net pay amount. ■ Double-click the paycheck entry in the check register; click in the To be printed checkbox. ■ Click the print button at the top of the window (use the next check number). ■ Click Save & Close; close the register. Document the lost check: ■ Choose Banking→Write Checks. ■ Create a check using the same check number and day as the one that was lost, payable to the employee. ■ Enter the net amount from the original check; note in the memo field that this check was replaced. ■ Choose Payroll Expenses as the Account on the Expenses tab; click Save & Close. ■ Choose Banking→Use Register; choose the same account into which you just entered the check. ■ Right-click on the check that you just created using the lost check number and date; choose to Void Check.
Issue an unscheduled payroll check	■ Choose Employees→Pay Employees→Unscheduled Payroll. ■ Choose the employees for whom you wish to create a paycheck. ■ Create the paycheck(s) using the same procedure you used to issue scheduled paychecks.
Void a regular check and replace it with a payroll liabilities check	■ Open the Checking register, and locate the check you wish to void. ■ Right-click the check; choose Void Check. ■ Choose Employees→Process Payroll Liabilities→Pay Payroll Liabilities. ■ Set the date range for the liabilities to be paid; click OK. ■ Set the bank account and the check date. ■ Select the payroll liabilities you need to pay; click Create.

Fix Payroll Errors

In this exercise, you will help Zoe take care of two paycheck "issues." She first needs to replace the paycheck for Samuel Jameson and issue an unscheduled payroll check to Stephen Johnston for an underpayment on the paycheck just produced.

1. Click the **Check Register** task icon in the Banking area of the Home page.

2. Click **OK** to choose to **10100•Checking** as the account to use.

3. Scroll up until you see **Samuel Jameson's paycheck, 10083**; double-click anywhere within the transaction.
   The Paycheck – Checking window displays.

4. Write down the check number (**10083**) and net amount (**$1,029.33**) for future reference.

5. Follow these steps to reprint the check:

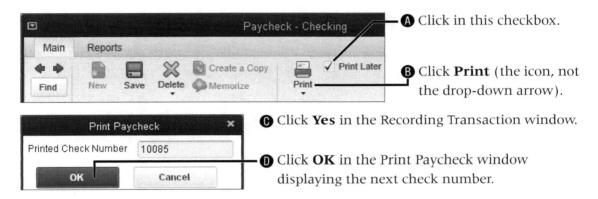

Ⓐ Click in this checkbox.

Ⓑ Click **Print** (the icon, not the drop-down arrow).

Ⓒ Click **Yes** in the Recording Transaction window.

Ⓓ Click **OK** in the Print Paycheck window displaying the next check number.

6. Ensure that the correct printer is selected (or choose to print to PDF), and then click **Print**.

7. Click **OK** in the Print Checks Confirmation window.
   This is the check you will give Samuel.

8. Click **Save & Close** in the Paycheck – Checking window.
   Leave the 10100•Checking register window open; you will need to use it again.

9. Choose **Banking→Write Checks**.

10. Click to choose for the check not to be printed later.

11. Follow these steps to create a check matching the one that was lost:

Ⓐ Enter **10083** as the No.   **Ⓑ** Tap [Tab], and then type **122914**.   **Ⓒ** Tap [Tab], type **sam**, and then **tap** [Tab] again.

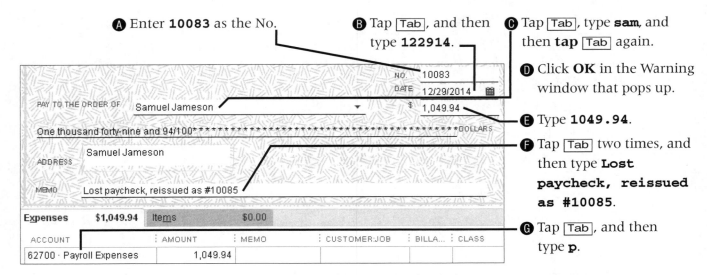

Ⓓ Click **OK** in the Warning window that pops up.

Ⓔ Type **1049.94**.

Ⓕ Tap [Tab] two times, and then type **Lost paycheck, reissued as #10085**.

Ⓖ Tap [Tab], and then type **p**.

12. Click **Save & Close**; click **Save Anyway** in the Items not assigned classes window.
You will be voiding the check in a moment, and the original transaction had a class assigned, so there is no reason to assign one here. The 10100•Checking window should be displayed.

13. Locate the check you just created (**10083**) in the 10100•Checking window, scrolling if necessary.

14. Right-click anywhere within the two lines of the **check 10083 transaction**, and then choose **Void Check**.
You will see VOID: preceding the memo you entered into the check, and the dollar amount will be zero.

15. Click **Record**; click **Yes** to record the transaction.

16. Click **No, just void the check**, and then close the **Checking register window**.

Issue an Unscheduled Payroll Check

To pay Stephen for the eight regular pay hours he worked, you will help Zoe create a special paycheck.

17. Click the **Payroll Center** task icon in the Employees area of the Home page.

18. Click the **Unscheduled Payroll** button in the Pay Employees area of the Payroll Center.

19. Follow these steps to create the paycheck for Stephen:

Ⓐ Type **123014**.   **Ⓑ** Tap [Shift]+[Tab], and then type **122914**.

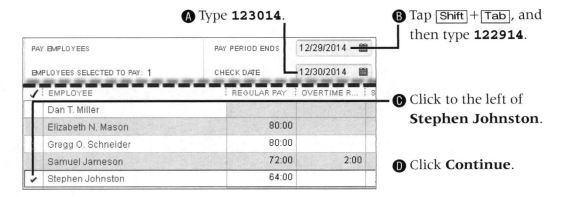

Ⓒ Click to the left of **Stephen Johnston**.

Ⓓ Click **Continue**.

20. Click **OK** in the window indicating some items may not have been assigned a class (you will assign it next).

21. Click on **Stephen Johnston's** name in the Review and Create Paychecks window.
The Preview Paycheck window appears with the Hours field selected.

22. Follow these steps to set up the paycheck:

Ⓐ Type **8**, and then tap Tab .   Ⓑ Click **OK** in the Special Calculation Situation window.   Ⓒ Click the **drop-down arrow**, and then choose **5645** for Carpentry.   Ⓓ Click the **drop-down arrow**, and then choose **Balak, Mike: Repair Deck**.

Ⓔ Click the **Class** drop-down arrow, and then choose **Remodel**.   Ⓕ Click in this **checkbox**.

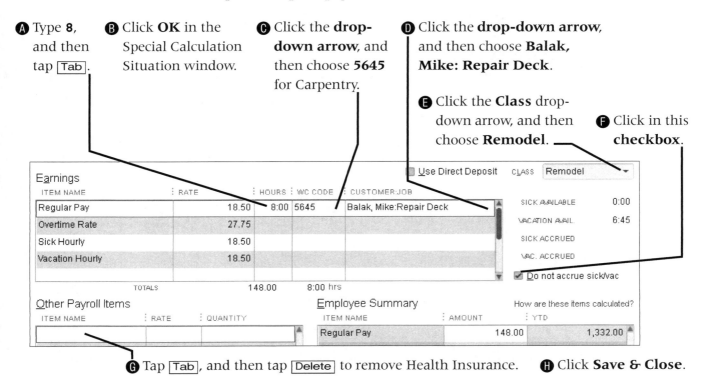

Ⓖ Tap Tab , and then tap Delete to remove Health Insurance.   Ⓗ Click **Save & Close**.

23. Click **Create Paychecks**.
The Confirmation and Next Steps window will be displayed.

24. Click **Print Paychecks**; click **OK** in the Select Paychecks to Print window.

BTS BRIEF

62700•Payroll Expenses DR 167.97; 24000•Payroll Liabilities CR <29.80>; 10100•Checking CR <138.17>

---

25. Ensure the correct printer is selected, and then click **Print**.

26. Click **OK** in the Print Checks – Confirmation window, and then close the **Confirmation and Next Steps** window.

27. Close the **Employee Center: Payroll Center**.

Working with 1099s and Processing Payroll Forms and Reports

The forms you are able to produce through QuickBooks depend on the payroll option you select. Look at a few basic payroll forms used in the United States and how QuickBooks supports each of them. If you live in Canada, check out www.quickbooks.ca to learn about payroll solutions and Intuit products available for the Canadian market.

W-2s and W-3s

W-2s are provided to each employee. They summarize earnings and deductions for the year. A W-3 form is what you prepare and submit to the government. It summarizes the W-2 information you provided to employees.

If you subscribe to one of the Enhanced payroll services you can print W-2s and W-3s on blank paper right from QuickBooks. If you subscribe to the Payroll Assisted Service, QuickBooks will provide the completed forms to you.

If you have chosen the Basic payroll service or will manually run payroll in QuickBooks, you can still purchase blank W-2 and W-3 forms and print them in QuickBooks.

940 and 941

Form 941 is the Employer's Quarterly Federal Tax Return. QuickBooks will fill in the appropriate amounts. You can edit the amounts if the IRS rules instruct you to do so.

Form 940 is the Employer's Annual Federal Unemployment (FUTA) Tax Return. QuickBooks stores forms for only one year at a time. You will need to subscribe to a payroll service to download the correct year's form. QuickBooks will fill in the appropriate amounts, which you can edit if necessary.

1099-MISC and 1096

When you have vendors who you subcontract work to, you will report their earnings on a 1099-MISC form that is provided to them. The 1096 form is something you prepare for the federal government. It summarizes the 1099 information you provided to subcontractors.

If you subscribe to the Enhanced payroll service, you can print 1099-MISC forms for your subcontractors right from QuickBooks. If you subscribe to the Payroll Assisted Service, Intuit will prepare the 1099-MISC forms for you.

If you have chosen the Basic payroll service or will manually run payroll in QuickBooks, you can purchase 1099-MISC and 1096 forms and print them in QuickBooks.

Before you can run 1099-MISC forms, you must turn on the preference in QuickBooks and properly set up your 1099 vendors. A wizard will walk you through 1099 and 1096 form preparation and filing.

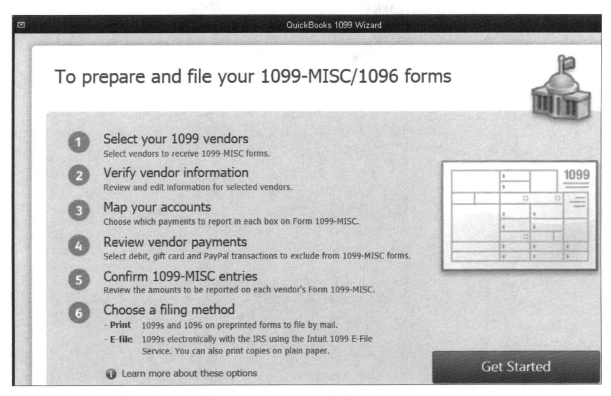

The QuickBooks 1099 Wizard walks you through form preparation and filing.

 Tab: Other Topics
Topic: File payroll tax forms

Other Payroll Reports

In addition to the reports you have already seen that deal with payroll, QuickBooks provides a variety of additional reports, including a number of them that can be run in Excel. All of these reports can be found in the Employees & Payroll category in the Report Center.

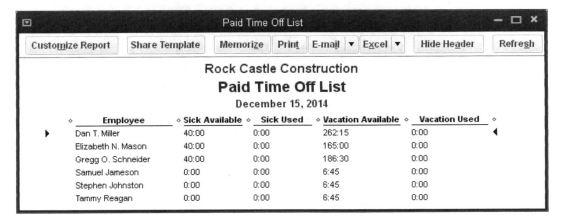

The Paid Time Off List report is just one report available when you use QuickBooks for payroll. It shows the amount of sick and vacation hours both available to and used by employees.

QUICK REFERENCE	PROCESSING PAYROLL FORMS
Task	**Procedure**
Turn on the 1099 preference	■ Choose Edit→Preferences. ■ Click the Tax:1099 category, and then the Company Preferences tab. ■ Click to choose Yes, that you file 1099-MISC forms; click OK.
Produce annual W-2 and W-3 reports	■ Choose Employees→Payroll Forms→Process Payroll Forms. ■ Click in the circle to the left of Federal Form; click OK. ■ Click Annual Form W-2/W-3 and enter the year for which you wish to create the forms; click OK. ■ Select the employees for whom you wish to produce W-2s, and then click the Review/Edit button so you can make sure the information is correct before printing. Continue to click Next through the screens displaying the company and employee W-2 information. ■ After reviewing the W-2s, click Next to view the W-3 form; click Next to view the Filing and Printing Instructions. ■ Check to make sure there are no errors; click Submit Form. ■ Use perforated paper or preprinted forms in the printer and choose to print the W-2s. ■ Choose to print the W-3 form.
Produce 1099-MISC and 1096 forms	■ Choose Vendors→Print 1099s/1096. ■ Work through the first three steps of 1099 production. ■ Click the Print 1099s button and specify the date range; click OK. ■ Click Print 1099 and ensure your printer settings are correct; click Print. ■ Click the Print 1096 button; enter your contact information. ■ Preview how the form will print; click Print.
Produce Form 940	■ Choose Employees→Payroll Forms→Process Payroll Forms. ■ Click in the circle to the left of Federal Form; click OK. ■ Click Annual Form 940/940EZ and enter the year; click OK. ■ Follow the series of steps to verify your data and print the forms.
Produce Form 941 and Schedule B	■ Choose Employees→Payroll Forms→Process Payroll Forms;. ■ Click in the circle to the left of Federal Form; click OK. ■ Click Annual Form 941/Schedule B, set the filing period, and then click OK. ■ Follow the series of steps to verify your data and print the forms.
Make adjustments to W-2 and 941 forms	■ Right-click the box that requires an adjustment; choose Override from the pop-up menu.
Produce a Paid Time Off List report	■ Choose Reports→Employees & Payroll→Paid Time Off List. ■ Set the correct date range.

Run 1099 Forms and W-2s

In this exercise, you will help Zoe print 1099-MISC forms for the subcontractors and W-2s for the employees for the 2014 tax year.

1. Choose **Vendors→Print/E-file 1099s→1099 Wizard**.
   The QuickBooks 1099 Wizard will launch.

2. Click the **Get Started** button.
   You will be asked to select your 1099 vendors.

3. Click **Continue** five times.
   You will move through several screens. Make sure to look at each as you continue through the wizard.

4. Click **Print 1099s**.

5. Choose **This Calendar Year** as the date range, and then click **OK**.
   The Select 1099s to Print window will appear.

6. Click the **Preview 1099** button, page through the forms, and then close the Print Preview window.

View the 1096 Form Which Is Submitted to the Government

The 1096 Form is what you provide to the government. It summarizes the information contained in all of the 1099s you issued.

7. Click the **Print 1096** button.

8. Type your name in the **Contact Name** field, and then click **OK**.

9. Click **Preview** to see how the form will print, and then close the **Print Preview** window.

10. Click **Cancel** in the Print 1096 window, close the **Select 1099s to Print** window, and then save and close the **QuickBooks 1099 Wizard** window.

Prepare to Print W-2s for Employees and a W-3 for the Government

You will wrap up employee payroll for the year next by producing W-2s for employees and then a W-3 for the government.

11. Click the **Process Payroll Forms** task icon in the Employees area of the Home page.

12. Click **OK** in the Select Form Type window to choose the default of **Federal** form.

13. Follow these steps to prepare to issue W-2s:

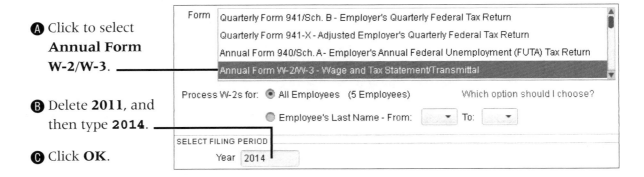

Ⓐ Click to select **Annual Form W-2/W-3**.

Ⓑ Delete **2011**, and then type **2014**.

Ⓒ Click **OK**.

14. Click **OK** in the Warning window, as we will work with the 2011 form for instructional purposes. Make sure you always have an up-to-date payroll service and forms when you do your own company's payroll!
The Payroll Tax Form window and the Select Employees for Form W-2/W-3 launch.

15. Click the **Review/Edit** button in the Select Employees for Form W-2/W-3 window.
Now you can see the Payroll Tax Form window a bit better. Notice that it functions as an interview, walking you through a series of steps to produce the W-2s and W-3.

Verify and Modify Company and Employee Information

16. Click **Next**; verify the company information in the next screen.
Since Zoe is doing all of the bookkeeping for Rock Castle now, she will replace Alan's name with her own.

17. Right-click **Alan Sun** in the Contact person field, and then choose **Override**.

18. Type **Zoe Minch**, and then tap Tab.

19. Click the **Next** button; take a look at the W-2 information for **Samuel**.

20. Click the **Next** button five more times, viewing each employee's information along the way.
You will now see a checklist that you can print and use for your own records, if you wish.

21. Click **Next**; take a look at the **W-3 form information** that is displayed.

22. Click **Next**; view the **Filing and Printing Instructions** that are displayed.

23. Click **Submit Form**, choosing to **Skip** viewing the errors.
Obviously, when working with your own company file, you would work through each error. The errors in this case are due to the fact that we are using a sample file and tax forms for an incorrect year.

Print W-2s

24. Click the **Print** button; click **Yes** in the Warning window.

25. Place the correct perforated paper in your printer, and then click the **Print** button to print the W-2 forms for your employees. (Print to PDF, if applicable.)
If you need to change the printer settings, you would click the Printer Setup button before clicking Print.

Print W-3

26. Click in the circle to the left of **W-3, 1 per page**, and then click **Print**.
This will print the form you need to file with the federal government for you.

27. Close the **Print W-2 and W-3 forms** window.

28. Click **Save & Close** in the Payroll Tax Form window; click **OK** in the Next Steps window.

29. When you are finished learning about Working with an Outside Payroll Service, choose the appropriate option for your situation:
   - If you are continuing on to the next lesson or to the end-of-lesson exercises, leave QuickBooks open.
   - If you are finished working in QuickBooks for now, choose **File→Exit**.

Working with an Outside Payroll Service

Some companies choose to go with an outside payroll service. If this is the case, you still need to enter the information into QuickBooks so you can create meaningful financial statements. The level of information you track in QuickBooks does not have to be as detailed when you use an outside service.

Information to Track

You will not need to worry about setting QuickBooks up for payroll or using the payroll features of the software, since you are not tracking specific withholdings and deductions. Your intent when working with an outside service is to track expenses, cash flow, and balances being held in liability accounts so that your balance sheet, profit & loss, and cash flow reports are accurate.

Do not turn on the QuickBooks payroll features to track payroll from an outside source.

Track Employees

You should enter your employees into the Employees List in QuickBooks. You will not need to enter information on the Payroll and Compensation Info tab, though, as that will be tracked by the service.

Track Expenses

To account for the payroll expenses for your company, you will need to set up an expense account, such as Payroll Expenses, and appropriate subaccounts for each type of payroll expense. Examples of subaccounts that you may wish to create are Gross Wages, Company-Paid Taxes, and Company-Paid Benefits.

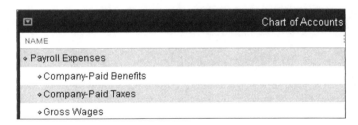

Notice the subaccounts that are set up for Payroll Expenses and used to track information from an outside payroll service.

Track Liabilities

You will still be holding deductions and withdrawals from employees that have to be paid to the appropriate agency at some time in the future. This means that you need to set up an Other Current Liability account, such as Payroll Liabilities, to track this information.

Enter Information from the Outside Service into QuickBooks

When you receive a report from the payroll service that shows the payroll activity for your company, you will need to enter it in to QuickBooks. You will see payments going to employees and then out to the agencies for which you are currently holding funds in the Payroll Liabilities account.

Enter Employee Paychecks

Employee paychecks should be entered in the Write Checks window since you are not worried about keeping the "other set of books" for payroll in QuickBooks. You will enter gross wages on the first line of the Expenses tab. All deductions will be entered on the second line with a minus sign and will flow to the Payroll Liabilities account.

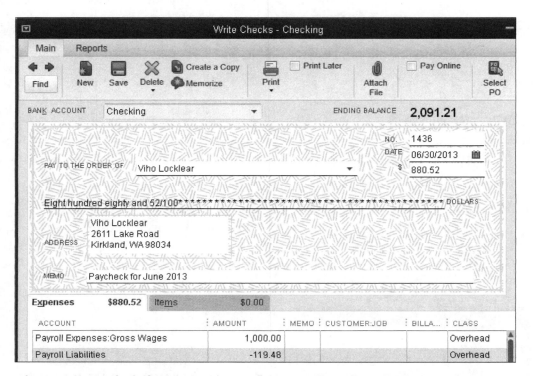

When entering paychecks from an outside payroll service, you use the Write Checks window and enter the gross wages as a positive amount and the payroll liabilities as a negative amount.

Enter Tax and Benefit Payments

When you use an outside payroll service, you will also use the Write Checks window to enter payments when you pay the payroll liabilities. On the Expense tab, you will enter the employee-paid taxes/deductions being held in Payroll Liabilities. Company-paid taxes and benefits will be entered on separate lines using the appropriate Payroll Expenses subaccounts.

Remember that, in this section, what we are talking about applies *only* when a company is using an outside payroll service! You should *never* use the Write Checks window for payroll transactions if you are completing your own payroll in QuickBooks!

QUICK REFERENCE	USING AN OUTSIDE PAYROLL SERVICE WITH QUICKBOOKS
Task	**Procedure**
Set up to track payroll expenses	■ Choose Lists→Chart of Accounts. ■ Set up the following expense account: Payroll Expenses. ■ Set up the following subaccounts for Payroll Expenses: Gross Wages, Company-Paid Taxes, and Company-Paid Benefits.
Set up to track payroll liabilities	■ Choose Lists→Chart of Accounts. ■ Inactivate the Payroll Liabilities account that was created for you. ■ Set up the following other current liability account: Payroll Liabilities-OS.
Enter an employee paycheck from an outside payroll service	■ Choose Banking→Write Checks. ■ Set the date of the check and fill in the employee in the Pay to the Order of field. ■ Enter the amount of the check. ■ On the Expenses tab, enter the total wages on the first line using the Payroll Expenses:Gross Wages account. ■ On the second line of the Expenses tab, enter the total taxes and deductions held from the employee's gross wages as a negative number using the Payroll Liabilities account.
Enter tax and benefit payments	■ Choose Banking→Write Checks. ■ Set the date of the check; fill in the vendor to whom you are paying the taxes or benefits in the Pay to the Order of field. ■ Enter the amount of the check. ■ On the Expenses tab, enter the employee deductions being paid on one line using Payroll Liabilities as the account. ■ On a separate line of the Expenses tab, enter the company-paid portion of the taxes or benefits using the appropriate subaccount, either Payroll Expenses:Company – Paid Taxes or Payroll Expenses Company – Paid Benefits.

 You will have the opportunity to work with an outside payroll service in the Apply Your Skills exercise at the end of this lesson since payroll is already set up for Rock Castle Construction.

Concepts Review

Concepts Review	http://labyrinthelab.com/qb13-level02

To check your knowledge of the key concepts introduced in this lesson, complete the Concepts Review quiz by going to the URL listed above.

Reinforce Your Skills

Before you begin the Reinforce Your Skills exercises, restore **Ginger's Gift Shop, Lesson 2 (Portable)** *from your file storage location.*

To complete payroll exercises in QuickBooks, we will be leaving Susie and Tea Shoppe at the Lake and switching to a QuickBooks sample file for Ginger's Gift Shop, which is also run as a sole proprietorship. This company file will always assume that the current date is 12/15/14, just as you have experienced with Rock Castle Construction.

REINFORCE YOUR SKILLS 2.1
Enter a New Employee

In this exercise, you will help add a new employee that Ginger just hired.

1. Choose **Employees→Employee Center**.
   The Employee Center will be displayed with three current employees.

2. Click the **New Employee** button.

3. Use the following information to set up Aiyana Harrison as a new employee.

Name	**Ms. Aiyana Harrison**
Address	**503 Oregon Place** **Bayshore, CA 92333**
Phone	**415-555-2134**
SS No.	**999-88-6666**
Gender	**Female**
Date of Birth	**04/13/86**
Hourly/Sick/Vacation Rate	**20.00**
Overtime Rate	**30.00**
Filing Status and Allowances	**Single, 0**
Vacation and Sick Leave	Use defaults

4. Close the **Employee Center** window.

Create Paychecks for Employees

In this exercise, you will create a paycheck for all of the employees for the period of 12/16/14–12/31/14.

1. Choose **Employees→Payroll Center**.

2. Click the **Pay Employees** button in the Pay Employees area of the Payroll Center.
   No scheduled payrolls have been set up for this company, so there is no Unscheduled Payroll button. Instead, you see a Pay Employees button.

3. Set the **Check Date** and the **Pay Period Ends** date both to **12/31/2014**.

4. Click the **Check All** button to choose to pay all employees; then, click **Aiyana Harrison's** name.
   The Preview Paycheck window for Aiyana appears.

5. Type **63** as the number of hours for Aiyana at the Hourly Regular Rate, and then tap Tab.
   Notice that all of the payroll tax information fills in for you once you move to the next field. You have no other entries for Aiyana, so her paycheck information is complete.

6. Click **Save & Next**.
   In this case, you are viewing the paycheck information for a salaried employee.

7. Click **Save & Next** two more times to view the paycheck information for the rest of the employees.
   Notice that QuickBooks fills in the information from the previous paycheck for you.

8. Change the number of hours worked by Regina French to **55**, and then click **Save & Close**.

Create and Print Paychecks

You will now review the information entered for each employee, and then create the paychecks.

9. Click **Continue**.
   The Review and Create Paychecks window will be displayed.

10. Click **Create Paychecks**.
    The Confirmation and Next Steps window will appear, showing a summary of how many paychecks were created as well as providing you with a shortcut to printing paychecks and pay stubs.

11. Click **Print Paychecks**, tap Tab, and then type **10733** as the First Check Number.

12. Click **OK** in the Select Paychecks to Print window; then, follow the desired step, depending on whether you wish to physically print the paychecks:

    ■ Click **Print**, and then retrieve the printout from the printer. You can also choose this option if you wish to print the checks as an electronic PDF file. Click **OK** to verify that all checks printed correctly.

    ■ Print choosing ***.pdf** as the printer, and then choose where to save the PDF file. Click **OK** to verify that all checks printed correctly.

13. Click the **Print Pay Stubs** button.

14. Tap `Tab`, type **123114**, tap `Tab` again, and then type **123114** (if necessary).

15. Click **Preview** to view how the pay stubs will print, and then close the **Print Preview** window.

16. Close the **Select Pay Stubs** window and the **Confirmation and Next Steps** window.

17. Close the **Payroll Center**.

REINFORCE YOUR SKILLS 2.3
Pay the Payroll Liabilities

In this exercise, you will pay all of the payroll liabilities due in January 2015.

1. Choose **Employees→Payroll Taxes and Liabilities→Pay Scheduled Liabilities**.

2. Click to the left of the two liability payments due in **January** to place checkmarks.

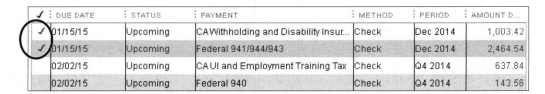

✓	DUE DATE	STATUS	PAYMENT	METHOD	PERIOD	AMOUNT D...
✓	01/15/15	Upcoming	CA Withholding and Disability Insur...	Check	Dec 2014	1,003.42
✓	01/15/15	Upcoming	Federal 941/944/943	Check	Dec 2014	2,464.54
	02/02/15	Upcoming	CA UI and Employment Training Tax	Check	Q4 2014	637.84
	02/02/15	Upcoming	Federal 940	Check	Q4 2014	143.56

3. Click the **View/Pay** button in the Pay Scheduled Liabilities area of the Payroll Center. *A Liability Payment – Checking window will be displayed for the first payment.*

4. Change the date to **12/31/14**, and then click **Save & Next** to view the next payment.

5. Change the date to **12/31/14**, and then click **Save & Close** to record the liability check.

6. Close the **Payment Summary** window, and then close the **Payroll Center**.

Process Form 941

In this exercise, you will follow the steps to produce the required Form 941 for Ginger's Gift Shop for this quarter.

1. Choose **Employees→Payroll Tax Forms & W-2s→Process Payroll Forms**.

2. Click **OK** to choose to prepare Federal forms.

3. Click **Quarterly Form 941/Sch. B**, set the filing period to **This Calendar Quarter ending 12/31/2014**, and then click **OK**.

4. Click **OK** in the Warning window.

5. Click **Next**.

6. Click **Submit Form**; click **Skip** in the Warning window.

You will receive warnings for a variety of reasons. You will skip them in this instance, but if there are errors discovered in your own company's federal tax forms, you must take the time to resolve them!

7. Click **Close** in the Submit Form window, close the **Payroll Tax Form** window, and then click **OK** in the Next Steps window.

8. Choose the appropriate option for your situation:

   ■ If you are continuing on to the next lesson or the rest of the end-of-lesson exercises, leave QuickBooks open.

   ■ If you are finished working in QuickBooks for now, choose **File→Exit**.

Apply Your Skills

Before you begin the Apply Your Skills exercises, complete one of these options:

- *Open* **[Your name] Wet Noses Veterinary Clinic, Lesson 1** *or* **Wet Noses Veterinary Clinic, Lesson 2** *from your file storage location.*

- *Restore* **Wet Noses Veterinary Clinic, Lesson 2 (Portable)** *from your file storage location. Make sure to place your name as the first word in the company filename (e.g., Sadie's Wet Noses Veterinary Clinic, Lesson 2).*

APPLY YOUR SKILLS 2.1

Set Up QuickBooks to Track Payroll from an Outside Service

Dr. James has been using an outside payroll service. In this exercise, you will help her verify that the correct accounts are set up to track expenses and liabilities properly. Then you will enter a new employee. You will need to have accounts set up in your Chart of Accounts to track your payroll expenses and liabilities.

The QuickBooks payroll features should not be turned on when entering payroll from an outside source.

1. Open the **Chart of Accounts**.

2. Verify that **Payroll Liabilities** is set up as an **Other Current Liability**.

3. Scroll down, and then verify that **Payroll Expenses** is set up as an **Expense** account.
   Dr. James has learned that she should set up subaccounts for the Payroll Expenses account, so you will help her to do this now.

4. Set up three subaccounts for Payroll Expenses: **Gross Wages**, **Company-Paid Taxes**, and **Company-Paid Benefits**.

Enter a New Employee

When you are entering a new employee and using an outside payroll service, you do not need to set up tax information.

5. Create a new employee for Wet Noses using the following information.

Name	Mr. Viho Locklear
Address	2611 Lake Road Kirkland, WA 98034
Phone	425-555-1066
SS No.	111-33-5555
Gender	Male
Date of Birth	04/24/83

6. Close the **Employee Center** window.

Create Paychecks Based on Information from an Outside Payroll Service

Dr. James has received a statement from the payroll service showing the amount to pay each employee (see below) and the amount that has been deducted. In this exercise, you will help her create the paychecks for the employees.

WET NOSES VETERINARY CLINIC JUNE 2013 PAYROLL

Employee	Gross Wages	Employee Federal Taxes Withheld	Net Pay	Company Federal Taxes Owed	Company Benefits Owed
Bentley Batson	$1,500.00	$234.62	$1,265.38	$174.55	$450.00
Carrie Jones	$2,166.00	$395.72	$1,770.28	$243.19	$450.00
Samantha Reese	$2,166.00	$324.21	$1,841.79	$228.61	$450.00
Viho Locklear	$1,000.00	$119.48	$880.52	$87.37	$225.00
Totals	$6,832.00	$1,074.03	$5,757.97	$733.72	$1,575.00

1. Create paychecks for the employees listed above dated 6/30/2013 using the Write Checks window. Look at the example below as a hint regarding how to create the checks.

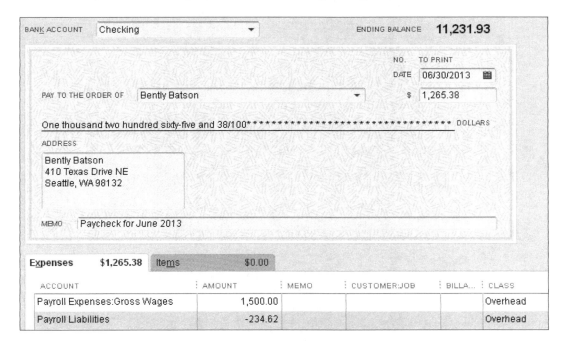

Remember, you only use the Write Checks window to create paychecks if you use an outside payroll service. *Never* use it if you are running payroll through QuickBooks!

Pay the Payroll Liabilities and Print Checks

In this exercise, you will use the information in the table shown in Apply Your Skills 2.2 to create a payroll liability check for June 2013.

1. Open the Write Checks window, and then set the date to 6/30/2013.

2. Create a liability check to the U.S. Treasury (Quick Add as a vendor) for all federal taxes owed. Use the illustration below as a guide.

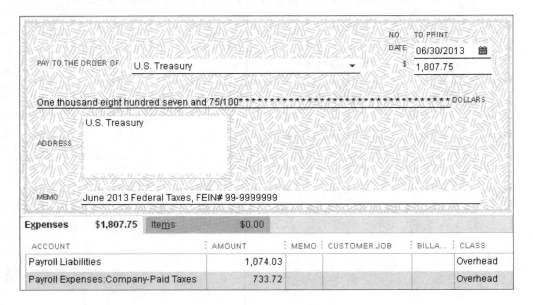

ACCOUNT	AMOUNT	MEMO	CUSTOMER:JOB	BILLA...	CLASS
Payroll Liabilities	1,074.03				Overhead
Payroll Expenses:Company-Paid Taxes	733.72				Overhead

3. Create a second check dated 6/30/2013, made payable to Kellerman Insurance, for the company-paid medical benefits owed.

4. Enter June 2013 Medical/Dental Insurance for Employees as the Memo, Company-Paid Benefits subaccount as the Account, and Overhead as the Class.

5. Choose to print all checks in the queue waiting to be printed, using 1431 as the first check number.

Answer Questions and Correct Information with Reports

In this exercise, you will answer questions for Dr. James by running reports. You may wish to display the Report Center in List View to help you answer the questions. Ask your instructor if you should print the reports, print (save) them as PDF files, export them to Excel, or simply display them on the screen.

1. How much has been paid in payroll to each employee? (Hint: Use a Quick Report for the Checking account, and then filter by Name, choosing All Employees.) Leave this report open for the next step.

   As you are creating this report, you realize that you just set up the Payroll Expenses subaccounts and that the 5/31/2013 payroll checks did not use the correct account. You will use QuickZoom to change the account on each of the three checks from 5/31/2013.

2. Double-click on each of the 5/31/2013 checks, using QuickZoom to open the transaction in the Write Checks window, and change the Payroll Expenses account to Payroll Expenses:Gross Wages, as indicated in the following illustration. Save the transactions without a class (you did not begin class tracking until after May).

Expenses	$1,265.38	Items	$0.00	
ACCOUNT		AMOUNT		MEMO
Payroll Expenses:Gross Wages		1,500.00		
Payroll Liabilities		-234.62		

3. How much was paid in Gross Wages from 5/1/2013–6/30/2013?

4. Would it be possible for you to print a list of all of the employees with their name, phone number, and address? Please make sure there is no information such as social security number or birthday displayed on the list, for privacy reasons. After the report is displayed, you notice that phone numbers were not entered for three employees. Using QuickZoom, add the following phone numbers to the employee records:

   - Bently Batson (206) 555-8789
   - Carrie Jones (425) 555-2052
   - Samantha Reese (425) 555-1742

5. Submit your reports based on the guidelines provided by your instructor.

6. Choose the appropriate option for your situation:

   - If you are continuing on to the next lesson or the Critical Thinking exercises, leave QuickBooks open.
   - If you are finished working in QuickBooks for now, choose **File→Exit**.

Critical Thinking

In the course of working through the following Critical Thinking exercises, you will be utilizing various skills taught in this and previous lesson(s). Take your time and think carefully about the tasks presented to you. Turn back to the lesson content if you need assistance.

2.1 Sort Through the Stack

Before You Begin: Restore the **Monkey Business, Lesson 2 (Portable)** file from your storage location. (Remember that you are to leave the password field blank for Mary.) You also have the option of opening either the final file from Critical Thinking 1.1 or Monkey Business, Lesson 2 from your storage location.

You have been hired by Mary Minard to help her with her organization's books. She is the owner of Monkey Business, a nonprofit organization that provides low-income students with help in preparing for college placement exams and applying for scholarships. You have just sat down at her desk and found a pile of papers. It is your job to sort through the papers and make sense of what you find, entering information into QuickBooks whenever appropriate and answering any other questions in a word-processing document saved as **Critical Thinking 2.1**. Remember, you are digging through papers on a desk, so it is up to you to determine the correct order in which to complete the tasks.

- Sticky note from Mary: Hired two part-time employees to provide training on 7/31/2013. Will use an outside payroll service. How will we enter the payroll information into QuickBooks? (Explain your answer.)

- Completed W-4 and I-9: Chelsea Sathrum; 8213 NW College Ct., Salem, OR, 97304; 503-555-2003; SS# 111-22-3333; Female; DOB 05/21/1988.

- Sticky note from Mary: Please prepare a check to pay all federal payroll liabilities that are owed. The amount in Payroll Liabilities that is owed to the U.S. Treasury is $80, but don't forget to pay the company's share!

- Note from accountant: Enter the accounts and subaccounts necessary to track an outside payroll service in QuickBooks.

- Statement from payroll service, dated 8/15/2013.

MONKEY BUSINESS AUGUST 15, 2013 PAYROLL					
Employee	Gross Wages	Employee Federal & State Taxes Withheld	Net Pay	Company Federal Taxes Owed	Company Unemployment Owed
Andy Martinez	$450.00	$78.00	$372.00	$34.42	$16.28
Chelsea Sathrum	$420.00	$48.71	$371.29	$32.13	$15.35

- Completed W-4 and I-9: Andy Martinez; 16932 SE Freedom Way, Salem, OR 97306; SS# 333-22-1111; Male; DOB 07/04/1987.

- Scribbled note from Mary: Can you produce a report for me that shows how much has been paid in payroll for each employee?

2.2 Tackle the Tasks

Now is your chance to work a little more with Rock Castle Construction and apply the skills that you have learned in this lesson to accomplish additional tasks. Open or restore the **Critical Thinking 2.2** company or portable company file from your file storage location, or open the company file you used in the Develop Your Skills exercises for this lesson. Then, enter the following tasks.

Add an employee	Add the following new employee:
	Tammy Reagan; 14896 Highridge Estates, Bayshore, CA 94326; 415-555-4004; SS# 333-22-1111; Female; DOB 6/17/1969; Hourly, sick, and vacation rate $20; Overtime rate $30; Filing status-Single with one exemption; Health insurance $25/paycheck.
Process a paycheck	Create a paycheck for Tammy as an unscheduled payroll for the pay period ending 12/29/2014. Date the paycheck 12/31/2014 for 56 hours of work, using Overhead as the Class, and 8810-Clerical as the WC Code.
Print a paycheck and pay stub	Print the paycheck you just created for Tammy; print a pay stub to go with it.
Pay liabilities	Run a Payroll Liabilities Report for December 2014 to view what is currently being held. Pay the payroll liabilities from Tammy's check as well as the extra paycheck that you issued Stephen that are due anytime in January 2015 on 12/31/2014.
Run a report	Create a report showing all of your employees and their withholding information.
Create a W-2	Create a W-2 for Tammy for the time worked in 2014.

You may use the company file from this exercise for the Develop Your Skills exercises in the next lesson if you wish.

2.3 Use the Web as a Learning Tool

Throughout this book, you will be provided with an opportunity to use the Internet as a learning tool by completing WebQuests. According to the original creators of WebQuests, as described on their website (WebQuest.org), a WebQuest is "an inquiry-oriented activity in which most or all of the information used by learners is drawn from the web." To complete the WebQuest projects in this book, navigate to the student resource center and choose the WebQuest for the lesson on which you are currently working. The subject of each WebQuest will be relevant to the material found in the lesson.

WebQuest Subject: Researching payroll regulations and determining the best payroll option

Working with Estimates and Time Tracking

LESSON OUTLINE

Creating an Estimate for a Job
Converting an Estimate to an Invoice
Dealing with Customer Deposits
Using QuickBooks' Time-Tracking and Mileage
    Features
Using Time-Tracking Hours to Create a Paycheck
Assessing Finance Charges
Reporting for Estimates, Time Tracking, and
    Mileage
Concepts Review
Reinforce Your Skills
Apply Your Skills
Critical Thinking

LESSON OBJECTIVES

After studying this lesson, you will be able to:

- Create an estimate for a job or customer and convert it to a progress invoice
- Apply the time-tracking feature and create a paycheck based on tracked time
- Work with customer deposits on account
- Assign finance charges to overdue accounts
- Work with reports for estimates and time tracking

QuickBooks allows you to create estimates for your jobs or for your customers if you don't have jobs assigned to them. Once you are awarded a job based on an estimate, QuickBooks makes it easy to convert the estimate to an invoice, saving you the time of having to reenter the information. Job costing is an important aspect for many businesses. In this lesson you will learn how to use jobs in QuickBooks to track profitability by those jobs. Also covered is the time-tracking feature, which allows you to track the time spent by each employee on each job. This feature allows you to track payroll expenses for each job much more accurately.

Rock Castle Construction

The president of Rock Castle Construction will be bidding for a job with the City of Bayshore to remodel the city's Lionello Community Center. Zoe has been asked to create an estimate in QuickBooks to be submitted with the bid.

Once the job is awarded, Zoe will need to convert the estimate to an invoice and bill the city for a portion of the amount using QuickBooks' progress invoicing feature. Zoe will receive the payment from the city and take some time to learn about how to deal with customer deposits for unearned income.

Time tracking allows a company to track employee time and create paychecks and invoices based on the data collected. You will look at how this QuickBooks feature works and help Zoe to create an invoice and a paycheck using the time data.

Finally, Zoe will assess finance charges for the customer and produce reports that will allow Alan to analyze job costing, estimate, and time-tracking data for the company.

You will continue to learn about the accounting cycle in this lesson, specifically the fourth step—how QuickBooks posts to ledger accounts.

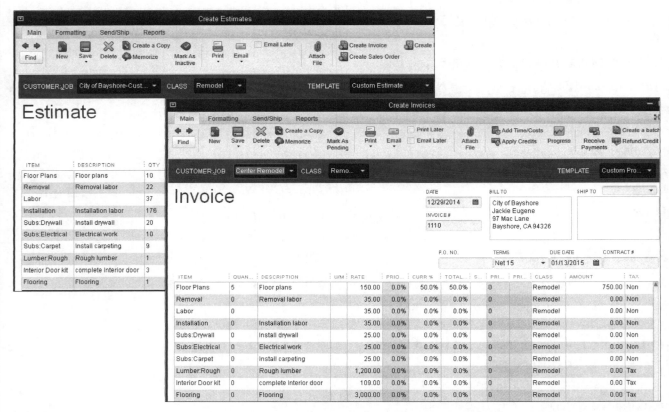

Notice that when you create a progress invoice from an estimate, the invoice includes all items on the estimate and shows the progress in regards to how much has been billed.

Creating an Estimate for a Job

When you create an estimate, QuickBooks creates a non-posting account that allows you to track your outstanding estimates. This account is displayed at the bottom of your Chart of Accounts. The non-posting account is created because estimates, like purchase orders, do not affect anything behind the scenes and, therefore, do not affect actual QuickBooks accounts.

You can create estimates for either customers or jobs. You can also create multiple estimates for a customer or a job. If a customer has no jobs created for it, there will be a Job Info tab available in the Edit Customer window with which you can work, but if at least one job has been created for a customer, that tab is no longer available. Before you can create any estimates, you must turn on the estimates feature in your Preferences window.

Job Costing in QuickBooks

In *QuickBooks Pro 2013: Level 1*, you learned that job information is stored with your customer data in the Customers & Jobs List, which is a component of the Customer Center. If you have multiple projects for an individual customer, you can create separate jobs for that customer. If you will perform just one job for a customer, you can track that information in the customer's record on the Job Info tab.

For Rock Castle Construction, all customers have a job associated with them, so you must always choose a job on a form, not just the customer.

FLASHBACK TO GAAP: MATCHING

Remember that expenses need to be matched with revenues. If a contractor buys a specific sink for a specific bathroom, it is matched to the cost of remodeling the bathroom. If there is no connection, then the cost may be charged as an expense to the project. This principle allows a better evaluation of the profitability and performance.

Preparing for Job Costing

For companies that deal with jobs, especially businesses such as construction companies, it is important to be able to look at the profitability of each job. To conduct job costing in Quick-Books, you need to take three basic steps.

1. Set up your data in the Customers & Jobs List.
2. Enter all job revenues and expenses.
3. Use QuickBooks reports to analyze job data.

The first two steps are covered as long as you set up your customers and jobs correctly and then enter them properly on sales and purchase forms. We will look at the job costing reports available in QuickBooks later in this lesson.

QUICK REFERENCE	CREATING AN ESTIMATE IN QUICKBOOKS
Task	**Procedure**
Add a job to a customer	■ Open the Customer Center; single-click the desired customer. ■ Click the New Customers & Jobs button; click Add Job. ■ Enter the information for the job; click OK.
Turn on estimating and progress invoicing	■ Choose Edit→Preferences. ■ Click the Jobs & Estimates category, and the Company Preferences tab. ■ Choose Yes to create estimates and do progress invoicing; click OK.
Create an estimate for a job	■ Choose Customers→Create Estimates. ■ Enter all of the information for the estimate; click Save & Close.

DEVELOP YOUR SKILLS 3.1

Create an Estimate

In this exercise, you will help Zoe create an estimate for a new customer. The first step is to open Quick-Books, and then either open a company file or restore a portable company file.

1. Start **QuickBooks 2013**.

   If you downloaded the student exercise files in the portable company file *format, follow Option 1 below. If you downloaded the files in the* company file *format, follow Option 2 below.*

If you choose, you may use the final company file from Critical Thinking 2.2. In this case, open the Critical Thinking 2.2 company file from your default storage location in Option 2 below.

Option 1: Restore a Portable Company File

2. Choose **File→Open or Restore Company**.

3. Restore the **Rock Castle Construction** portable file for this lesson from your file storage location, placing your name as the first word in the filename (e.g., Zoe's Rock Castle Construction, Lesson 3).

   It may take a few moments for the portable company file to open. Once it does, continue with step 4.

Option 2: Open a Company File

2. Choose **File→Open or Restore Company**, ensure that **Open a regular company file** is selected, and then open the **Rock Castle Construction** company file for this lesson from your file storage location.

   The QuickBooks company file will open.

3. Click **OK** to close the QuickBooks Information windows. If necessary, click **No** in the Set Up External Accountant User window.

Verify the Estimates and Progress Invoicing Preferences

Now you need to make sure that the preferences are set up correctly for Rock Castle to use estimates and progress invoicing.

4. Choose **Edit→Preferences**.

5. Follow these steps to turn on the estimates and progress invoicing features:

Ⓐ Click the **Jobs & Estimates** category.　　Ⓑ Click the **Company Preferences** tab.　　Ⓒ Verify that **Yes** is selected for both estimates and progress invoicing.　　Ⓓ Click **OK**.

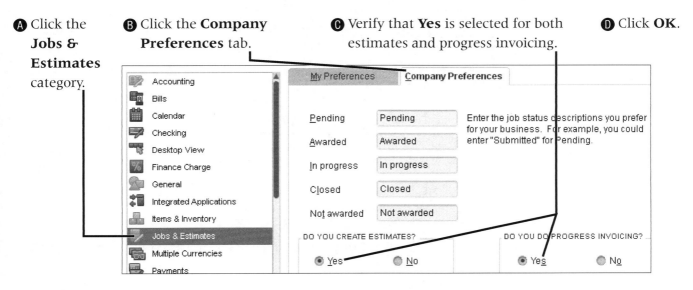

Create a New Customer

The City of Bayshore is not yet set up as a customer, so you will help Zoe create a new customer and a job for the customer.

6. Click the **Customers** button on the Icon Bar.

7. Tap Ctrl + n to open a New Customer window.

8. Type **City of Bayshore-Cust**, and then tap Tab three times.

The City of Bayshore is already an entry on the Vendors List and you cannot have the same name in multiple lists. Therefore, you need to modify how the name will be displayed in one list or the other. In this case, adding "-Cust" to the end will differentiate the customer and vendor list entries.

9. Follow these steps to create the new customer:

Ⓐ Type **City of Bayshore**.   **Ⓑ** Type this text, tapping Tab to move from field to field.

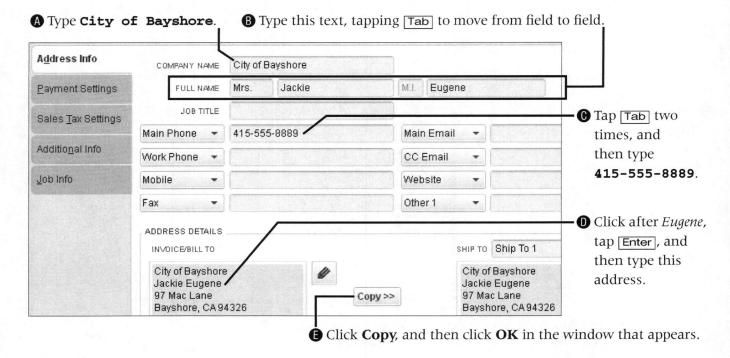

Ⓒ Tap Tab two times, and then type **415-555-8889**.

Ⓓ Click after *Eugene*, tap Enter, and then type this address.

Ⓔ Click **Copy**, and then click **OK** in the window that appears.

10. Click the **Payment Settings** tab, and then follow these steps to add information:

Ⓐ Click the **drop-down arrow**, and then choose **Net 15**.

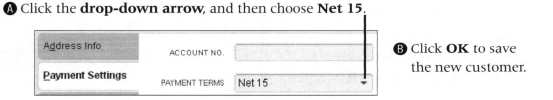

Ⓑ Click **OK** to save the new customer.

You will see your new customer displayed on the list; it is selected.

Create a New Job for the Customer

11. Click the **New Customer & Job** button, and then choose **Add Job**.

12. Follow these steps to add information for the new job:

A Type **Comm Center Remodel**.

B Click the **Job Info** tab.

C Type **Remodel Community Center** here.

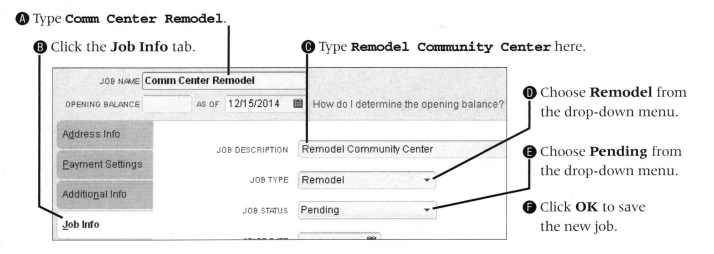

D Choose **Remodel** from the drop-down menu.

E Choose **Pending** from the drop-down menu.

F Click **OK** to save the new job.

JOB NAME Comm Center Remodel

OPENING BALANCE   AS OF 12/15/2014   How do I determine the opening balance?

Address Info

Payment Settings

Additional Info

Job Info

JOB DESCRIPTION Remodel Community Center

JOB TYPE Remodel

JOB STATUS Pending

Create an Estimate for a Job

The newly created job now appears in the Customers & Jobs List and is selected, ready for you to create a new transaction for it.

13. Click the **New Transactions** button, and then choose **Estimates**. *The Create Estimates window opens with the Community Center Remodel job already filled in.*

New Transactions ▼
Estimates

14. Follow these steps to complete the estimate:

A Tap ⌨Tab, and then type **r**.

B Tap ⌨Tab two times, and then type **122214**.

C Choose each **Item** listed, and then enter the **quantity** and **cost** displayed.

D Click **Save & Close**.

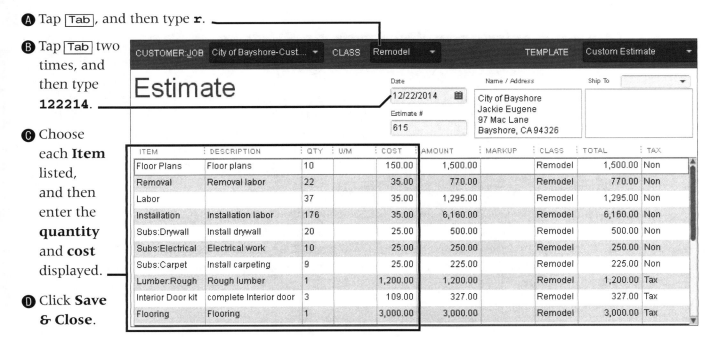

CUSTOMER:JOB City of Bayshore-Cust....   CLASS Remodel   TEMPLATE Custom Estimate

Estimate

Date 12/22/2014

Estimate # 615

Name / Address
City of Bayshore
Jackie Eugene
97 Mac Lane
Bayshore, CA 94326

Ship To

ITEM	DESCRIPTION	QTY	U/M	COST	AMOUNT	MARKUP	CLASS	TOTAL	TAX
Floor Plans	Floor plans	10		150.00	1,500.00		Remodel	1,500.00	Non
Removal	Removal labor	22		35.00	770.00		Remodel	770.00	Non
Labor		37		35.00	1,295.00		Remodel	1,295.00	Non
Installation	Installation labor	176		35.00	6,160.00		Remodel	6,160.00	Non
Subs:Drywall	Install drywall	20		25.00	500.00		Remodel	500.00	Non
Subs:Electrical	Electrical work	10		25.00	250.00		Remodel	250.00	Non
Subs:Carpet	Install carpeting	9		25.00	225.00		Remodel	225.00	Non
Lumber:Rough	Rough lumber	1		1,200.00	1,200.00		Remodel	1,200.00	Tax
Interior Door kit	complete Interior door	3		109.00	327.00		Remodel	327.00	Tax
Flooring	Flooring	1		3,000.00	3,000.00		Remodel	3,000.00	Tax

The estimate is created. Now you will wait to hear if you have been awarded the job before doing anything else with it. Remember that nothing happens behind the scenes here!

15. Close the **Customer Center**.

Converting an Estimate to an Invoice

QuickBooks makes it very easy for you to convert an estimate to an invoice once a job has been awarded. When you choose a customer or job with an existing estimate in the Create Invoices window, you have the opportunity to choose to create the invoice based on the estimate.

Progress Invoicing

QuickBooks allows you to invoice from an estimate in stages rather than for the entire estimate amount. You can either invoice a customer for the entire amount or for a percentage of the entire amount. You can even specify different percentages for each line item or which items to include. You must turn on the progress invoicing feature in the Preferences window before you can use it.

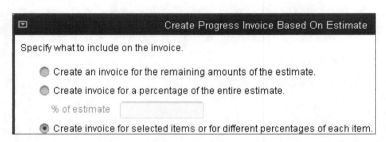

When the progress invoicing feature is turned on, you will see the Create Progress Invoice Based On Estimate window appear after you choose the estimate on which you will base an invoice.

Once you have chosen how much you wish to include on the invoice, you will see an invoice based on the Progress Invoice template. You will see new columns included on this invoice template: Est Amt, Prior Amt, and Total %.

Using Estimates for Change Orders

If you are using the contractor or accountant version of QuickBooks Premier, you can use estimates to track change orders. If you are using a different version, you can make changes to estimates, but they will not be called out as change orders. The change order feature will detail the amount of each change, exactly what changed, and the net change to the amount of the estimate. It will also document the change order for you in the description field of the estimate window.

Working with Sales Reps

For many businesses, being able to track sales by employee or representative is important, and QuickBooks provides a way to track this information by providing a Sales Rep List as one of the Customer & Vendor Profile Lists that you learned about in *QuickBooks Pro 2013: Level 1*. Sales Reps may be employees, a partner in the business, or independent contractors to whom you issue 1099s.

You will be creating a progress invoice based on the estimate for 50 percent of the design work on the floor plans. Take a look at the following T-accounts to see what is happening behind the scenes in this transaction.

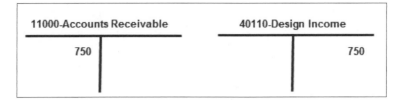

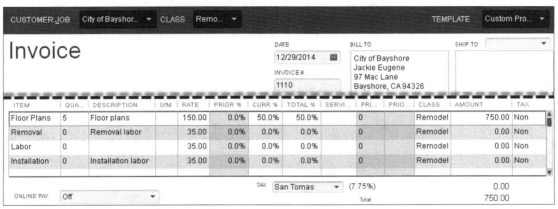

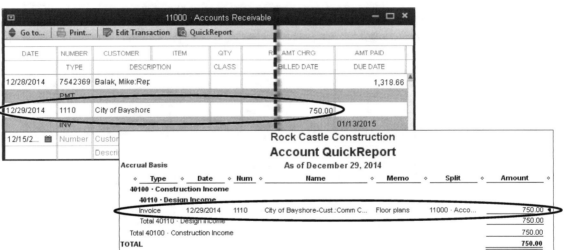

Notice that QuickBooks posted the journal entries that occurred behind the scenes when you created the invoice to the individual ledger accounts.

Task	Procedure
Use an estimate to create an invoice	■ Open the Create Invoices window; choose the desired customer/job.
	■ Select the desired estimate; choose whether to use progress invoicing.
	■ Enter any additional information, including selecting a price level if appropriate; click Save & Close.
Add a new sales rep	■ Choose Lists→Customer & Vendor Profile Lists→Sales Rep List.
	■ Click the Sales Rep menu button; choose New.
	■ Click the drop-down arrow; choose the name from the Vendors, Employees, or Other Names List.
	■ Enter the initials of the sales rep and the sales rep type; click OK.

DEVELOP YOUR SKILLS 3.2

Create a Progress Invoice Based on an Estimate

Zoe has just learned that Rock Castle Construction has been awarded the job for the remodel of the Community Center. In this exercise, you will update the job information and create a progress invoice based on the estimate. The first step is to open the Edit Job window for the Community Center Remodel and change the status of the job on the Job Info tab.

1. Click the **Customers** button on the Icon Bar.

2. Double-click the **Comm Center Remodel** job for the **City of Bayshore** to open it for editing.

3. Follow these steps to edit the job:

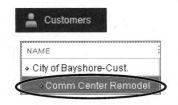

Ⓐ Click the **Job Info** tab.   Ⓑ Choose **Awarded** from the drop-down menu.

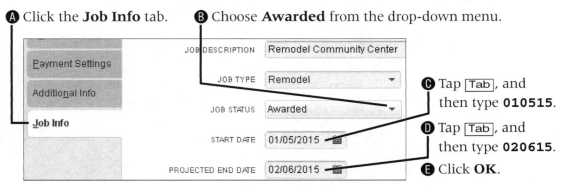

Ⓒ Tap ⟦Tab⟧, and then type **010515**.

Ⓓ Tap ⟦Tab⟧, and then type **020615**.

Ⓔ Click **OK**.

The Edit Job window closes after recording the changes to the job information.

4. Close the **Customer Center** window.

Create a Progress Invoice Based on an Estimate

Now you will create a progress invoice based on the estimate. Rock Castle will bill the city for 50 percent of the cost of the floor plans upfront.

5. Click the **Create Invoices** task icon in the Customers area of the Home page.

6. Choose the **Comm Center Remodel** job as the Customer:Job, and then tap ⟦Tab⟧. *The Available Estimates window appears, displaying all of the available estimates for the job.*

7. Single-click to select **Estimate 615** in the Available Estimates window, and then tap Enter .
   The Create Progress Invoice Based on Estimate window appears.

8. Click to the left of **Create invoice for selected items or for different percentages of each item**, and then click **OK**.

The Specify Invoice Amounts for Items on Estimate window appears.

9. Follow these steps to identify what should be included on the invoice:

Ⓐ Click in the checkbox to deselect **Show Quantity and Rate**.

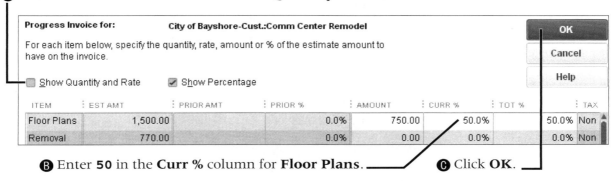

Ⓑ Enter **50** in the **Curr %** column for **Floor Plans**. ——— Ⓒ Click **OK**. ——

The Create Invoices window displays with 50 percent of the Floor Plans charge filled in for you.

10. Follow these steps to complete the invoice:

Ⓐ Click the **drop-down arrow** and choose **Custom Progress Invoice**. ——

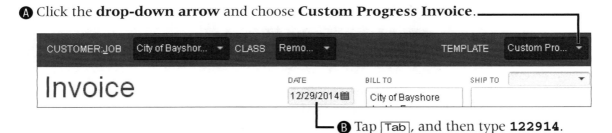

Ⓑ Tap Tab , and then type **122914**.

BTS BRIEF

11000•Accounts Receivable DR 750.00; 40110•Design Income CR <750.00>

11. Click **Save & Close**.
    The progress invoice is recorded. The next time you choose to create an invoice based off of the estimate for the Community Center Remodel job, the 50 percent that you just invoiced for will show as a prior amount.

Dealing with Customer Deposits

When you collect money from a customer as a deposit or sell a gift certificate, you need to record the receipt as unearned income, since no work has been performed and no product has been sold.

Unearned Income

If you receive funds before they are earned, they are considered unearned income or unearned revenue. You may also hear this called customer deposits or deferred revenue. You shouldn't credit unearned income to an income account. The proper way to deal with it is to hold it in a liability account such as Customer Deposits or Unearned Revenues. Once you have delivered the goods or performed the service, you can then decrease the liability account and credit, or increase, an income account.

Customer Deposits or Gift Certificates, Oh My!

No worries! Both customer deposits and gift certificates are tracked the same way in Quick-Books. And they both require you to go through the three steps of setting up, collecting, and recording. In this lesson, we will deal specifically with customer deposits, but you can apply the same principles if you need to account for gift certificates.

Set Up to Track Customer Deposits

The first step in dealing with unearned income is to set up an Other Current Liability account and two items (an Other Charge and a Payment type) because, by accepting a customer deposit or a payment for a gift certificate, you essentially are accepting the liability to turn the deposit into a payment or to redeem the gift certificate for goods or services. By setting up a liability account, you will be able to show that you are holding the funds in a separate account until the income becomes "earned."

Receiving a Customer Deposit

You will use an invoice to record the receipt of the deposit, but you will use the item that you created to direct the funds to a liability account. In essence, you are "liable" for doing something in return for the funds you are receiving, and you will hold onto the funds in a special account until you have done what is promised. You will not record the income until the service is performed, the product is delivered, or the gift certificate is redeemed.

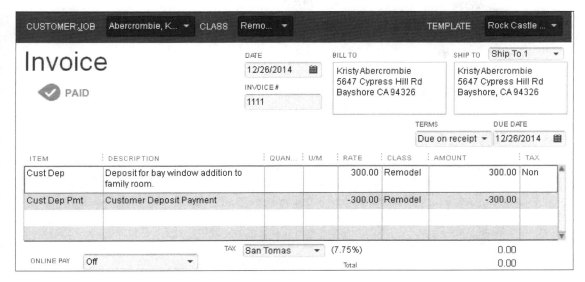

Notice the invoice created when a customer deposit is received. It does not affect an income account or Accounts Receivable (since the balance owing on the invoice is zero).

Presto! Turning a Deposit into a Payment

Once you have delivered on your promise and have traded goods or services for the gift certificate, you will use an invoice to record the income. The invoice will increase an income account and then reduce the liability account when the income becomes "earned" and you are no longer liable to perform or deliver.

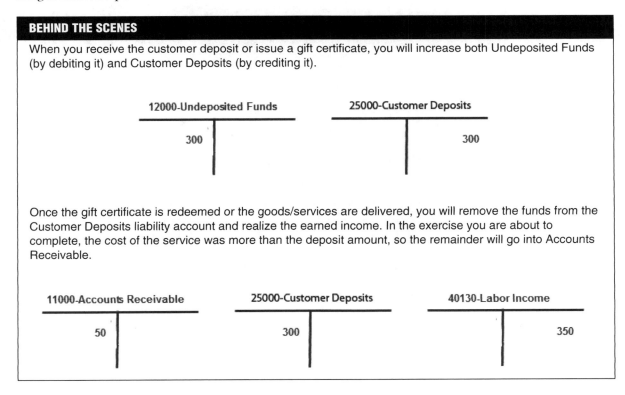

BEHIND THE SCENES

When you receive the customer deposit or issue a gift certificate, you will increase both Undeposited Funds (by debiting it) and Customer Deposits (by crediting it).

12000-Undeposited Funds	25000-Customer Deposits
300	300

Once the gift certificate is redeemed or the goods/services are delivered, you will remove the funds from the Customer Deposits liability account and realize the earned income. In the exercise you are about to complete, the cost of the service was more than the deposit amount, so the remainder will go into Accounts Receivable.

11000-Accounts Receivable	25000-Customer Deposits	40130-Labor Income
50	300	350

Task	Procedure
Set up to track customer deposits	Create a liability account: ■ Choose Lists→Chart of Accounts. ■ Create a new Other Current Liability account named Customer Deposits with the proper account number (if applicable). Create two new items: ■ Choose Lists→Item List. ■ Create a new Other Charge item named Cust Dep. ■ Direct the item to Customer Deposits (amount is blank; item is nontaxable). ■ Create a new Payment item named Cust Dep Pmt.
Collect a customer deposit	■ Choose Customers→Create Invoices. ■ Enter the Customer:Job, Date, Class, and Terms in the top area of the invoice. ■ First line: Enter the Cust Dep Other Charge and deposit amount; fill in the Description field. ■ Second line: Enter the Cust Dep Pmt item and the deposit amount. ■ Click Save & Close; the net amount of the invoice should be zero.
Turn a customer deposit into a payment	■ Choose Customers→Create Invoices. ■ Enter the Customer:Job, Date, Class, and Terms in the top area of the invoice. ■ Enter all of the sales items, line by line, into the invoice. ■ Enter the Cust Dep Other Charge item in the next line of the invoice after the sales items. If the deposit is for more than the amount of the invoice, enter only the total invoice amount for the deposit. If the deposit is for less than the amount of the invoice, then enter the full amount of the deposit. ■ Click Save & Close.

DEVELOP YOUR SKILLS 3.3

Account for a Customer Deposit

In this exercise, you will assist Zoe in preparing to track customer deposits, receiving a deposit from a customer, and turning the deposit into a payment.

Before you can even think about dealing with unearned income and, in Rock Castle's case, customer deposits, you must set up the proper account and items.

1. Click the **Chart of Accounts** task icon in the Company area of the Home page.

2. Click the **Account** menu button, and then choose **New**.

Chart of Accounts

3. Follow these steps to create the new account:

Ⓐ Click in the circle for **Other Account Types**.

Ⓑ Click to choose **Other Current Liability**.

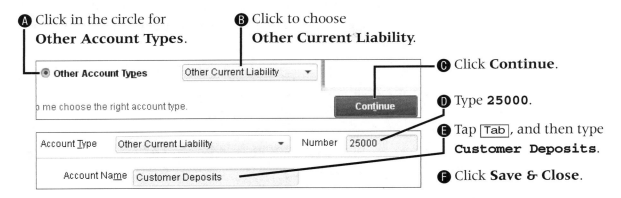

Ⓒ Click **Continue**.

Ⓓ Type **25000**.

Ⓔ Tap ⟦Tab⟧, and then type **Customer Deposits**.

Ⓕ Click **Save & Close**.

4. Close the **Chart of Accounts**.

5. Click the **Items & Services** task icon in the Company area of the Home page.

6. Click the **Item** menu button, and then choose **New**.

Items & Services

7. Follow these steps to create the first item:

Ⓐ Click to choose **Other Charge** as the type of item.

Ⓑ Tap ⟦Tab⟧, and then type **Cust Dep**.

Ⓒ Tap ⟦Tab⟧ three times, and then type **Customer Deposit**.

Ⓓ Click the **drop-down arrow**, and then choose **Non** as the Tax Code.

Ⓔ Tap ⟦Tab⟧, and then type **cu**.

The Amount field is left as 0.00; you will fill that in at the time of sale.

8. Click **Next**.

9. Follow these steps to create the second new item:

Ⓐ Type **p**.

Ⓑ Tap ⟦Tab⟧, and then type **Cust Dep Pmt**.

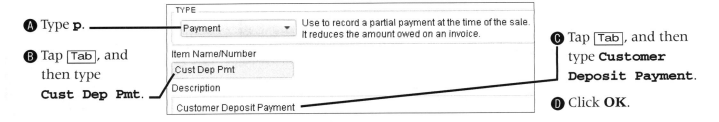

Ⓒ Tap ⟦Tab⟧, and then type **Customer Deposit Payment**.

Ⓓ Click **OK**.

10. Close the **Item List** window.

Collect a Customer Deposit

Kristy Abercrombie just called and asked for a bay window to be installed in the family room that you remodeled for her earlier in the year. Alan asked for a deposit to be made before the work begins. You will help Zoe record this deposit.

11. Click the **Create Invoices** task icon in the Customers area of the Home page.

Create Invoices

12. Click the **Customer:Job field drop-down arrow**, and then choose **Abercrombie, Kristy:Family Room** from the list.
The Billable Time/Costs window will appear.

13. Click to the left of the option to **Exclude outstanding billable time and costs**, and then click **OK**.

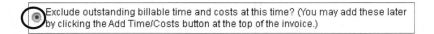
Exclude outstanding billable time and costs at this time? (You may add these later by clicking the Add Time/Costs button at the top of the invoice.)

14. Follow these steps to complete the invoice:

Ⓐ Click the **drop-down arrow,** and then choose **Remodel.**

Ⓑ Tap Tab two times, and then type **122614.**

Ⓒ Click on the **Terms drop-down arrow,** and then choose **Due on receipt.**

Ⓓ Click the **drop-down arrow** in the first line of the Item field, and then choose **Cust Dep.**

Ⓔ Tap Tab, delete the **description** that filled in, and then **type** the description displayed.

Ⓕ Tap Tab two times, and then type **300.**

Ⓖ Click the **drop-down arrow** in the second line of the Item field, and then choose **Cust Dep Pmt.**

Ⓗ Tap Tab two times, and then type **–300.**

Ⓘ Click **Save & Close.**

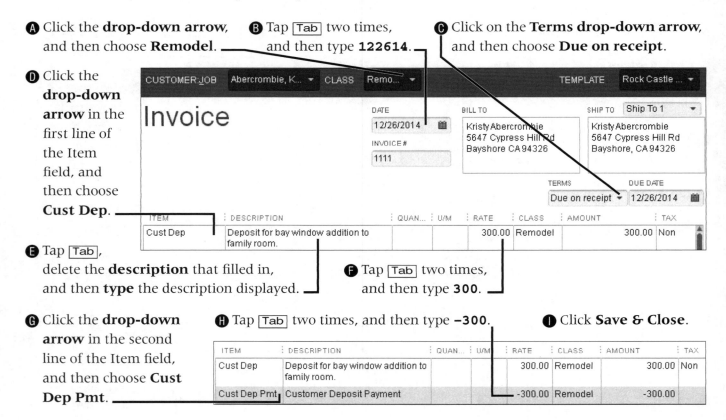

The total due for the invoice should be 0.00 because the net effect to Accounts Receivable is 0.00. In other words, the customer doesn't owe anything as a result of the transaction. What you have accomplished behind the scenes, though, is that you collected $300 that debited Undeposited Funds and credited Customer Deposits.

BTS BRIEF
12000•Undeposited Funds DR 300.00; 25000•Customer Deposits CR <300.00>

15. Click **No** in the Name Information Changed window.

You changed the terms to Due upon receipt for this one transaction, but you want the default terms you have set for the customer to remain the same.

Turn a Deposit into a Payment

The final step when working with customer deposits is to do a little magic and turn the deposit into a payment!

16. Click the **Create Invoices** task icon in the Customers area of the Home page.

17. Click the **Customer:Job field drop-down arrow**, and then choose **Abercrombie, Kristy:Family Room** from the list.
The Billable Time/Costs window will appear.

18. Click to the left of the option to **Exclude outstanding billable time and costs**, and then click **OK**.

19. Follow these steps to complete the invoice:

Ⓐ Click the **drop-down arrow**, and then choose **Remodel**.

Ⓑ Tap ⸢Tab⸥ two times, and then type **123114**.

Ⓒ Click the **drop-down arrow** in the first line of the Item field, and then choose **Installation**.

Ⓓ Tap ⸢Tab⸥, delete the default description, and then type **Installation of bay window**.

Ⓔ Tap ⸢Tab⸥, and then type **10**.

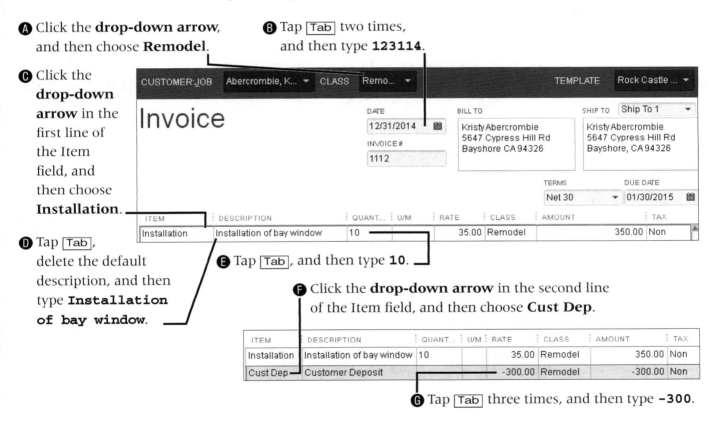

Ⓕ Click the **drop-down arrow** in the second line of the Item field, and then choose **Cust Dep**.

Ⓖ Tap ⸢Tab⸥ three times, and then type **-300**.

Note that it is up to you to type in the amount of the deposit that will apply to the invoice. In this case, the invoice was for more than the deposit, so the customer owes $50 (see the following illustration) and Accounts Receivable will be debited for this net amount owing on the invoice. If the deposit was for more than the total invoice amount, you would only enter that amount for the Customer Deposit on the invoice; the rest would remain in the liability account.

ITEM	DESCRIPTION	QUAN...	U/M	RATE	CLASS	AMOUNT	TAX
Installation	Installation of bay window	10		35.00	Remodel	350.00	Non
Cust Dep	Customer Deposit			-300.00	Remodel	-300.00	Non

				TAX	San Tomas ▼	(7.75%)	0.00
ONLINE PAY	Off ▼					Total	50.00

BTS BRIEF

25000•Customer Deposits DR 300.00; 11000•Accounts Receivable DR 50.00; 40130•Labor Income CR <350.00>

---

20. Click **Save & Close**.

The invoice is recorded. There are no longer funds on deposit in the liability account for this customer.

Using QuickBooks' Time-Tracking and Mileage Features

The Time-Tracking feature allows you to create weekly timesheets so you can break down the hours by customer/job or to record single activities for a customer/job. In addition to these payroll benefits, time tracking also allows you to:

■ Invoice customers for number of hours worked (If you recall, in Lesson 2, Using Quick-Books for Payroll, the billable costs were classified as expenses rather than time; with this feature, you can bill customers based on time)

■ Automatically fill in the hours worked on paychecks

■ Track time for subcontractors by automatically filling in time data on bills and checks

■ Track payroll costs by job, class, or type of work performed

■ Track billable versus non-billable time

Once you have used time data, you can run reports such as the Time by Job Summary to view how many man-hours you are putting into each job. Time tracking also allows you to allocate the appropriate payroll costs to a job, making your job costing reports more accurate and meaningful.

Methods of Entering Time

When you enter a single activity, it is recorded on that employee's weekly timesheet. A single activity can be entered by typing in the amount of time or by using the timer feature to actually track the exact amount of time on a task. If you choose to use the timer feature, you can use it only for timed activities on the current day.

There are two methods by which you can enter time data in QuickBooks:

■ **As a single activity when it occurs:** You can either type the amount of time in the single activity window or use the built-in timer to record the exact amount of time.

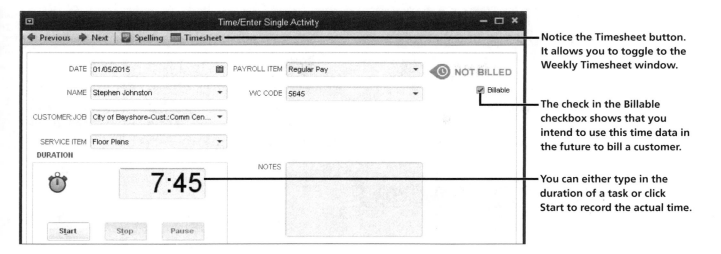

Notice the Timesheet button. It allows you to toggle to the Weekly Timesheet window.

The check in the Billable checkbox shows that you intend to use this time data in the future to bill a customer.

You can either type in the duration of a task or click Start to record the actual time.

- **On a weekly timesheet:** The weekly timesheet allows you to enter time data for multiple customer/jobs, service items, and payroll items for a single employee. You can use this information to create paychecks when you process payroll.

The column to the far right is the "billable" column. If a checkmark is in this field, you can bill the customer for the time. If an invoice icon appears, it means the time has already been invoiced.

Fields Available in Both Time Data Entry Windows

Regardless of whether you choose to enter time as single activities or on a weekly timesheet, notice that each window provides the following fields:

- **Customer:Job:** Information entered in this field allows you to bill a customer for the time and to keep track of information required for accurate job costing.
- **Service Item:** Information entered in this field allows you to track services performed.
- **Payroll Item:** Information entered in this field allows you to create paychecks from your time data.
- **Billable:** If you choose this field, the information is made available for you to bill the customer for the time.
- **Notes:** Information entered in this field is displayed in the description field on reports and invoices.

Batch Timesheets

Some businesses may find that they have employees or vendors who work the same hours for a job, for instance, if you are a construction company with crews who work together on the same jobs each day. These businesses can create one timesheet for multiple payroll names (employees for whom you have chosen to use time data to create paychecks) or multiple non-payroll names (can be vendors and/or employees). Something to keep in mind if you choose to work with batch timesheets, though, is that all workers for whom you are creating a timesheet must have the following criteria in common: job, number of hours worked per day, payroll item(s), and service item(s).

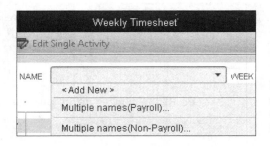

Notice that when you go to choose a name for a weekly timesheet, you have the option to choose multiple payroll or multiple non-payroll names in order to create a batch timesheet.

Tracking Mileage

The mileage tracking feature in QuickBooks allows you to track mileage for your business vehicle—but not for the purpose of reimbursing your employees. If you do track mileage, you can use the data to bill customers for the expense or for tax reporting purposes. It will be up to you to keep on top of the IRS mileage reimbursement rates, and QuickBooks will calculate the mileage expense based on the approved rate on the specific day. To track mileage for a particular vehicle, you need to enter the vehicle into the Vehicle List first.

To view your mileage information once you have start tracking it, QuickBooks provides mileage reports from which you can choose to display your data. You can also choose to pass on the mileage expense to your customers and create reports to view the amount that has been billed.

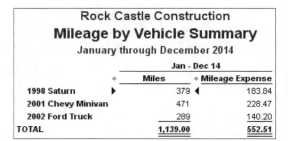

The Mileage by Vehicle Summary displays the total number of miles and the expense based on the approved IRS mileage rate. If you choose to track the mileage by customer and/or job, you can also view the mileage expense billed to each customer and job.

QUICK REFERENCE	USING QUICKBOOKS TIME AND MILEAGE TRACKING FEATURES
Task	**Procedure**
Create a single time activity	■ Choose Employees→Enter Time→Time/Edit Single Activity. ■ Choose the desired Name; enter the Date, Customer:Job, Service Item, and Payroll Item information. ■ Enter the of time spent, and any appropriate note; click Save & Close.
Enter hours on a weekly timesheet	■ Choose Employees→Enter Time→Use Weekly Timesheet. ■ Choose the desired Name. ■ Click the Set Date button, and then type the appropriate week; enter the Customer:Job, Service Item, and Payroll Item for each line. ■ Enter the time worked for each day; click Save & Close.
Create a batch timesheet for multiple people	■ Choose Employees→Enter Time→Use Weekly Timesheet. ■ Choose to select from either Payroll or Non-Payroll multiple names. ■ Choose the desired Names. ■ Click the Set Date button, and then type the appropriate week; enter the Customer:Job, Service Item, and Payroll Item (if appropriate) for each line. ■ Enter the time worked for each day; click Save & Close.
Enter vehicle mileage	Enter the current mileage rate: ■ Choose Company→Enter Vehicle Mileage. ■ Click the Mileage Rates button. ■ Type in the Effective Date and the Rate; click Close. Add a vehicle to the list: ■ Choose Lists→Customer & Vendor Profile Lists→Vehicle List. ■ Click the Vehicle menu button; choose New. ■ Enter the vehicle's name and description; click OK. Add an item, if you wish to pass mileage expenses on to customers: ■ Choose Lists→Item List. ■ Create a new service or other charge item called Mileage or Delivery Charges, leaving the rate field as zero. ■ Choose the appropriate expense account; click Save & Close. Enter mileage: ■ Choose Company→Enter Vehicle Mileage. ■ Choose the Vehicle; enter the start and end dates for the trip. ■ Type in the odometer readings from the start and end of the trip. ■ If passing this expense on to a customer or job, mark the Billable checkbox, choose the appropriate Customer:Job, and choose Mileage or Delivery Charges as the Item. ■ Enter any appropriate notes, if desired; click Save & Close.

Track Time for a Job

In this exercise, you will help Zoe record the time spent on the Lionello Community Center job for the City of Bayshore and track the mileage for the job.

1. Click the **Enter Time** task icon in the Employees area of the Home page, and then choose **Time/Enter Single Activity**.

2. Follow these steps to enter Stephen's billable time:

A Type **010515** as the date.

B Tap Tab, and then type **ste**.

C Tap Tab, and then click **Yes** to use time data.

D Type **com**.

E Tap Tab, and then type **fl**.

F Tap Tab, and then type **7.75**.

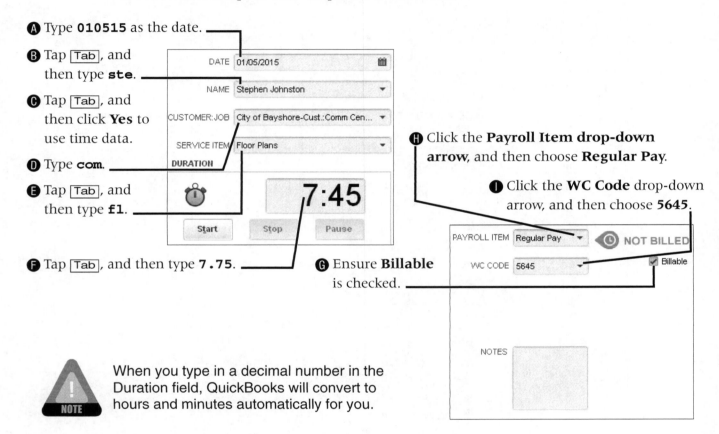

H Click the **Payroll Item drop-down arrow**, and then choose **Regular Pay**.

I Click the **WC Code** drop-down arrow, and then choose **5645**.

G Ensure **Billable** is checked.

> **NOTE**
> When you type in a decimal number in the Duration field, QuickBooks will convert to hours and minutes automatically for you.

3. Click **Save & Close**.

Enter Time Using a Weekly Timesheet

You will now enter the rest of Stephen's time for the week.

4. Click the **Enter Time** task icon in the Employees area of the Home page, and then choose **Use Weekly Timesheet**.

5. Type **ste**, and then tap Tab to fill in Stephen Johnston as the Name.

6. Follow these steps to set the time frame for the timesheet:

Ⓐ Click this **button** to display a calendar.

Ⓑ Click the **right arrow** to display **January 2015**.

Ⓒ Click the **5** on the calendar.

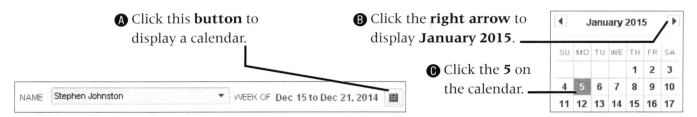

QuickBooks sets the week of Jan 5 to Jan 11, 2015 as the date range for the timesheet. Notice that the time data you just entered as a single activity appears on the weekly timesheet for the week of 1/5/2015.

7. Follow these steps to enter the rest of Stephen's time data for the Community Center job:

Ⓐ Click in the first line under **7**, and then type **2**.

Ⓑ Click under **City of Bayshore**, and then type **com**.

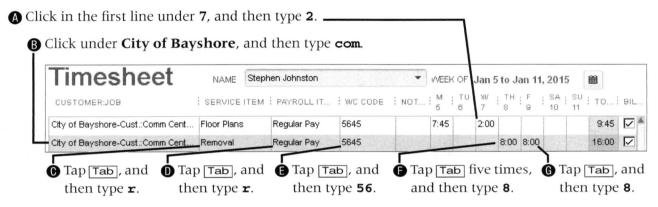

Ⓒ Tap Tab, and then type **r**.

Ⓓ Tap Tab, and then type **r**.

Ⓔ Tap Tab, and then type **56**.

Ⓕ Tap Tab five times, and then type **8**.

Ⓖ Tap Tab, and then type **8**.

Ⓗ Click here, and then click the **drop-down arrow** and choose the **Barley, Renee: Repairs** job.

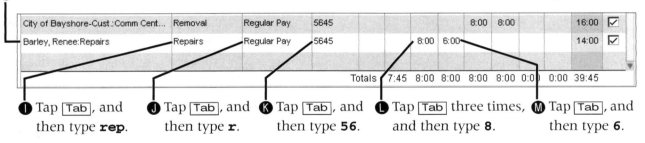

Ⓘ Tap Tab, and then type **rep**.

Ⓙ Tap Tab, and then type **r**.

Ⓚ Tap Tab, and then type **56**.

Ⓛ Tap Tab three times, and then type **8**.

Ⓜ Tap Tab, and then type **6**.

8. Click **Save & Close**.

Enter Vehicle Mileage

Finally, you will enter the mileage Stephen put on the Ford truck while doing some repair work for Renee Barley. You will need to update the mileage rate before you enter the miles driven.

9. Choose **Company→Enter Vehicle Mileage**.

10. Click the **Mileage Rates** button on the toolbar.

11. Follow these steps to enter a new mileage rate:

A Click in the second line of the **Effective Date** column, and then type **010114**.

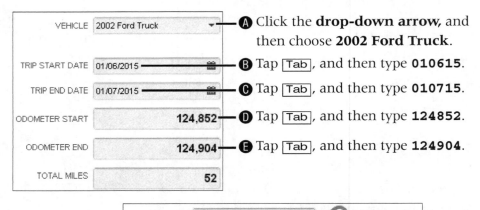

EFFECTIVE DATE	RATE
01/01/2007	0.485
01/01/2014	0.515

B Tap Tab, and then type **.515**.

C Click **Close**.

Do not use this mileage rate for your own company—unless it is the rate that is currently being used by the IRS!

12. Follow these steps to enter the mileage driven:

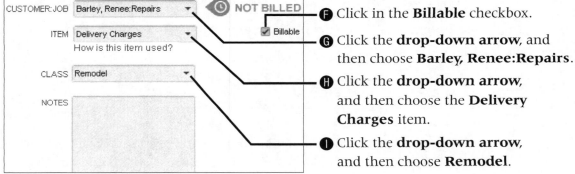

VEHICLE	2002 Ford Truck
TRIP START DATE	01/06/2015
TRIP END DATE	01/07/2015
ODOMETER START	124,852
ODOMETER END	124,904
TOTAL MILES	52

A Click the **drop-down arrow,** and then choose **2002 Ford Truck**.

B Tap Tab, and then type **010615**.

C Tap Tab, and then type **010715**.

D Tap Tab, and then type **124852**.

E Tap Tab, and then type **124904**.

CUSTOMER:JOB	Barley, Renee:Repairs
ITEM	Delivery Charges
	How is this item used?
CLASS	Remodel
NOTES	

NOT BILLED

☑ Billable

F Click in the **Billable** checkbox.

G Click the **drop-down arrow**, and then choose **Barley, Renee:Repairs**.

H Click the **drop-down arrow**, and then choose the **Delivery Charges** item.

J Click the **drop-down arrow**, and then choose **Remodel**.

13. Click **Save & Close**.

Using Time-Tracking Hours to Create a Paycheck

You can use time data for employees to create their paychecks. If you recall from the last exercise, the first time you entered time data for Stephen Johnston, you were prompted to set him up to use time data during paycheck creation.

There are two ways to use class tracking when it comes to payroll. You can choose a class for an entire paycheck or for each earning item. The default setting is a class for an entire paycheck. You should determine which option works best for your company based on what you track with classes.

Allocating Salaried Pay to an Individual Customer or Job

To accurately determine the cost of a job, you need to account for the time spent by salaried employees, too. You can record their time using the time-tracking features and choosing to "use time data to create paychecks" in the Preview Paycheck window.

Invoicing a Customer for Time Spent on a Job

In Lesson 2, Using QuickBooks for Payroll, you learned how to pass on billable payroll expenses to customers. You can also use the time-tracking feature to pass on billable time to customers. In addition, you can use the same procedure to include the billable mileage. Regardless of what type of cost you are passing on to the customer, the process is virtually the same—and you can even choose to specify a markup amount for the hours.

QUICK REFERENCE	USING TIME DATA TO CREATE A PAYCHECK
Task	**Procedure**
Use time tracking to create a paycheck	■ Choose Employees→Pay Employees. ■ Enter the check date, pay period end date, and the payee; click Create. ■ Enter any Class information or modifications, if appropriate; click Create.
Create an invoice for a customer using time and mileage information	■ Choose Customers→Create Invoices. ■ Choose the Customer:Job you wish to bill; indicate that you wish to include the outstanding billable time and costs to the invoice. ■ Click the Time tab and select any time data; click the Mileage tab and select any mileage data.

Create a Paycheck and Invoice from Time and Mileage Data

In this exercise, you will help Zoe create a paycheck for Stephen based on the time data that was entered. The first step is to set the preference that will allow you to assign classes by earnings item rather that just for an entire paycheck.

1. Choose **Edit→Preferences**.

2. Follow these steps to set the preference:

🅐 Click the **Payroll & Employees** category.   🅑 Click the **Company Preferences** tab.

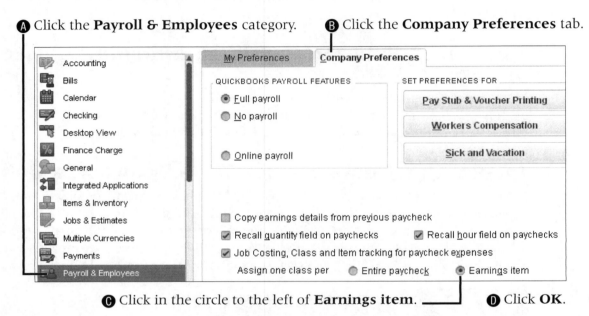

🅒 Click in the circle to the left of **Earnings item**. ────   🅓 Click **OK**.

3. Click the **Pay Employees** task icon in the Employees area of the Home page.

4. Click the **Unscheduled Payroll** button in the Pay Employees area of the window.

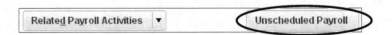

The Enter Payroll Information window displays. Look at the Regular Pay column for Stephen Johnston and notice that the amount is in blue, which indicates it is for the amount of billable time that you have entered.

5. Follow these steps to choose to pay Stephen:

Ⓐ Type **011215**.

Ⓑ Click to the left of **Stephen Johnston**.

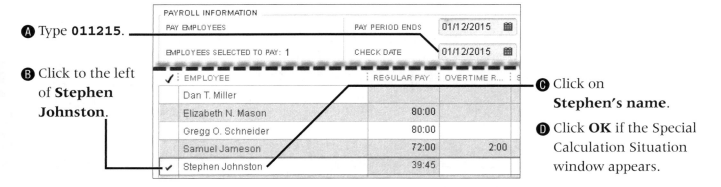

Ⓒ Click on **Stephen's name**.

Ⓓ Click **OK** if the Special Calculation Situation window appears.

The Preview Paycheck window appears. Stephen also worked in the office while another staff member was on vacation, so you will add that time to his paycheck.

6. Follow these steps to complete the paycheck for Stephen:

Ⓐ Click below the last entry in the **Item Name** column, and then type **r**.

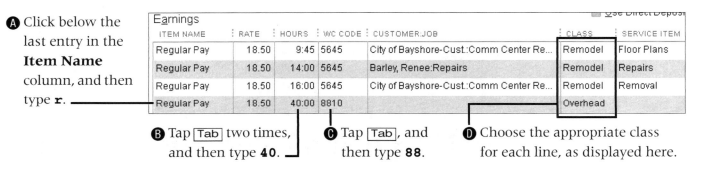

Ⓑ Tap Tab two times, and then type **40**.

Ⓒ Tap Tab, and then type **88**.

Ⓓ Choose the appropriate class for each line, as displayed here.

The following BTS Brief section shows the "parent accounts," not the various subaccounts.

BTS BRIEF

62700•Payroll Expenses DR 1,674.55; 24000•Payroll Liabilities CR <457.52>; 10100•Checking CR <1,217.03>

7. Click **Save & Close**; then, click **Continue**.

8. Click **Create Paychecks**; then, close the **Confirmation and Next Steps** window as well as the **Payroll Center**.

Create an Invoice from Time and Mileage Data

You will now create an invoice for Renee Barley that includes the time and mileage costs for the repair work Stephen completed for her.

9. Click the **Create Invoices** task icon in the Customers area of the Home page.

10. Click the **Customer:Job field drop-down arrow** and choose the **Repairs** job for Renee Barley.
The Billable Time/Costs window appears.

Create Invoices

11. Click **OK** in the Billable Time/Costs window to choose the default of selecting outstanding billable time and costs to add to the invoice.
The Time tab of the Choose Billable Time and Costs window displays.

12. Follow these steps to choose the billable time and costs to pass on:

Ⓐ Click the **Select All** button. ⟶

Ⓑ Click the **Mileage** tab. ⟶

Ⓒ Click the **Select All** button. ⟶

Ⓓ Click **OK**.

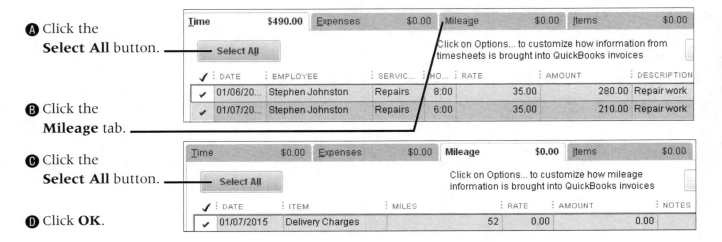

The Create Invoices window displays.

13. Follow these steps to complete the invoice:

Ⓐ Tap Tab three times, and then type **010715**.

Ⓑ Choose **Remodel** as the class.

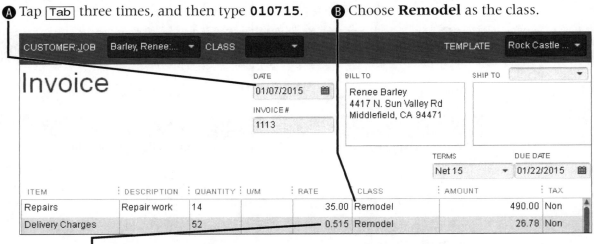

Ⓒ Drag to select **0.00**, and then type **.515** as the rate for the Delivery Charges.

BTS BRIEF

11000•Accounts Receivable DR 516.78; 40130•Labor Income CR <490.00>; 40530•Reimbursed Freight & Delivery CR <26.78>

---

14. Click **Save & Close**.

Assessing Finance Charges

If you are invoicing customers, you will inevitably find that not all of your customers pay their invoices on time. You may wish to assess finance charges for these late-paying customers.

Lending laws vary by jurisdiction, so you will need to research those applicable to you regarding whether you can assess finance charges on overdue balances. After you've performed this research, you are ready to set your preferences in QuickBooks.

Finance charge laws are different in different locations! Do *not* use the specifics provided in this book; rather, find out the laws that apply to you and apply them to the principles you have been taught.

QuickBooks allows you to set several finance charge preferences in the Finance Charge category on the Company Preferences tab. The following illustration shows an example of the types of preferences you can control.

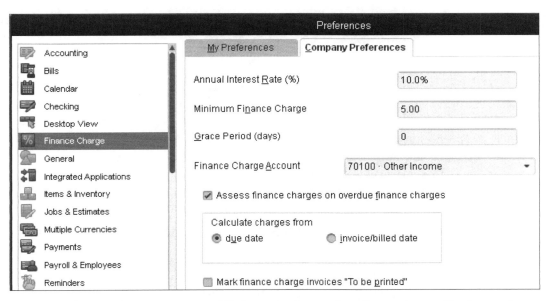

Note the preferences that you are responsible for setting in regards to finance charges. The finance charge account is an Other Income account as the income received is not the result of your normal business practices (unless you are a bank!). Before you set whether you will assess finance charges on overdue finance charges or when to calculate charges from, understand the laws where you do business.

The Assess Finance Charges Window

The Assess Finance Charges window does more than provide you with a means to determine which customers are overdue and should be charged a finance charge. It also calculates the charge due (based on the preferences set) and gives you a quick way to view the preferences and customize the finance charge invoice template.

Once you set the Assessment Date, QuickBooks determines the overdue balance and calculates the finance charge based on the preferences you have set.

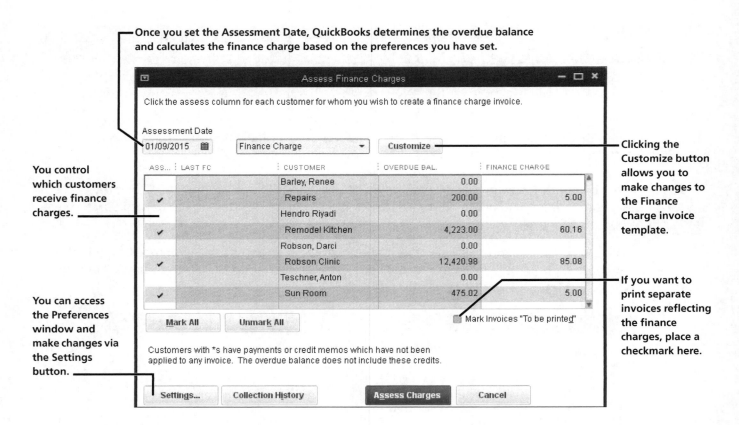

You control which customers receive finance charges.

You can access the Preferences window and make changes via the Settings button.

Clicking the Customize button allows you to make changes to the Finance Charge invoice template.

If you want to print separate invoices reflecting the finance charges, place a checkmark here.

Once you view the Assess Finance Charges window, you may also see customers that need friendly collections calls or may need to have their balances written off as bad debt. You learned how to deal with collections in Lesson 1, Dealing with Physical Inventory and bad debt in Lesson 5, Correcting and Customizing in QuickBooks.

Using a Batch of Statements to Bill for Finance Charges

You can send an invoice reflecting assessed finance charges to your customers. To do this, you need to ensure that there is a checkmark in the "To be printed" checkbox in the Preferences window.

The more common way to alert customers to finance charges that they owe is to produce a statement that reflects the finance charge, outstanding invoices, and aging information. You can produce a statement for just one customer, if you wish (as you did in Lesson 5, Correcting and Customizing in QuickBooks, when dealing with a NSF check). In the following exercise, you will produce a batch of statements for multiple customers, though.

When you assess finance charges, you need to debit Accounts Receivable and the appropriate accounts receivable customer subregister (you can see the example for Dr. Darci Robson below), as well as indicate the account credited by the charge (in this case, 70000•Other Income).

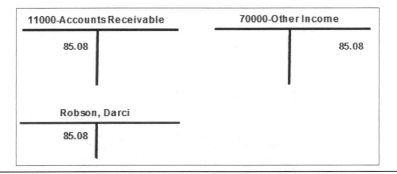

Task	Procedure
Set a company's finance charge preferences	■ Choose Edit→Preferences. ■ Click the Finance Charge category, and then the Company Preferences tab. ■ Enter the appropriate finance charge preferences; click OK.
Assess finance charges	■ Choose Customers→Assess Finance Charges. ■ Set the date from which to assess the charges; choose which customers should be assessed charges. ■ Verify and modify, if necessary, the information; click Assess Charges.
Produce a batch of statements	■ Choose Customers→Create Statements. ■ Choose the appropriate date range and customers, as well as any additional options. ■ Click Print or Email to deliver the statements.

DEVELOP YOUR SKILLS 3.6
Assess Finance Charges

In this exercise, you will help Zoe assess finance charges for any customers who have overdue balances. The finance charge preferences have already been set, but Zoe wants to take a look at them to make sure they match what she just looked up for the jurisdiction in which Rock Castle Construction operates.

1. Choose **Edit→Preferences**.

2. Click the **Finance Charge** category on the left, and then the **Company Preferences** tab.
   You will see the finance charge preferences that have been set up for Rock Castle Construction.

3. Click **Cancel** to close the Preferences window without making any changes.

Assess Finance Charges

Now that you have verified that the finance charge preferences are correct, you will choose to assess finance charges on all overdue invoices.

Finance
Charges

4. Click the **Finance Charges** task icon in the Customers area of the Home page.
   The Assess Finance Charges window will be displayed.

5. Type **010915** as the Assessment Date, and then tap ⎡Tab⎤.
   All customers with open invoices that are past due as of January 9 display, along with the calculated finance charge.

6. Click **Assess Charges** and then click **Yes** in the Assess Finance Charges window.
   The finance charges are now reflected in Accounts Receivable for each customer assessed.

> **BTS BRIEF**
>
> **11000•Accounts Receivable DR 155.24 (each customer's subregister is also debited for the finance charge amount); 70000•Other Income CR <155.24>**

Produce a Batch of Statements

You will now help Zoe create statements for the four customers to whom you just assessed finance charges (Renee Barley, Riyadi Hendro, Darci Robson, and Anton Teschner).

Statements

7. Click the **Statements** task icon in the Customers area of the Home page.

8. Follow these steps to produce a batch of statements:

A Type **010915**.

B Click to choose the **All open transactions** option.

C Click to choose the **Multiple Customers** option.

D Click the **Choose** button.

The Print Statements window appears.

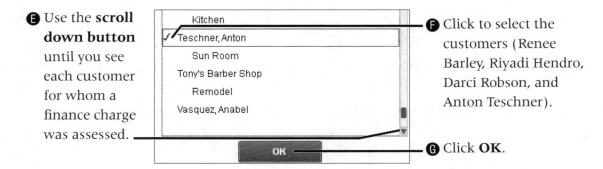

E Use the **scroll down button** until you see each customer for whom a finance charge was assessed.

F Click to select the customers (Renee Barley, Riyadi Hendro, Darci Robson, and Anton Teschner).

G Click **OK**.

9. Click the **Preview** button at the bottom left of the Create Statements window.
   You can now see what each statement will look like printed.

10. Click the **Close** button at the top of the Print Preview window.

At this point, you would choose to print or email the statements by clicking the appropriate button at the bottom of the window.

11. Close the **Create Statements** window, unless your instructor wishes for you to print the statements for review.

Reporting for Estimates, Time Tracking, and Mileage

QuickBooks' job costing, estimating, mileage, and time-tracking features include many preset reports that you can run to learn more about your business. Notice in the figure below the reports available in the QuickBooks Pro version for the Jobs, Time & Mileage category on the Reports menu. Many other reports are available for your use if you use a Premier version of QuickBooks that is specialized for your type of company.

There are a large number of standard reports available to QuickBooks users to help with tracking jobs, time, and mileage.

QUICK REFERENCE	PRODUCING REPORTS ABOUT ESTIMATES, TIME AND MILEAGE TRACKING, AND JOB COSTING
Task	**Procedure**
Produce a report to show the amount of an estimate invoiced	■ Choose Reports→Jobs, Time & Mileage→Job Progress Invoices vs. Estimates. ■ Set the date range.
Produce a report to show time tracked for each job	■ Choose Reports→Jobs, Time & Mileage→Time by Job Summary. ■ Set the date range.

Task	Procedure
Produce a report to show the profitability of all jobs	■ Choose Reports→Jobs, Time & Mileage→Job Profitability Summary.
Produce a report to show the detailed mileage expenses for all vehicles	■ Choose Reports→Jobs, Time & Mileage→Mileage by Vehicle Detail.

DEVELOP YOUR SKILLS 3.7

Produce Job, Estimate, Mileage, and Time-Tracking Reports

In this exercise, you will work with Zoe to produce a variety of reports for Rock Castle Construction.

1. Choose **Reports→Jobs, Time & Mileage→Job Progress Invoices vs. Estimates**.

2. Click the **Dates drop-down arrow**, and then choose **This Fiscal Year**.
   The Job Progress Invoices vs. Estimates report for 2014 displays.

3. Take a look at the first entry on the report and notice the result of the **estimate and progress invoice** that you entered in this lesson.

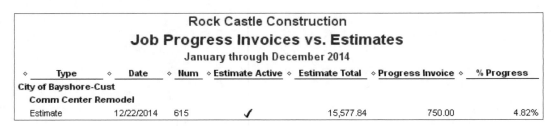

Rock Castle Construction
Job Progress Invoices vs. Estimates
January through December 2014

Type	Date	Num	Estimate Active	Estimate Total	Progress Invoice	% Progress
City of Bayshore-Cust						
Comm Center Remodel						
Estimate	12/22/2014	615	✓	15,577.84	750.00	4.82%

4. Close the **Job Progress Invoices vs. Estimates** window.

Report on Time Tracking

The next report will show the time spent on each job.

5. Choose **Reports→Jobs, Time & Mileage→Time by Job Summary**.

6. Tap Ⓐ to set the date range to All.
The Time by Job Summary report displays for all dates. Take a look down the report and notice the time for which you invoiced Renee Barley, as shown in the following illustration.

7. Close the **Time by Job Summary** window.

Report on Job Costing

The third report will show the profitability of each job.

8. Choose **Reports→Jobs, Time & Mileage→Job Profitability Summary**.
The Job Profitability Summary report displays with the default date range of all dates.

9. Take a look at the **profitability** so far for the Lionello Community Center remodel for the City of Bayshore.

10. Close the **Job Profitability Summary** window.

Report on Mileage

The final report that you will produce in this exercise will detail the mileage expenses for all vehicles.

11. Choose **Reports→Jobs, Time & Mileage→Mileage by Vehicle Detail**.

12. Tap $\boxed{a}$ to set the date range to All.

    The Mileage by Vehicle Detail report displays for all dates. Scroll down to see the entries for the Ford truck and notice the mileage expense that you entered on 1/7/2015, as displayed in the following illustration.

Rock Castle Construction
Mileage by Vehicle Detail
All Transactions

Vehicle	Trip End Date	Total Miles	Mileage Rate	Mileage Expense
2002 Ford Truck				
2002 Ford Truck	06/15/2014	18	0.515	9.27
2002 Ford Truck	06/17/2014	35	0.515	18.03
2002 Ford Truck	06/22/2014	71	0.515	36.57
2002 Ford Truck	06/22/2014	15	0.515	7.73
2002 Ford Truck	07/02/2014	44	0.515	22.66
2002 Ford Truck	07/07/2014	11	0.515	5.67
2002 Ford Truck	08/14/2014	31	0.515	15.97
2002 Ford Truck	08/19/2014	7	0.515	3.61
2002 Ford Truck	09/06/2014	9	0.515	4.64
2002 Ford Truck	09/23/2014	48	0.515	24.72
2002 Ford Truck	01/07/2015	52	0.515	26.78
Total 2002 Ford Truck		341		175.65
TOTAL		**1,191**		**613.46**

13. Close the **Mileage by Vehicle Detail** window.

14. Choose the appropriate option for your situation:

    - If you are continuing on to the next lesson or to the end-of-lesson exercises, leave QuickBooks open.

    - If you are finished working in QuickBooks for now, choose **File→Exit**.

Concepts Review

Concepts Review	http://labyrinthelab.com/qb13-level02

To check your knowledge of the key concepts introduced in this lesson, complete the Concepts Review quiz by going to the URL listed above.

Reinforce Your Skills

Before you begin the Reinforce Your Skills exercises, complete one of these options:

- *Open* **[Your name]'s Tea Shoppe at the Lake, Lesson 1** *from your file storage location that you used for Lesson 1 (not Lesson 2, as we used a different company file to learn about payroll). Or, open Tea Shoppe at the Lake, Lesson 3 if you are working with company files instead of portable company files.*

- *Restore* **Tea Shoppe at the Lake, Lesson 3 (Portable)** *from your file storage location.*

REINFORCE YOUR SKILLS 3.1

Create a Job and an Estimate for a Customer

In this exercise, you will produce a job for Lisa Silvers and then create an estimate for her. Lisa is getting married and has asked Susie for an estimate to cater her reception. Before Susie can create estimates and conduct progress invoicing, the preferences must be set.

1. Choose **Edit→Preferences**.

2. Click the **Jobs & Estimates** category, and then the **Company Preferences** tab.

3. Click in the circle to the left of **Yes** to turn on both the estimate creation and progress invoicing features, and then click **OK**. Click **OK** to close all windows to set the preference.

Create a Job for a Customer

Next you will create a job for Lisa Silvers for her reception.

4. Choose **Customers→Customer Center**.

5. Right-click on **Lisa Silvers**, and then choose **Add Job** from the pop-up menu.

6. Type **Wedding Catering** as the Job Name, and then click **OK**.
   The new job appears on the Customers & Jobs List; it is selected.

Create an Estimate for a Job

Now that you have a job set up for Lisa's wedding reception, you will create an estimate for it. The Wedding Catering job should still be selected.

7. Click the **New Transactions** button, and then choose **Estimates**.

8. Enter Catering as the **Class**, and then **7/16/2013** as the **Date**.

9. Choose Catering as the **Item**, and then tap Tab.

10. Delete the displayed description, and then **type the description and cost** displayed in the following illustration.

ITEM	DESCRIPTION	QTY	COST	CLASS	TOTAL	TAX
Catering	Catering for wedding on Lady of San Marcos boat for 65 people. Buffet-style with appetizers, salads, entree, side dish, non-alcoholic beverages, and champagne toast.		3,575.00	Catering	3,575.00	Non

11. Click **Save & Close** for the estimate.

12. Close the **Customer Center**.

Create a Progress Invoice Based on an Estimate

In this exercise, you will create a progress invoice to collect a down payment for the catering job for Lisa's wedding reception, as she liked your quote. Susie has decided to collect 25 percent up front.

1. Choose **Customers→Create Invoices**, and then choose **Lisa Silvers:Wedding Catering** as the Customer:Job.

2. Click the estimate for **7/16/2013** in the Available Estimates window, and then click **OK**.

3. Click to choose to create the invoice based on a percentage of the estimate, enter **25%** as the percent of estimate, and then click **OK**.
   Note that once that selection is made, everything will fill into the Create Invoices window, including the Class.

   > Specify what to include on the invoice.
   >
   > ○ Create invoice for the entire estimate (100%).
   >
   > ● Create invoice for a percentage of the entire estimate.
   >
   > % of estimate   25.0%

4. Choose **Due on receipt** as the Terms, and set the date to 7/22/2013.

5. Click **Save & Close**, choosing to not have the Terms permanently changed.

Enter Mileage for a Job

In this exercise, you will help Susie enter a car in the Vehicle List and track mileage for a catering job. You will first enter the current IRS-approved mileage rate. Susie has chosen to not pass on mileage expenses to customers, so you will not set up a separate item.

1. Choose **Lists→Customer & Vendor Profile Lists→Vehicle List**.

2. Click the **Vehicle** menu button, and then choose **New**.

3. Type **Honda CR-V** as the vehicle name, and then click **OK**.

4. Close the **Vehicle List**.

Enter the Current Mileage Rate

Now you will enter the current mileage rate.

5. Choose **Company→Enter Vehicle Mileage**, and then click the **Mileage Rates** button.

6. Click below the last **Effective Date** entry, and then type **070113**.

7. Tap [Tab], and then type **.515** as the Rate.

8. Close the **Mileage Rates** window, leaving the **Enter Vehicle Mileage** window open for the next step.

Enter Mileage for a Vehicle

Now you will help Susie enter mileage for the catering job for Peggy Oceans on 7/4/2013.

9. Type **h**, and then tap [Tab] to choose **Honda CR-V** as the Vehicle.

10. Type **070413**, tap [Tab], and then type **070413** again.

11. Tap [Tab], and then type **22167** as the Odometer Start.

12. Tap [Tab], and then type **22302** as the Odometer End.

13. Choose **Catering** as the Class, tap [Tab], and then type **Catering for 4th of July party** in the **Notes** field.

14. Click **Save & Close**.
    In this case, you have not indicated a customer as you do not plan to pass on the expense.

REINFORCE YOUR SKILLS 3.4

Display Reports for Estimates and Mileage Tracking

In this exercise, you will help Susie create estimate and mileage reports.

1. Choose **Lists→Chart of Accounts**.

2. Scroll to the bottom of the list, right-click on **Estimates**, and then choose **QuickReport: Estimates** from the pop-up menu.
   Take a look at the report to view the estimate you created.

3. Set the date range to **All**, and then close the **Account QuickReport** and the **Chart of Accounts** windows.

View the Progress of Invoicing an Estimate

You will now run a report that will show you the percentage of the estimate that has been invoiced.

4. Choose **Reports→Jobs, Time & Mileage→Job Progress Invoices vs. Estimates**.

5. Tap [a] to set the date range to All.
   Notice that this report shows the 25 percent of the estimate that you have invoiced.

6. Close the **Job Progress vs. Estimates** window, choosing not to memorize report.

Create a Vehicle Mileage Report

Finally, you will create a report that shows the details of the mileage for the Honda CR-V.

7. Choose **Reports→Jobs, Time & Mileage→Mileage by Vehicle Detail**.

8. Tap [a] to set the date range to All.
   You will see a report that displays the mileage for the catering job that you just entered.

9. Close the **Mileage by Vehicle Detail** report, choosing to not memorize the report.

10. Choose the appropriate option for your situation:

    ■ If you are continuing on to the next lesson or the rest of the end-of-lesson exercises, leave QuickBooks open.

    ■ If you are finished working in QuickBooks for now, choose **File→Exit**.

Apply Your Skills

Before you begin the Apply Your Skills exercises, complete one of these options:

- *Open* **[Your name] Wet Noses Veterinary Clinic, Lesson 2** *or* **Wet Noses Veterinary Clinic, Lesson 3** *from your file storage location.*

- *Restore* **Wet Noses Veterinary Clinic, Lesson 3 (Portable)** *from your file storage location. Make sure to place your name as the first word in the company filename (e.g., Sadie's Wet Noses Veterinary Clinic, Lesson 3).*

APPLY YOUR SKILLS 3.1
Set the Preferences and Create a New Job

In this exercise, you will set the necessary preferences to be able to use QuickBooks' estimating and progress invoicing features. Then you will create a new "job" for Amy Ridgeway's new kitten, Autumn.

1. Open the **Preferences** window, and display the **Company Preferences** tab for the Jobs & Estimates category.

2. Choose to both create estimates and do progress invoicing.

3. Click **OK** in the **Preferences** window to save the changes.

Create a New Job

Now that the preferences have been set, you will create the job for Amy's new kitten.

4. Create a new job for Amy Ridgeway called **Cat-Autumn**.

5. On the **Additional Info** tab, enter the following information into the custom fields: **Feline**, **DMH** (for domestic medium hair), **Tortoise Shell**, and **Female**.

6. Click **OK**.
   Dr. James has decided that it is not important for her to track "job status" for her customers, so you will leave the fields on the Job Info tab blank.

APPLY YOUR SKILLS 3.2
Create an Estimate for a Job

Amy knows that she needs to bring in her new kitten to be spayed, tested for FIV and feline leukemia, and vaccinated, but she is concerned about the total cost and needs to budget the services. In this exercise, you will create an estimate for her so she can see the full cost for all of the services. Remember that all service and non-inventory items are not taxable; only inventory items are taxable.

ITEM	DESCRIPTION
New Patient	New Patient Exam
Vaccine	Vaccine Injection Fee
Pre-A Blood Wk	Pre-Anesthesia Blood Work
Spay Cat	Feline Spay Procedure
IV Fluids	Intravenous Fluids
Pain Meds	Pre- & Post-Surgical Pain Medication
FIV/FeLV	FIV/Feline Leukemia Test
F Leuk	Feline Leukemia Vaccine
Feline DHC	Feline DHC Vaccine
Rabies	Rabies Vaccine
Rev-Cat/Sm Dog	Revolution-Cat/Small Dog

1. Create an estimate on 7/15/2013 for Amy Ridgeway: Cat-Autumn, using Routine/Scheduled as the class for the items displayed in illustration to the right.

2. Click **Save & Close**.

Create an Invoice from the Estimate

Amy Ridgeway has decided to get Autumn the care she needs in phases. In this exercise, you will create a progress invoice for the first set of items.

1. Open the **Create Invoices** window, and choose **Amy Ridgeway:Cat-Autumn** as the Customer:Job. Set the date to **7/17/13**.

2. Choose to create the invoice based on the estimate created on 7/15/2013, and then to create an invoice for selected items.

3. In the Specify Invoice Amount for Items on Estimate, click in the Show Percentage checkbox, and then choose the following items to include on the invoice: New Patient, FIV/FeLV, Vaccine, and Rabies by typing **100%** in the Curr % column. Click **OK** when you are finished.

Once you enter 100 in the Curr % column for the first item, you can use the ⬇ key to move down the column to enter the percentage for the other three items.

4. Read the warning message; click **OK** in the Zero Amount Items window.

5. Click **Save & Close** on the invoice.
   The invoice is created for the customer. The rest of the estimate will still be available, from which you can create future invoices.

Answer Questions with Reports

In this exercise, you will answer questions for Dr. James by running reports. You may wish to display the Report Center in List View to help you answer the questions. Ask your instructor if you should print the reports, print (save) them as PDF files, export them to Excel, or simply display them on the screen.

1. What is the balance still outstanding on the estimate created for Amy Ridgeway?

2. How much does each customer currently owe?

3. Is it possible to see a pie chart that shows the income by account for May 2013?

4. Will you please show me, graphically, the income by class for Wet Noses for July 2013?

5. Submit your reports based on the guidelines provided by your instructor.

6. Choose the appropriate option for your situation:
   - If you are continuing on to the next lesson or the Critical Thinking exercises, leave QuickBooks open.
   - If you are finished working in QuickBooks for now, choose **File→Exit**.

Critical Thinking

In the course of working through the following Critical Thinking exercises, you will be utilizing various skills taught in this and previous lesson(s). Take your time and think carefully about the tasks presented to you. Turn back to the lesson content if you need assistance.

3.1 Sort Through the Stack

Before You Begin: Restore the **Monkey Business, Lesson 3 (Portable)** *file from your storage location. (Remember that you are to leave the password field blank for Mary.) You also have the option of opening either the final file from Critical Thinking 2.1 or Monkey Business, Lesson 3 from your storage location.*

You have been hired by Mary Minard to help her with her organization's books. She is the owner of Monkey Business, a nonprofit organization that provides low-income students with help in preparing for college placement exams and applying for scholarships. You have just sat down at her desk and found a pile of papers. It is your job to sort through the papers and make sense of what you find, entering information into QuickBooks whenever appropriate and answering any other questions in a word-processing document saved as **Critical Thinking 3.1**. Remember, you are digging through papers on a desk, so it is up to you to determine the correct order in which to complete the tasks.

- Handwritten receipt: Dated 8/19/2013 for a $329.50 donation from Matthew Drill to provide College 101 books to ten children who are not able to afford them. Sticky note from Mary on the receipt: Can you please figure out a way to account for this donation since the books have not been distributed to the kids yet?

- Handwritten estimate: Dated 8/17/2013 for a series of workshops (College 101, FAFSA preparation, SAT preparation, and Searching for Scholarships) for a local home-school group, Expanding Opportunities Together. (They are asking for bids from three different groups before choosing a provider.) Each of the four workshops was on a separate line: College 101 $875; FAFSA $450; SAT $895; Scholarships $370. Also included were 35 College 101 texts and 35 SAT Prep books, both at 10 percent off regular retail.

- Message from Mary: "We should probably think about what we should do if customers do not pay their bill on time…Can we assess finance charges in QuickBooks? If so, please set it up so we charge 12 percent interest on overdue invoices. I think we need to have a nice grace period, though, so please set that at 30 days. Don't worry about charging a minimum finance charge or charging interest on overdue finance charges."

- Printed email: Received the contract from Expanding Opportunities Together. Could you please bill them for 50 percent up front?

- Scribbled note from Mary: Is there a report you can create for me that will show how much of the estimate has been invoiced?

3.2 Tackle the Tasks

Now is your chance to work a little more with Rock Castle Construction and apply the skills that you have learned in this lesson to accomplish additional tasks. Open or restore the **Critical Thinking 3.2** company or portable company file from your file storage location, or open the company file you used in the Develop Your Skills exercises for this lesson. Then, enter the following tasks.

Create an estimate for a new job	Create a new job for Paula Easley called Family Room, as you will be bidding on the opportunity to remodel it.
	Create an estimate for the remodel job on 01/05/2015 for 8 hours of removal labor, 40 hours of labor at $25/hour, 20 hours of installation labor, 12 hours of sub-drywall work, 8 hours of sub-electrical work, 8 hours of sub-carpeting work, flooring in the amount of $1,000, and rough lumber in the amount of $850.
Create a progress invoice based on an estimate	You have been awarded the family room remodel job for Paula Easley, so edit the job to show this. The dates for the job will be 1/19/2015 to 2/13/2015.
	Create an invoice dated 1/12/2015 for 50 percent of the entire estimate. Set the terms for the invoice as Net 15 (do not make the change permanent).
Receive a customer deposit	Chris Baker would like you to install some cabinetry that he has purchased for his garage. Receive a deposit from Chris using the Garage Repair job on 1/7/2015 for $500 for the work.
Apply a customer deposit as a payment	The garage cabinets for Chris Baker were installed on 1/15/2015 and 1/16/2015. The job took 16 hours. Create an invoice on 1/19/2015 for the work, using Installation as the item. Apply the $500 customer deposit to the invoice.
Enter time worked on a job	Samuel worked on the City of Bayshore's Lionello Community Center job for 8 hours a day from 1/12/2015 to 1/16/2015. Enter the time using a weekly timesheet. The first 22 hours were spent on removal labor; the last 18 hours were for regular labor. Choose to use time data for Samuel and use 5645 as the WC code. The class is New Construction.

You may use the company file from this exercise for the Develop Your Skills exercises in the next lesson if you wish.

3.3 Use the Web as a Learning Tool

Throughout this book, you will be provided with an opportunity to use the Internet as a learning tool by completing WebQuests. According to the original creators of WebQuests, as described on their website (WebQuest.org), a WebQuest is "an inquiry-oriented activity in which most or all of the information used by learners is drawn from the web." To complete the WebQuest projects in this book, navigate to the student resource center and choose the WebQuest for the lesson on which you are currently working. The subject of each WebQuest will be relevant to the material found in the lesson.

WebQuest Subject: Working with gift certificates

Working with Balance Sheet Accounts and Budgets

LESSON OBJECTIVES

After studying this lesson, you will be able to:

- Work with other current assets and transfer funds between accounts
- Track petty cash
- Work with fixed asset accounts and items
- Set up a long term liability
- Work with equity accounts
- Set up and use QuickBooks budgets

In previous lessons you learned to work with banking and credit card accounts, along with two current liabilities—sales tax payable and payroll liabilities. Also, you worked with an Other Current Liability account when dealing with customer deposits in the last lesson. In this lesson, you will tackle the other balance sheet accounts in QuickBooks: Other Current Assets, Fixed Assets, Long Term Liabilities, and Equity. These other balance sheet accounts allow you to track the various assets owned by your business, loans that span more than one year, prepaid expenses, and owner/shareholder investment in a company. Finally, you will learn how to use the budgeting feature in QuickBooks.

Rock Castle Construction

Rock Castle Construction has decided to rent a new office space in Millbrae. The landlord has approached Alan and offered a discount on the monthly rent amount if the company will pay six months of rent up front. Alan has decided to take advantage of this offer and has asked Zoe to set QuickBooks up to track this rent prepayment.

The president of the company has decided to purchase a new truck that will be located at the Millbrae office since business is doing so well. Zoe will be setting up a fixed asset item for the truck and a long term liability to track the loan for it.

Finally, Zoe will explore how to work with budgets in QuickBooks, creating a budget for 2015 and running a budget vs. actual report for 2014.

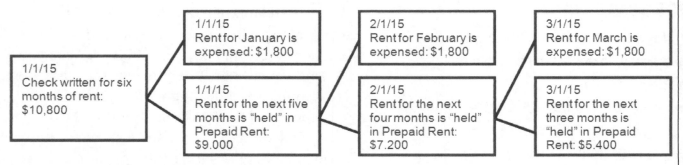

Notice how the Prepaid Insurance account "holds" funds that you have prepaid so you can expense them in the month they are actually used.

Rock Castle Construction
Profit & Loss Budget vs. Actual
January through December 2014

	Jan - Dec 14	Budget	$ Over Budget	% of Budget
Ordinary Income/Expense				
Income				
40100 · Construction Income				
40110 · Design Income	▶ 37,479.25 ◀			
40130 · Labor Income	211,149.42	93,500.00	117,649.42	225.8%
40140 · Materials Income	120,859.67	110,400.00	10,459.67	109.5%
40150 · Subcontracted Labor Income	82,710.35	192,500.00	-109,789.65	43%
40199 · Less Discounts given	-76.98	1,100.00	-1,176.98	-7%
40100 · Construction Income - Other	0.00			
Total 40100 · Construction Income	452,121.71	397,500.00	54,621.71	113.7%

The Profit & Loss Budget vs. Actual shows you how the company performed in relation to the budget prepared at the beginning of the year. This illustration displays only the income aspect of the budget.

Working with Other Current Assets

Companies use other current assets to help them match their expenses to income within the same reporting period. This is a particularly important aspect when you use the accrual basis of accounting. You will recall from *QuickBooks Pro 2013: Level 1* that a company using the accrual basis of accounting records expenses when accrued, not when cash is paid. This means that even if you pay a six-month insurance policy up front, you must expense it during the month that it covers.

Balance Sheet Accounts

Remember, the balance sheet accounts are the asset, liability, and equity accounts. You have already learned about many balance sheet accounts: bank, credit card, current liabilities (sales tax payable and payroll liabilities), Accounts Receivable, and Accounts Payable. Now you will focus on the remaining balance sheet accounts. Refer to the following table to learn more about these other accounts.

ADDITIONAL TYPES OF BALANCE SHEET ACCOUNTS

Account Type	Description	Examples
Other Current Asset	Assets you plan to either use or convert to cash within one year	■ Prepaid Insurance ■ Security Deposit
Fixed Asset	Assets you do not plan to convert to cash within one year; they are usually depreciable	■ Vehicle ■ Equipment
Long Term Liabilities	Liabilities (loans) you do not plan to pay off within the next year	■ Mortgage ■ Auto Loan
Equity	The owner's equity in the company, whether it is a sole proprietor, a partner, or shareholders	■ Owner's Equity ■ Retained Earnings

BEHIND THE SCENES

When writing a check for six months of rent, you expense the current month's coverage and hold the rest in the Prepaid Rent account.

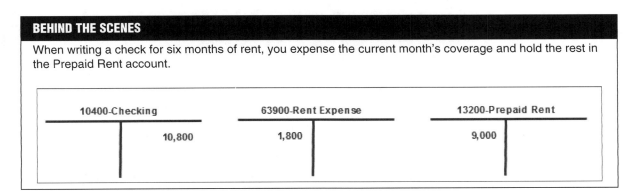

QUICK REFERENCE	USING OTHER CURRENT ASSET ACCOUNTS
Task	**Procedure**
Create an Other Current Asset account	■ Choose Lists→Chart of Accounts. ■ Click the Account menu button, and choose New. ■ Choose Other Account Types, select Other Current Asset from the drop-down list, and then click Continue. ■ Type the account number and the name of the new account.
Fund an Other Current Asset account	■ Choose Banking→Write Checks. ■ Choose Checking as the bank account; complete the rest of the vendor information. ■ Enter the amount for the current month as an expense and the remaining amount as a debit to the other current asset account you created to track it (such as Prepaid Rent).

DEVELOP YOUR SKILLS 4.1

Create and Fund a Prepaid Rent Account

In this exercise, you will help Zoe set QuickBooks up to be able to track the prepayment of rent for the company. The first step is to open QuickBooks, and then either open a company file or restore a portable company file.

1. Start **QuickBooks 2013**.

   If you downloaded the student exercise files in the portable company file *format, follow Option 1 below. If you downloaded the files in the* company file *format, follow Option 2 below.*

 If you choose, you may use the final company file from Critical Thinking 3.2. In this case, open the Critical Thinking 3.2 company file from your default storage location in Option 2 below.

Option 1: Restore a Portable Company File

2. Choose **File→Open or Restore Company**.

3. Restore the **Rock Castle Construction** portable file for this lesson from your file storage location, placing your name as the first word in the filename (e.g., Zoe's Rock Castle Construction, Lesson 4).

   It may take a few moments for the portable company file to open. Once it does, continue with step 4.

Option 2: Open a Company File

2. Choose **File→Open or Restore Company**, ensure that **Open a regular company file** is selected, and then open the **Rock Castle Construction** company file for this lesson from your file storage location.

   The QuickBooks company file will open.

3. Click **OK** to close the QuickBooks Information windows. If necessary, click **No** in the Set Up External Accountant User window.

Create a Prepaid Rent Account

Now you will create a prepaid rent account.

4. Click the **Chart of Accounts** task icon in the Company area of the Home page.

5. Click the **Account** menu button and then choose **New**.

6. Follow these steps to create the new account:

Chart of Accounts

Ⓐ Click to choose **Other Account Types**. ⟶

Ⓑ Click to choose **Other Current Asset**.

Ⓒ Click **Continue**.

Ⓓ Type **13200** as the Number.

Ⓔ Tap Tab, and then type **Prepaid Rent**.

7. Click **Save & Close**; close the **Chart of Accounts** window.

Fund the Prepaid Rent Account

Zoe will now write the check for the rent payment, expensing the current month and placing the rest in the prepaid rent account.

8. Click the **Write Checks** task icon in the Banking area of the Home page.

9. Follow these steps to write the rent check:

Write Checks

Ⓐ Set the date to **01/01/2015**. ⟶

Ⓑ Tap Tab, and then type **re**.

Ⓒ Tap Tab, and then type **10800**. ⟶

Ⓓ Tap Tab two times, and then type **Rent for January-June 2015**. ⟶

Ⓔ Tap Tab two times, and then type **1800**. ⟶

Ⓕ Tap Tab three times, and then type **o**.

Ⓖ Tap Tab, and then type **132**.

Ⓗ Tap Tab four times, and then type **o**.

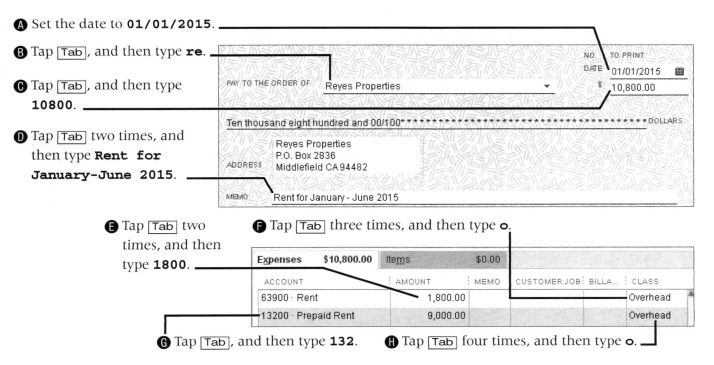

10. Click **Save & Close**.

Transferring Funds Between Accounts

Once you place funds in an Other Current Asset account, you must be able to expense them when they are used. This is important, as you need to make sure to match expenses to income during the period in which they are utilized. Another term for this transfer of funds from the asset to the expense account is *amortization*. Amortization is likely familiar to you; it is simply the process of a balance decreasing over time. For instance, if you have a home mortgage, the way that the balance that you owe decreases over, say 30 years, is amortization. You can accomplish this transfer in the register window of the asset; you do not have to use a formal journal entry.

Memorizing Transactions

FROM THE KEYBOARD

Ctrl+t to open the
Memorized
Transactions List

There are many transactions (such as the expensing of other current assets) that you have to repeat over and over again. You can choose to have QuickBooks memorize these transactions to increase your efficiency. When QuickBooks memorizes a transaction, you can choose:

- To be reminded about the transaction
- To not be reminded and simply have it listed on the Memorized Transaction List
- To have QuickBooks automatically enter it as frequently as you wish

By default, QuickBooks will choose for you to be reminded of the memorized transaction. You must make sure to choose one of the other options if you want the transaction to be listed or to occur automatically.

TRANSACTION NAME ▲	TYPE	SOURCE ACCOUNT	AMOUNT	FREQUENCY	AUTO	NEXT DATE
◆ **Monthly**	**Group**			**Monthly**	✔	**03/01/2015**
◆ Rent Txfr	General Journal	13200 · Prepaid Rent	1,800.00			
◆ Overhead	General Journal	13100 · Pre-paid Insurance	675.00	Never		
◆ Recurring Depr Entry - Monthly	General Journal	54599 · Less Discounts Taken	19.60	Monthly	✔	12/31/2014
◆ Sergeant Insurance	Check	10100 · Checking	675.00	Monthly		01/15/2015

The Memorized Transaction List keeps track of all of your memorized transactions for you. Access it via the Lists option on the menu bar.

Recurring Transactions

When you are creating a new memorized transaction that you want QuickBooks to enter automatically for you, you can now group it with other transactions you have memorized.

The Enter Memorized Transactions window appears whenever you open QuickBooks and have transactions that are scheduled to be entered. This detailed list of automatic transactions helps you stay on top of which transactions are slated to be entered. And, if you enter all of them, you will have a reminder of exactly what QuickBooks is doing for you behind the scenes when entering automatic transactions.

Using Memorized Transactions for Common Transactions

You can also use the Memorized Transaction List for transactions that you complete on a regular basis. For instance, if you often pay bills electronically you can memorize a Write Checks window with BPOL (Bill Pay Online) in the check number field, and then just double-click it from the Memorized Transaction List when you need to enter another online bill payment.

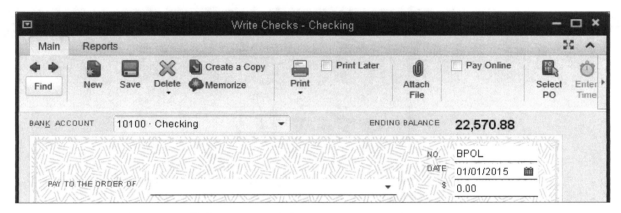

To set up a common transaction to be memorized, add the entries in the correct transaction window. Here, note that "BPOL" has been entered as the check number.

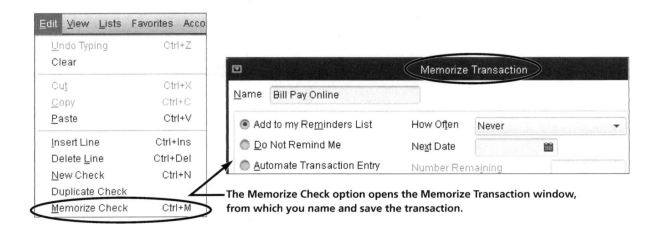

The Memorize Check option opens the Memorize Transaction window, from which you name and save the transaction.

Each month the amount for the current month's rent should be expensed.

13200-Prepaid Rent		63900-Rent	
	1,800	1,800	

QUICK REFERENCE | **TRANSFERRING FUNDS AND MEMORIZING TRANSACTIONS**

Task	Procedure
Transfer funds between accounts using a register	■ Choose Lists→Chart of Accounts. ■ Double-click the desired account; enter the date and amount of the transfer. ■ Choose the desired account; record the transaction.
Memorize a transaction	■ Ensure that the desired transaction is currently displayed, and then single-click within it to select it. ■ Choose Edit→Memorize General Journal (or whatever type of transaction it is). ■ Enter the information regarding how you want QuickBooks to deal with the memorized transaction; click OK.

DEVELOP YOUR SKILLS 4.2
Make and Memorize a Transfer of Funds

In this exercise, you will help Zoe record the first transfer of funds from Prepaid Rent to Rent Expense. Once the transfer is set up, you will memorize it to occur automatically.

Before you set up your first recurring monthly transaction in your Memorized Transaction List, you will create a group called "Monthly" for this list entry. You can then add new monthly transactions as they are created.

1. Choose **Lists→Memorized Transaction List**.
   The Memorized Transaction List window will appear.

2. Click the **Memorized Transaction menu button**, and then choose **New Group**.
   The New Memorized Transaction Group window will be displayed.

3. Follow these steps to create the new group:

Ⓐ Type **Monthly**.

Ⓑ Click to the left of **Automate Transaction Entry.**

Ⓒ Click the **drop-down arrow** and choose **Monthly**.

Ⓓ Tap Tab, and then type **030115**.

4. Click **OK** to record the new memorized group.

Record Next Month's Insurance Expense

5. Choose **Lists→Chart of Accounts**.

6. Double-click the **13200•Prepaid Rent** account.

The register for the asset will open. Notice that QuickBooks has registered an increase in the Prepaid Rent account for $9,000.

7. Follow these steps to record a transfer of $1,800 from Prepaid Rent to the Rent expense account:

Ⓐ Type **020115** as the date.   **Ⓑ** Tap ⌷Tab⌷ three times, and then type **1800**.   **Ⓒ** Tap ⌷Tab⌷, and then type **ren**.

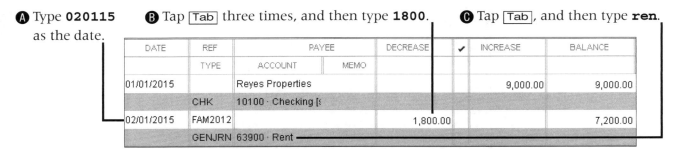

DATE	REF	PAYEE		DECREASE	✔	INCREASE	BALANCE
	TYPE	ACCOUNT	MEMO				
01/01/2015		Reyes Properties				9,000.00	9,000.00
	CHK	10100 · Checking [					
02/01/2015	FAM2012			1,800.00			7,200.00
	GENJRN	63900 · Rent					

> **BTS BRIEF**
>
> 63900•Rent Expense DR 1,800.00; 13200•Prepaid Rent CR <1,800.00>

8. Click **Record** at the bottom right of the register window.

Memorize the Transaction

So that Zoe will not have to sit down at the computer at the first of each month and record this transfer, she will memorize it and choose for QuickBooks to include it in the Enter Memorized Transactions window.

9. Click anywhere within the two lines of the transaction you just recorded.

10. Choose **Edit→Memorize General Journal**.

This transaction is considered a general journal entry because it is a basic transfer between accounts.

11. Follow these steps to memorize the transaction in the Monthly group:

Ⓐ Type **Rent Txfr**.

Ⓑ Click to the left of **Add to Group**.

Ⓒ Click the **drop-down arrow** and choose **Monthly**.

Ⓓ Click **OK** to memorize the transaction.

12. Close the **Prepaid Insurance** account register and the **Chart of Accounts** window.

Take a look at the Memorized Transaction List and notice the new group and rent transfer entries.

13. Close the **Memorized Transaction List** window.

Tracking Petty Cash

Most businesses keep cash around for small expenditures. This is known as petty cash. In QuickBooks, you set up Petty Cash as a bank account in your Chart of Accounts. You fund it by transferring money from another account or by keeping cash back when you make a deposit.

Recording Methods

QuickBooks offers two methods to record petty cash expenditures:

- **Write Checks Method:** You can choose Petty Cash as the account and use the Write Checks window to record your petty cash expenses.
- **The Register Method:** You can enter petty cash expenditures directly into the register.

The register method allows you to enter your petty cash expenditures more quickly, as you can tab through it faster.

BEHIND THE SCENES

When you use the checking account to fund the petty cash account, you debit Petty Cash and credit Checking.

10100-Checking		10400-Petty Cash	
	200	200	

When you use petty cash for a purchase, you debit the expense account (in this example Postage) and credit Petty Cash.

63100-Postage		10400-Petty Cash	
44			44

QUICK REFERENCE	TRACKING PETTY CASH
Task	**Procedure**
Create a Petty Cash account	▪ Choose Lists→Chart of Accounts. ▪ Click the Account menu button; choose New. ▪ Choose Bank as the account type; click Continue. ▪ Type the account number, and then name the account Petty Cash.
Fund the Petty Cash account	▪ Choose Banking→Write Checks. ▪ Enter a check to cash for the amount, with Petty Cash as the account, and then record the transaction.

	TRACKING PETTY CASH (continued)
Task	**Procedure**
Enter petty cash expenditures	■ Choose Banking→Write Checks. ■ Choose Petty Cash as the Bank Account, enter the details, and then record the transaction.

DEVELOP YOUR SKILLS 4.3

Work with a Petty Cash Account

In this exercise, you will help Zoe fund and use a petty cash account.

Rock Castle already has a Petty Cash account on the books, so you do not need to create it before transferring funds into it.

1. Click the **Write Checks** task icon in the Banking area of the Home page.

2. Tap ⎡Tab⎤ once you have ensured that Checking is the account; then, follow these steps to complete the check:

Write Checks

Ⓐ Type **010215** as the Date.

Ⓑ Tap ⎡Tab⎤, type **Cash**, and then tap ⎡Tab⎤, Quick Adding it as a vendor.

Ⓒ Type **200** as the amount.

Ⓓ Click in the **Account** column, and then type **pe**.

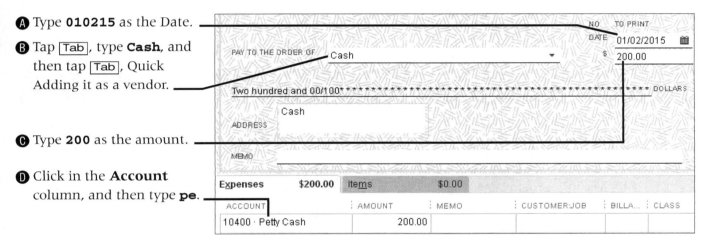

> **BTS BRIEF**
>
> 10400•Petty Cash DR 200.00; 10100•Checking CR <200.00>

3. Click **Save & Close**, and then click **Save Anyway**.

Pay for Stamps Using the Petty Cash Register

Zoe will now purchase a roll of stamps with petty cash and record the transaction in the Petty Cash register.

4. Click the **Chart of Accounts** task icon in the Company area of the Home page.

5. Double-click the **Petty Cash** account in the Chart of Accounts window.

Chart of Accounts

6. Follow these steps to record the charge to petty cash:

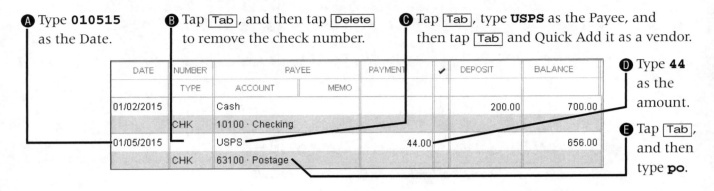

Ⓐ Type **010515** as the Date.

Ⓑ Tap Tab, and then tap Delete to remove the check number.

Ⓒ Tap Tab, type **USPS** as the Payee, and then tap Tab and Quick Add it as a vendor.

Ⓓ Type **44** as the amount.

Ⓔ Tap Tab, and then type **po**.

DATE	NUMBER	PAYEE		PAYMENT	✔	DEPOSIT	BALANCE
	TYPE	ACCOUNT	MEMO				
01/02/2015		Cash				200.00	700.00
	CHK	10100 · Checking					
01/05/2015		USPS		44.00			656.00
	CHK	63100 · Postage					

> **BTS BRIEF**
>
> 63100•Postage DR 44.00; 10400•Petty Cash CR <44.00>

7. Click **Record**; close the **Petty Cash** register window.

8. Close the **Chart of Accounts** window.

Working with Fixed Asset Accounts

As you saw in the Additional Types of Balance Sheet Accounts table on page 157, a fixed asset is one that you don't plan to use up or turn into cash within the next year. A business uses fixed assets in a productive capacity to promote the main operations of the company. Fixed assets are also depreciable, which means that you don't expense the assets when you purchase them but rather over the useful life of the asset.

Look at the following list to see the main types of fixed assets:

- Land
- Furniture & Equipment
- Buildings
- Vehicles
- Leasehold Improvements

Setting Up Fixed Assets in QuickBooks

There are many correct ways to set up your fixed assets in QuickBooks. You should ask your accountant which method she prefers that you use. In this lesson, you will look at one method that involves creating a fixed asset account for each major type of fixed asset and then an account to track accumulated depreciation for all fixed assets. This is displayed in the following illustration.

Chart of Accounts				
NAME	$	TYPE	BALANCE TOTAL	ATTACH
◇ 15000 · Furniture and Equipment		Fixed Asset	34,326.00	
◇ 15100 · Vehicles		Fixed Asset	78,936.91	
◇ 15200 · Buildings and Improvements		Fixed Asset	325,000.00	
◇ 15300 · Construction Equipment		Fixed Asset	15,300.00	
◇ 16900 · Land		Fixed Asset	90,000.00	
◇ 17000 · Accumulated Depreciation		Fixed Asset	-110,344.60	

Depreciation

Depreciation provides a business with a way to match income to expenses. A fixed asset is used to produce income over a period of time, and depreciation allows you to record the appropriate expense for the same period. Many small businesses record depreciation transactions just once a year, but they can be entered monthly or quarterly if the business produces financial statements for those periods.

FLASHBACK TO GAAP: MATCHING

Remember that expenses need to be matched with revenues.

Accumulated Depreciation

Each accounting period, a business records a depreciation expense for the fixed asset(s). These depreciation expenses "accumulate" in an account called Accumulated Depreciation, which is also a fixed asset account. Accumulated Depreciation is a *contra account*, which means it offsets the balance of the related fixed asset accounts by entering a negative amount so that the book value is displayed rather than the original cost on the balance sheet report.

Fixed Asset Items

Fixed asset items provide a convenient way to track your fixed assets. After creating your fixed asset account and subaccounts, you should set up the fixed asset item. These items help you consolidate all of the important information about each fixed asset in a convenient place. In addition, your accountant can transfer the information from your Fixed Asset List to the Fixed Asset Manager, if they use that feature of QuickBooks.

In the Fixed Asset Item List QuickBooks allows you to track the following information:

- Purchase information/cost basis
- Sales information
- Corresponding asset account
- Serial number
- Warranty information
- Notes and descriptions

NAME	LOCATION OF FI...	PURCHASE...	ACCOUNT ▲	COST	COST/BASIS	ACCUMULAT...	BOOK VALUE	SAL...	PRI...	A...
Desktop PC (5) - 8		05/01/2010	15000 · Furniture a...	13,000.00	13,000.00	2,600.00	10,400.00		0.00	
Copier/Printer - 15	Main Office	04/26/2010	15000 · Furniture a...	5,000.00	5,000.00	1,000.00	4,000.00		0.00	
Chairs - 3		11/15/2009	15000 · Furniture a...	475.00	475.00	247.00	228.00		0.00	
Conference Table - 4		11/15/2009	15000 · Furniture a...	3,500.00	3,500.00	1,820.00	1,680.00		0.00	
Desks - 5		12/20/2009	15000 · Furniture a...	2,100.00	2,100.00	1,092.00	1,008.00		0.00	
Desktop computer - 6	MV	10/15/2009	15000 · Furniture a...	2,000.00	2,000.00	1,040.00	960.00		0.00	
Desktop PC - 7		10/01/2009	15000 · Furniture a...	5,000.00	5,000.00	2,600.00	2,400.00		0.00	
Laser Printer - 9		10/01/2009	15000 · Furniture a...	2,001.00	2,001.00	1,040.52	960.48		0.00	
Metal filling cabinets - ...		10/29/2009	15000 · Furniture a...	1,250.00	1,250.00	484.69	765.31		0.00	
Server - 13		10/01/2009	15000 · Furniture a...	6,500.00	6,500.00	3,380.00	3,120.00		0.00	
2015 Ford Truck - 18	Millbrae, CA	01/02/2015	15100 · Vehicles	30,649.00					0.00	
Lexus - 16		04/26/2010	15100 · Vehicles	75,000.00	75,000.00	15,000.00	60,000.00		0.00	
2005 pickup - 2	Bayshore, CA	02/14/2007	15100 · Vehicles	28,602.91	28,602.91	12,585.00	16,017.91		0.00	
2005 Van - 14		10/15/2007	15100 · Vehicles	26,000.00	26,000.00	21,507.20	4,492.80		0.00	
Utility Truck - 1	Bayshore, CA	06/01/2007	15100 · Vehicles	24,334.00	24,334.00	12,585.00	11,749.00		0.00	
Office Building - 11	1735 County Ro...	09/22/2007	15200 · Buildings a...	325,000.00	325,000.00	27,430.54	297,569.46		0.00	
Equipment - 17		12/31/2009	15300 · Constructio...	15,300.00	15,300.00	5,932.65	9,367.35		0.00	
Office Land - 12	1735 Country R...	09/22/2007	16900 · Land	90,000.00	90,000.00		90,000.00		0.00	

The Fixed Asset Item List helps you to track your fixed assets and compile all of the essential information for them in one convenient place.

Creating Fixed Asset Items

There are two ways that a new fixed asset item can be set up:

■ Create the new item when entering the purchase transaction
■ Open the Fixed Asset Item List and create a new item

When you enter fixed assets upon creation of a new company, you will debit the fixed asset account and credit Opening Balance Equity. If you recall from *QuickBooks Pro 2013: Level 1*, this account is created by QuickBooks when the first balance sheet account is created so you have an accurate balance sheet from the beginning. If a loan is associated with the fixed asset, the loan amount will be entered in a Long Term Liability account and the difference in an equity account.

When you set up a fixed asset item, you indicate the account into which it has been entered. This does not enter it into the account or affect what happens behind the scenes. You must also complete the appropriate transaction to make sure and enter the fixed asset properly.

Accountant Tool: Fixed Asset Manager

If your accountant uses the Premier Accountant version of QuickBooks, he can pull the fixed asset information from your Fixed Asset Item list into the Fixed Asset Manager in order to work with your fixed assets. This tool will help him determine how to depreciate the fixed assets as well as the amount that needs to be posted back to the company file as an adjusting entry.

> **FLASHBACK TO GAAP: COST**
>
> Remember that when a company purchases assets, it should record them at cost, not fair market value. For example, if you bought an item worth $750 for $100, it should be recorded at $100.

Task	Procedure
Create a fixed asset item from a transaction	■ Enter the purchase transaction information; click the Items tab. ■ Click the Item column drop-down arrow; choose <Add New>. ■ Enter all of the fixed asset information, choosing the correct fixed asset account, and then click OK.
Create a fixed asset item using the Fixed Asset Item List	■ Choose Lists→Fixed Asset Item List. ■ Click the Item menu button; choose New. ■ Enter all of the fixed asset information, choosing the correct fixed asset account, and then click OK.

DEVELOP YOUR SKILLS 4.4
Create a Fixed Asset Item

In this exercise, you will help Zoe create a new fixed asset item for the new truck that was purchased.

1. Choose **Lists→Fixed Asset Item List**.

2. Click the **Item** menu button, and then choose **New**.

3. Follow these steps to create the new item:

Ⓐ Type **2015 Ford Truck - 18**.

Ⓑ Tap ⎡Tab⎦ three times, and then type **Ford F-150 Truck**.

Ⓒ Tap ⎡Tab⎦, and then type **010215**.

Ⓓ Tap ⎡Tab⎦, and then type **30649**.

Ⓔ Tap ⎡Tab⎦, and then type **Bayshore Ford**.

Ⓕ Tap ⎡Tab⎦, and then type **v**.

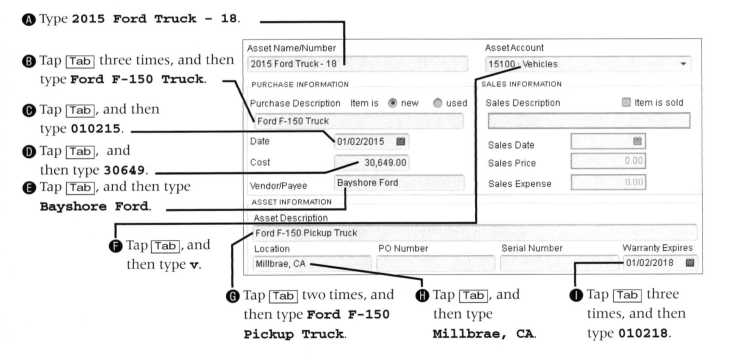

Ⓖ Tap ⎡Tab⎦ two times, and then type **Ford F-150 Pickup Truck**.

Ⓗ Tap ⎡Tab⎦, and then type **Millbrae, CA**.

Ⓘ Tap ⎡Tab⎦ three times, and then type **010218**.

4. Click **OK**.

5. Close the **Fixed Asset Item List**.
   You did not affect anything behind the scenes in this exercise, but in the next exercise you will see how the purchase of the new fixed asset is entered behind the scenes.

Setting Up a Long Term Liability

Most companies have to take out a loan for a fixed asset (or a loan for some other item for a period longer than a year) at some time or another. In this section, you will create a Long Term Liability account to track the new truck loan. A company uses a Long Term Liability to track a loan that is scheduled to take longer than a year to pay off.

The QuickBooks Loan Manager

QuickBooks provides a tool for you to track your loans, similar to the Fixed Asset Item List that allows you to track your fixed assets. The Loan Manager allows you to set up loans based on information that you have entered in a long term liability or other current liability account. The Loan Manager tracks the principle and interest payments without having to set up separate amortization schedules. You can also use the Loan Manager to compare different loan scenarios. In addition, you have the opportunity to print loans from the Loan Manager.

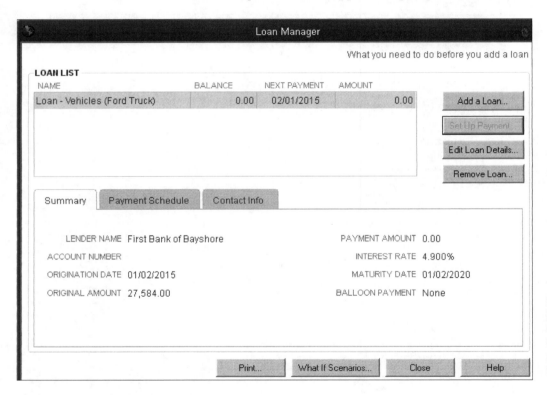

The Loan Manager provides you with a place to track your long term liabilities. You can even click the What If Scenarios button to explore possible loan situations before you make a decision.

Preparing to Use the Loan Manager

There are a number of items you should prepare before you set up a loan in the Loan Manager:

- **Set Up Your Accounts:** Make sure to set up any liability (i.e., 23300•Loan – Vehicles (Ford Truck)), expense (i.e., 62420•Loan Interest), and escrow (only if required) accounts that will be affected by the loan.

- **Check Previous Transactions:** If you are working with an existing (rather than new) loan, you will also need to confirm that all of the transactions related to it are entered into QuickBooks before setting up the loan in the Loan Manager.

- **Gather Loan Documents:** Make sure you have all of your original loan documents handy before you begin to set up the loan. It is important that you enter the opening balance and other information properly.

Once all transactions are up to date and the loan has been entered into the Loan Manager, you will be able to record future loan payments in the Set Up Payment window.

Feature update - reboot required to use this feature ✕

QuickBooks updated this feature to work with your version of Internet Explorer. Please reboot your computer to use this feature. You can continue using other features of QuickBooks if you don't reboot.

If this window appears when you use the Loan Manager, you will have to reboot your computer in order for the feature to work.

BEHIND THE SCENES

When you pay for the truck with your new loan and down payment, the offsetting account will be the fixed asset account.

10100-Checking	15100-Vehicles	23300-Loan - Vehicles (Ford Truck)
3,065	30,649	27,584

Making a payment affects three accounts (unless you have a 0 percent interest loan): the loan account, the bank account, and the interest expense account.

10100-Checking	62420-Loan Interest	23300-Loan - Vehicles (Ford Truck)
519.28	112.63	406.65

QUICK REFERENCE	DEALING WITH LONG TERM LIABILITIES
Task	**Procedure**
Enter the funds for the loan	■ Choose Lists→Chart of Accounts.
	■ Double-click the desired Long Term Liability account.
	■ Enter the transaction date and the amount.
	■ Choose the correct fixed asset to debit; click Record.
Enter a loan in the Loan Manager	■ Gather all of your loan documents and information.
	■ Set up the liability and expense accounts required to track the loan.
	■ Choose Banking→Loan Manager; click the Add a Loan button.
	■ Enter the information on each screen, clicking Next to move through the setup screens and clicking Finish once all information has been entered.
Set up a loan payment with the Loan Manager	■ Choose Banking→Loan Manager.
	■ Click to select the loan for which you need to set up a payment; click Set Up Payment.
	■ Make any necessary changes in the Set Up Payment window; click OK.
	■ Look over the bill or check to ensure its accuracy; click Save & Close.

Create a Long Term Liability

In this exercise, you will assist Zoe with setting up the loan account for the new truck, funding the loan, and setting up the loan in the Loan Manager.

First, you will create the new liability account.

1. Click the **Chart of Accounts** task icon in the Company area of the Home page.

2. Click the **Account** menu button, and then choose **New**.

3. Follow these steps to create the new Long Term Liability account:

Chart of Accounts

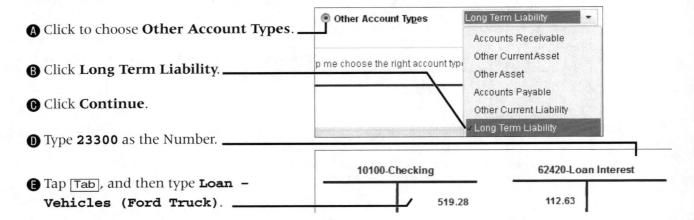

Ⓐ Click to choose **Other Account Types**.

Ⓑ Click **Long Term Liability**.

Ⓒ Click **Continue**.

Ⓓ Type **23300** as the Number.

Ⓔ Tap Tab, and then type **Loan – Vehicles (Ford Truck)**.

4. Click **Save & Close** to record the new account.

Fund the Long Term Liability Account

Rock Castle has just received the new truck and the First Bank of Bayshore has issued the funds on your behalf to Bayshore Ford. It's now time for Zoe to record the starting balance for the loan and the cost of the truck.

5. Double-click the **Loan – Vehicles (Ford Truck)** account in the Chart of Accounts window.

6. Follow these steps to record the funding of the loan:

Ⓐ Type **010215** as the Date.

Ⓑ Tap Tab three times, and then type **27584** as the amount.

Ⓒ Tap Tab, and then type **v** to choose the Vehicles account.

Ⓓ Click **Record**.

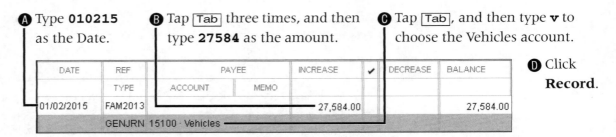

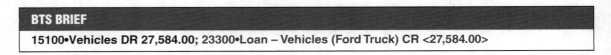

BTS BRIEF

15100•Vehicles DR 27,584.00; 23300•Loan – Vehicles (Ford Truck) CR <27,584.00>

7. Close the **register** window; close the **Chart of Accounts** window.

Write a Check for the Down Payment

Alan has asked Zoe to prepare a check for the 10 percent that the company put down on the new truck.

8. Click the **Write Checks** task icon in the Banking area of the Home page.

Write Checks

9. Check **Print Later** from the Ribbon, and then follow these steps to create the check for the down payment:

Ⓐ Tap Tab, and then type **010215**.

Ⓑ Tap Tab, type **First Bank of Bayshore**, tap Tab, and then **Quick Add** it as a vendor.

Ⓒ Type **3065** as the amount.

Ⓓ Tap Tab two times, and then type **Down payment, Ford F-150 truck**.

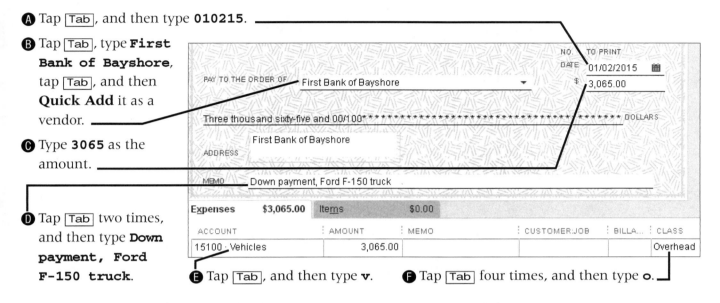

Ⓔ Tap Tab, and then type **v**.   **Ⓕ** Tap Tab four times, and then type **o**.

BTS BRIEF

15100•Vehicles DR 3,065.00; 10100•Checking CR <3,065.00>

10. Click **Save & Close** to record the transaction.
The 15100•Vehicles account will be increased by total cost of the truck ($27,584 from the loan and $3,065 from the down payment).

Enter a Loan in the Loan Manager

11. Choose **Banking→Loan Manager**.

12. If the Feature update window appears, click **OK**, and then reboot your computer.

If you had to reboot your computer, you will need to launch QuickBooks, open [Your name]'s Rock Castle Construction, Lesson 4 company file, and then choose Banking→Loan Manager before continuing.

13. Click the **Add a Loan** button [Add a Loan...] .

14. Follow these steps to enter the account information for the loan:

A Choose this account from this drop-down menu.

B Choose First Bank of Bayshore from this drop-down menu.

C Tap [Tab], and then type **010215**.

D Tap [Tab], and then type **27584**.

E Tap [Tab], and then type **60**.

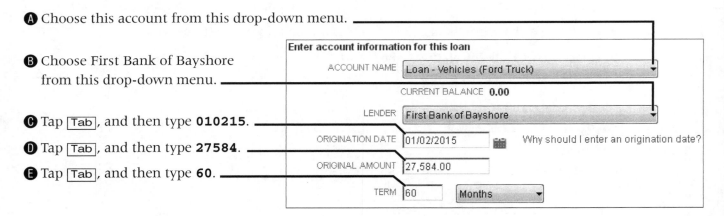

15. Click **Next**, and then follow these steps to enter the payment information:

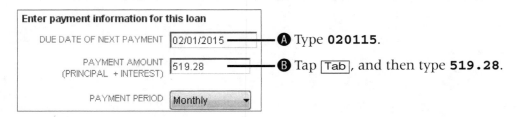

A Type **020115**.

B Tap [Tab], and then type **519.28**.

16. Click **Next**, and then follow these steps to enter the interest information:

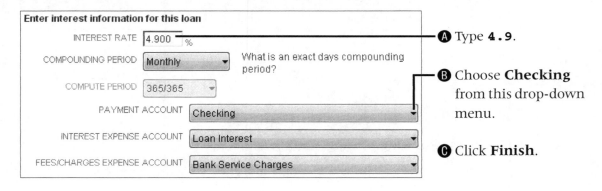

A Type **4.9**.

B Choose **Checking** from this drop-down menu.

C Click **Finish**.

The loan is now set up in the Loan Manager, ready for you to track.

17. Close the **Loan Manager** window.

Working with Equity Accounts

Equity accounts reflect the net worth of a company. Take another look at Appendix A, Need to Know Accounting and notice that the accounting equation teaches that the sum of the equity accounts is equal to assets (what you own) less liabilities (what you owe):

Equity = Assets – Liabilities

An equity account has a credit normal balance. It represents how viable your company is since it shows how much you would have left if you sold all of your assets and then paid off the liabilities.

Owner's Equity / Capital Stock

In a sole proprietorship, the equity is what the owner has invested in the company. In a corporation, the equity is what the shareholders have invested in the company. An owner's investment occurs when an owner deposits funds into the company or shareholders purchase stock. An owner's withdrawal of funds from the company is known as a draw; if it is a corporation you will see shareholder distributions.

Retained Earnings

At the end of the fiscal year, a business will show either a net income or a net loss. When the books are closed, this amount is transferred into the Retained Earnings account to clear out all income and expense accounts for the next year. When the fiscal year ends, QuickBooks automatically makes this transfer.

Opening Balance Equity

QuickBooks creates the Opening Balance Equity account when you first create your company. As you enter opening balances into the accounts, QuickBooks uses Opening Balance Equity as the offset account so you can have a working balance sheet right from the beginning. You may need to enter a transfer between accounts if there is a balance in the Opening Balance Equity account once all of your new accounts are entered into QuickBooks. In addition, there are other times when QuickBooks may use the Opening Balance Equity account and an adjustment must be made. For instance, when you set QuickBooks up to track inventory in Lesson 1, Dealing with Physical Inventory and entered a beginning number of inventory items on hand, you debited 12100 • Inventory Asset, and 30000 • Opening Bal Equity was credited behind the scenes.

Equity transactions can be a bit tricky. You should talk to your accountant about how to deal with them for your unique company.

FLASHBACK TO GAAP: BUSINESS ENTITY

Remember that the first assumption of GAAP is that the business is separate from the owners and from other businesses. Revenues and expenses of the business should be kept separate from the personal expenses of the business owner.

QUICK REFERENCE	DEALING WITH EQUITY TRANSACTIONS
Task	**Procedure**
Record an Owner's Investment	▪ Choose Banking→Make Deposits.
	▪ Choose the account into which the deposit will be made, and the owner's equity account in the From Account field.
	▪ Enter the payment information and amount; click Save & Close.
Record an Owner's Draw	▪ Choose Banking→Write Checks.
	▪ Enter the owner as the payee, as well as the date and amount of the check.
	▪ Choose Owners draw in the Account column on the Expenses tab.
	▪ Choose whether to print the check; click Save & Close.

The Audit Trail

The audit trail feature of QuickBooks allows you to track every entry, modification, or deletion to transactions in your file. The audit trail feature is always on to make sure that an accurate record of your QuickBooks data is kept. The audit trail does not track changes to lists, only to transactions. This can help you research transaction history and determine whether certain types of fraudulent activity are occurring. To view the audit trail, you can run a QuickBooks report called "Audit Trail," which is available from the Accountant & Taxes category of the Report Center. In fact, the QuickBooks Audit Trail report has even been reported to have helped determine a fraud case in court!

Creating Budgets & Forecasts in QuickBooks

QuickBooks includes a budgeting feature that allows you to create account-based budgets for Balance Sheet or Profit & Loss accounts. Budgets can be created based on a previous year's budget or from scratch—or, if you have been using QuickBooks for a year, the actual figures from the previous year.

Forecasting the Future

In addition to budgets, QuickBooks also supplies you with a forecasting feature that assists you with making predictions about the future; for instance, it allows you to conduct "what-if" analyses as well as look at future cash flow or revenue. Forecasts can be based on actual figures from the last year or from scratch.

Once you have created a budget or a forecast, you will run a report to view the information. QuickBooks provides several reports that will allow you to use the information in your budget(s) or forecast(s).

The Report Center lists all of the budget and forecast reports available for you to create.

Email Functionality in Reports

QuickBooks allows you to email reports from any report window. You have a chance to choose whether the recipient will receive the report as an Adobe Acrobat (PDF) or Microsoft Excel file. The report will appear the same as it would as if you printed it from QuickBooks.

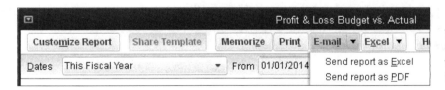

When you click the Email button on the toolbar, you can choose the type of file that will be attached to your email message.

You cannot send a report by email when using a sample company file, but you will have a chance to explore this feature in the Reinforce Your Skills exercises at the end of this lesson.

QUICK REFERENCE	CREATING BUDGETS & FORECASTS IN QUICKBOOKS AND EMAILING REPORTS
Task	**Procedure**
Create a budget in QuickBooks	▪ Choose Company→Planning & Budgeting→Set Up Budgets. ▪ Click the Create New Budget button. ▪ Choose the budget year and type; click Next. ▪ Choose to base the budget on a customer:job or class, or neither; click Next. ▪ Choose whether you wish to create the budget from scratch or by using the previous year's actual data, and then click Finish.
Create a forecast in QuickBooks	▪ Choose Company→Planning & Budgeting→Set Up Forecast. ▪ Click the Create New Forecast button. ▪ Choose the year for the forecast; click Next. ▪ Choose whether the forecast will use customer:job, class, or neither of them as additional criteria; click Next. ▪ Choose whether you wish to create the forecast from scratch or by using the previous year's actual data, and then click Finish.
Email a report from QuickBooks	▪ Produce the report you wish to email. ▪ Click the Email button, and choose to send it as a PDF or an Excel file. ▪ Using your email program, enter the recipients and make any desired modifications to the message. ▪ Send the email.

DEVELOP YOUR SKILLS 4.6

Produce a Budget and a Budget Report

In this exercise, you will help Zoe create a budget for 2015 based on the actual figures from 2014.

1. Choose **Company→Planning & Budgeting→Set Up Budgets**.
   The Set Up Budgets window appears with the FY2014-15 Profit & Loss by Account budget displayed.

2. Click the **Create New Budget** button.

Create New Budget

3. Ensure that **2015** and **Profit and Loss** are selected; click **Next**.

4. Ensure that **No additional criteria** is selected; click **Next**.
   Your budget will be based on all classes and all customers:jobs, so you do not need to add additional criteria at this time.

5. Click to the left of **Create budget from previous year's actual data**; click **Finish**.

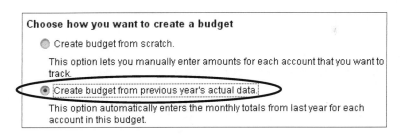

The new budget that you just created displays. Alan has told you that based on projections, the company plans to increase the labor income by 25 percent. You will make a change to Jan 15 reflecting this increase and then copy the amount across to every month.

6. Follow these steps to make the change to the budget:

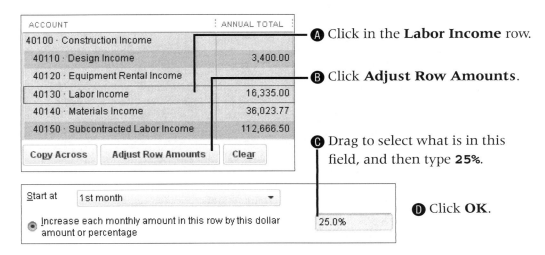

Ⓐ Click in the **Labor Income** row.

Ⓑ Click **Adjust Row Amounts**.

Ⓒ Drag to select what is in this field, and then type **25%**.

Ⓓ Click **OK**.

7. Click **OK** to save the budget with the changes.
The Set Up Budget window closes with the changes you made intact.

Produce a Budget Report

Now that the budget for 2015 has been produced, Alan would like to see a report showing the amount budgeted for 2014 compared to the actual amount earned or spent.

8. Choose **Reports→Budgets & Forecasts→Budget vs. Actual**.
A Budget Report "wizard" will appear to walk you through selections that will help you create the report you desire.

9. Click the **drop-down arrow**, and then choose to use the **FY2014-15** budget; click **Next**.

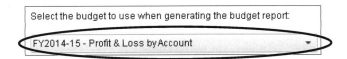

10. Click **Next** to choose for the layout to be Account by Month.

11. Click **Finish** to create the report.
Now you will modify the report so that it shows the information for the entire year.

12. Follow these steps to view the actual vs. budget for all of 2014:

Ⓐ Click the **Dates drop-down arrow**, and then choose **This Fiscal Year**.

Ⓑ Click the **Columns drop-down arrow**, and then choose **Year**.

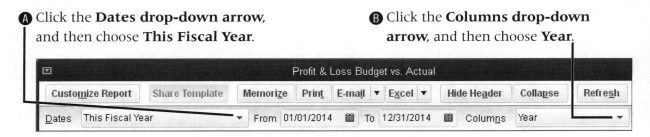

The top portion of your report should resemble the following illustration.

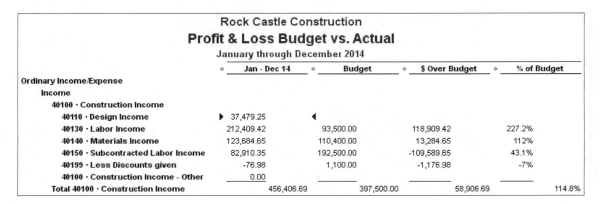

13. Close the **budget report** window.

14. Choose the appropriate option for your situation:

- If you are continuing on to the next lesson or to the end-of-lesson exercises, leave QuickBooks open.

- If you are finished working in QuickBooks for now, choose **File→Exit**.

Concepts Review

Concepts Review   http://labyrinthelab.com/qb13-level02

To check your knowledge of the key concepts introduced in this lesson, complete the Concepts Review quiz by going to the URL listed above.

Reinforce Your Skills

Before you begin the Reinforce Your Skills exercises, complete one of these options:

- *Open* **[Your name]'s Tea Shoppe at the Lake, Lesson 4** *or Tea Shoppe at the Lake, Lesson 3 from your file storage location that you used for Lesson 3.*

- *Restore* **Tea Shoppe at the Lake, Lesson 4 (Portable)** *from your file storage location.*

REINFORCE YOUR SKILLS 4.1

Use a Prepaid Rent Account

In this exercise, you will help Susie set up and use a Prepaid Rent account. The first step is to set up an Other Current Asset account.

1. Choose **Lists→Chart of Accounts**.

2. Click the **Account** menu button, and then choose **New**.

3. Create a new **Other Current Asset** account called **Prepaid Rent**.

Write the Rent Check

The next step is to write the check for the rent.

4. Choose **Banking→Write Checks**.

5. Write a **$6900** check to **Palomar Property Management** on **6/1/13** for six months of discounted rent ($1,150/month).

6. Choose for the check to be printed and enter a Memo of **Rent for June–November 2013**; expense the first month (**$1,150**) to Rent Expense and the rest (**$5,750**) to Prepaid Rent.

7. Enter **Other** as the Class for both lines of the transaction.

8. Save the **check** and close the **Write Checks** window.

Memorize a Funds Transfer

Now you will help Susie make the first transfer from Prepaid Rent to Rent Expense. The Chart of Accounts should still be open. If it isn't, choose Lists→Chart of Accounts.

9. Double-click the **Prepaid Rent** account to open the register.

10. Record a transfer of **$1,150** to Rent Expense on **7/1/13**.

11. Click within the transaction and choose **Edit→Memorize General Journal**.

12. Create a memorized transaction called **Rent Transfer** that is a monthly automated transaction entry. The next transfer will be on **8/1/13** and there are **4** remaining.

13. Close the **Prepaid Rent** register window.

Track Petty Cash

In this exercise, you will help Susie set up and use a petty cash account for her minor expenses, and to make a purchase with it.

If necessary, choose Lists→Chart of Accounts.

1. Click the **Account** menu button, and then click **New**.

2. Create a new **Bank** account called **Petty Cash**; choose to not set up online services.

3. Choose **Banking→Write Checks**, and then choose **Checking**.

4. Enter the next check number, **1109**, and then set the date to **7/06/13**.

5. Write the check to **Cash** (Quick Add as a vendor) for **$200**, choose **Petty Cash** as the account, and then choose **Other** as the Class.

Make a Purchase with Petty Cash

Now that the Petty Cash account is set up, you will use it to purchase whipped cream. (You ran out with many more drinks to make!)

6. Double-click **Petty Cash** from the Chart of Accounts window.

7. Enter **7/08/13** as the date, tap ⟦Tab⟧, and then tap ⟦Delete⟧ to remove the Number.

8. Tap ⟦Tab⟧ again, and then type **Grissom's Grocery** as the Payee.

9. Tap ⟦Tab⟧ and choose to **Quick Add** it as a vendor, type **$21.87** as the Payment, and then choose **Food Purchases** as the Account.

10. Enter **whipped cream** as the Memo; save the transaction, and then close the **Petty Cash** window.

Deal with a New Fixed Asset Item

Susie purchased a new milk steamer machine for Tea Shoppe at the Lake so she can make her famous Earl Grey non-fat misto with sugar-free vanilla syrup en masse. In this exercise, you will set up this purchase as a fixed asset item in her QuickBooks company file.

1. Choose **List→Fixed Asset Item List**.

2. Create a new **Fixed Asset Item** for the equipment using the following information:
   - Asset Name: **Espresso Steamer**
   - Purchase Description: **New Standalone Steamer**
   - Date: **7/8/2013**
   - Cost: **$2,569**
   - Vendor: **Poway Restaurant Supply**
   - Asset Account: Furniture and Equipment
   - Asset Description: **BUNN 35800.0401 Standalone Steamer Unit**

3. Save the new **Fixed Asset Item**; close the **Fixed Asset Item List**.
   Leave the Chart of Accounts open for the next exercise.

Track a Long Term Liability

Susie took out a loan for a portion of the cost of the new steamer unit. In this exercise, you will help her set up the Long Term Liability account and record the purchase transaction. The Chart of Accounts window should still be open. If it is not, choose Lists→Chart of Accounts.

1. Click the **Account** menu button, and then choose **New**.

2. Choose to create a new **Long Term Liability** account (which is an Other Account Type), and then click Continue.

3. Type **Steamer Loan** as the Account Name.

4. Click **Save & Close**.

Enter the Down Payment Transaction

You will now enter the two transactions to account for the full purchase price of the steamer unit.

5. Choose **Banking→Write Checks**, and then choose **Checking** as the account.

6. Choose for the **check to be printed later**, and then set the date to **7/8/13**.

7. Enter **Poway Restaurant Supply** as the payee, and **$569** as the amount of the down payment.

8. Type **Steamer Unit Down Payment** as the Memo, and then choose **Furniture and Equipment** as the Account.

9. Choose **Beverages** as the Class; click **Save & Close**.

Enter the Loan Transaction

The loan has been funded, so now you need to account for it in QuickBooks. The Chart of Accounts should still be open. If it is not, choose Lists→Chart of Accounts.

10. Double-click the **Steamer Loan** Long Term Liability account.
    The Steamer Loan register window opens.

11. Ensure that the date is set to **7/8/2013**, and then tap ⌷Tab⌷ three times.

12. Type **$2,000** as an Increase and choose **Furniture and Equipment** as the Account; **record** the transaction.

13. Close the **Steamer Loan** and **Chart of Accounts** windows.

Email a Report

In this exercise, you will help Susie create a report that shows all of the accounts in her Chart of Accounts to send to her accountant, who has requested it since she created the new asset and liability accounts. You will take the steps necessary to email the report but will not be able to hit send unless your computer is set up with email capability.

1. Choose **Reports→List→Account Listing**.

2. Click the **Email** button on the report toolbar, and then choose **Send report as PDF**.

3. Click **OK** in the Email Security box after reading the message.
   The report will be saved for you as a PDF file and attached to an email message. What happens at this point will depend on how the computer on which you are working is set up for email. At this stage, if you were working with your own company file, you would enter the email address of the recipient, make any edits to the message, and then click Send.

4. Close the email window that may have appeared; choose **Window→Close All**.

5. Choose the appropriate option for your situation:

   ■ If you are continuing on to the next lesson or the rest of the end-of-lesson exercises, leave QuickBooks open.

   ■ If you are finished working in QuickBooks for now, choose **File→Exit**.

Apply Your Skills

Before you begin the Apply Your Skills exercises, complete one of these options:

- *Open* **[Your name] Wet Noses Veterinary Clinic, Lesson 3** *or* **Wet Noses Veterinary Clinic, Lesson 4** *from your file storage location.*

- *Restore* **Wet Noses Veterinary Clinic, Lesson 4 (Portable)** *from your file storage location. Make sure to place your name as the first word in the company filename (e.g., Sadie's Wet Noses Veterinary Clinic, Lesson 4).*

APPLY YOUR SKILLS 4.1
Deal with Prepaid Web Hosting

Dr. James has decided that her business needs a website, and she has found a company to host it. She can get a deal if she pays for a year in advance, so she has decided to take that option. In this exercise, you will set up an Other Current Asset account for her to track the prepaid web hosting expense.

1. Open the **Chart of Accounts,** and then choose to create an **Other Current Asset** account.

2. Name the account **Prepaid Web Hosting**, and then **save** it.

Pay for the Prepaid Expense
You will now pay for the entire year, expensing one month's worth and placing the rest in the prepaid expense account you just created.

3. Open the **Write Checks** window, ensure that it is set for the **check to be printed later**, and then set the date to **7/22/2013**.

4. Type **Zoom Web Services** as the payee (Quick Add it as a vendor), and then **$1,068** as the amount (the deal is for $89/month).

5. Type **One year web hosting, July 2013-June 2014** as the Memo.

6. Choose to expense **$89** to Computer and Internet Expenses, and the rest to Prepaid Web Hosting. Choose **Overhead** as the Class for each line. Finally, save the transaction.

Make and Memorize a Transfer of Funds

You will now enter the transfer of $89 from the other current asset account to the expense account for August and set it up to happen automatically for the rest of the 12-month period.

7. Open the **Prepaid Web Hosting** register window from the Chart of Accounts.

8. Enter **8/22/2013** as the date and **89** in the Decrease field. Set **Computer and Internet Expenses** as the Account.

9. Choose to **memorize the transaction**.

10. Type **Web Host Txfr** as the Name.

11. Choose to have the transaction entry automated every month, with the next transfer occurring on **9/22/2013** and **10** more remaining.

12. Save the **memorized transaction** and the **register entry**; close the **Prepaid Web Hosting** window.
    Leave the Chart of Accounts window open for the next exercise.

APPLY YOUR SKILLS 4.2
Track and Use Petty Cash

In this exercise, you will create a petty cash account and use it to pay for an expense.

1. Open the **Chart of Accounts**, and then create a new bank account called **Petty Cash**.

2. Write a check to fund the **Petty Cash** account on **7/8/13** for **$300**. Enter the next check number, **1440**, and indicate **Overhead** as the class.

3. Purchase an appetizer platter for **$44.95** from Laura's Café for an office party on **7/12/13**. Use **Petty Cash** to pay for it.

4. Close the **Write Checks** or **Petty Cash** register window.

APPLY YOUR SKILLS 4.3
Buy a New Ultrasound Machine (Fixed Asset)

In this exercise, you will help Sadie enter a new ultrasound machine into the Fixed Asset Item List.

1. Open the **Fixed Asset Item List**.

2. Use the following information to create a new fixed asset item:
   - Asset Name: **Ultrasound Machine**
   - Purchase Description: **New Health Power Ultrasound Machine**
   - Date: **7/21/2013**
   - Cost: **$2,050**
   - Vendor: **Seattle Vet Supply**
   - Asset Account: Furniture and Equipment
   - Asset Description: **High Performance +7.5 MHz Vet Ultrasound**

3. Save the new **Fixed Asset Item**; close the **Fixed Asset Item List**.

Create and Fund a Long Term Liability Account

In this exercise, you will use the Loan Manager to track the loan that you took out for the x-ray machine.

1. Create a new **long term liability** account called **Ultrasound Loan**.

2. Fund the loan by entering an increase to the Ultrasound Loan account for **$2,050** on 7/22/13.

3. Open the **Loan Manager**.

4. Create a new loan using the following information:
   - Account Name: Ultrasound Loan
   - Lender: Bank of Bothell
   - Origination Date: **7/21/2013**
   - Original Amount **$2,050**
   - Term: **36** months
   - Due Date of Next Payment: **8/21/2013**
   - Payment Amount: **$64.05**
   - Payment Period: Monthly
   - Interest Rate: **7.8%**
   - Payment Account: Checking
   - Interest Expense Account: Interest Expense
   - Fees/Charges Expense Account: Bank Service Charges

5. Close the **Loan Manager** and the **Chart of Accounts**.

Answer Questions with Reports

In this exercise, you will answer questions for Dr. James by running reports. You may wish to display the Report Center in List View to help you answer the questions. Ask your instructor if you should print the reports, print (save) them as PDF files, export them to Excel, or simply display them on the screen.

1. Will you please print a list of all of the accounts that are set up in the Chart of Accounts for the accountant?

2. If we were to take out a five-year loan at 8.75 percent interest for a new piece of equipment for $5,000, what would the monthly payments be? (Hint: The Loan Manager has a feature that can help with this! If the Loan Manager is not working for you, go online and use a free loan calculator.)

3. Create a report that shows the entries of the Fixed Asset Item List.

4. Prepare a report that shows all transactions affecting the Prepaid Web Hosting account.

5. Submit your reports based on the guidelines provided by your instructor.

6. Choose the appropriate option for your situation:

   ■ If you are continuing on to the next lesson or the Critical Thinking exercises, leave QuickBooks open.

   ■ If you are finished working in QuickBooks for now, choose **File→Exit**.

Critical Thinking

In the course of working through the following Critical Thinking exercises, you will be utilizing various skills taught in this and previous lesson(s). Take your time and think carefully about the tasks presented to you. Turn back to the lesson content if you need assistance.

4.1 Sort Through the Stack

Before You Begin: Restore the **Monkey Business, Lesson 4 (Portable)** *file from your storage location. (Remember that you are to leave the password field blank for Mary.) You also have the option of opening either the final file from Critical Thinking 3.1 or Monkey Business, Lesson 4 from your storage location.*

You have been hired by Mary Minard to help her with her organization's books. She is the owner of Monkey Business, a nonprofit organization that provides low-income students with help in preparing for college placement exams and applying for scholarships. You have just sat down at her desk and found a pile of papers. It is your job to sort through the papers and make sense of what you find, entering information into QuickBooks whenever appropriate and answering any other questions in a word-processing document saved as **Critical Thinking 4.1**. Remember, you are digging through papers on a desk, so it is up to you to determine the correct order in which to complete the tasks.

- Receipt from USPS: Dated 8/15/2013, $44.00 for 100 first-class stamps, paid for with petty cash.

- Deposit slip: Check #578 for $5,000 from the House Foundation, deposited in the Checking account on 8/12/2013; $200 was kept back for petty cash.

- Bill from landlord for six months of rent at a discount: Mary wrote a note on the bill stating she wants to take advantage of a discounted rent by prepaying it for six months. The amount per month is $875, payable to Keely Amaral Properties, LLC. Pay the rent for August 2013 on 8/5/2013 and then set it up for the remaining months of rent to automatically transfer the on the fifth of each month for the remainder of the six-month term.

- Note from the accountant: Need to set up account for loan for new computer equipment. Total financed is $3,029. Loan was funded on 8/10/2013. Please set up the equipment as a fixed asset item as well, using Furniture & Equipment as the account. Description of equipment is two new Sony desktop computers, two 21-inch dual monitors, and a new laser printer. The vendor is Lancaster Computer Sales. It was financed by Cherry City Finance.

- Scribbled note from Mary: I would like to set up a budget for the rest of the fiscal year (September 2013–June 2014) based on the amounts spent and received in July and August. Is that something you could do in QuickBooks for me? If so, please create the budget for me and save it for me as a PDF file so I can send it by email.

4.2 Tackle the Tasks

Now is your chance to work a little more with Rock Castle Construction and apply the skills that you have learned in this lesson to accomplish additional tasks. Open or restore the **Critical Thinking 4.2** company or portable company file from your file storage location, or open the company file you used in the Develop Your Skills exercises for this lesson. Then, enter the following tasks.

Create and fund a prepaid utilities account	Rock Castle has decided to prepay the water bill for the next six months. Create 13300•Prepaid Utilities as an Other Current Asset account. Write a check to City of Bayshore on 1/1/15 for $1,200, expensing $200 in January to 65130•Water, placing the rest in the Prepaid Utilities account. Use Overhead as the Class.
Record and memorize a transfer of funds	Record a transfer of $200 from 13300•Prepaid Utilities to 65130•Water on 2/1/15. Memorize the transaction in the Monthly group.
Make a petty cash expenditure	Use 10400•Petty Cash to purchase a birthday cake on 1/30/15 for Samuel's birthday. The total amount is $33.75, payable to Billy's Bakery, expensed to 69000•Miscellaneous.
Create a new fixed asset item	Rock Castle Construction purchased furniture for the Millbrae office on 1/8/15 for $2,639 from Pa's Custom Furniture. Create a new fixed asset item called Millbrae Office Furniture – 19, and use 15000•Furniture and Equipment as the Asset Account.
Create a long term liability	Create a long term liability account for the new furniture for the Millbrae office called 28300•Loan – Furniture (Millbrae). On 1/8/15, enter the total amount of the furniture as an increase in the new liability account you just created, using 15000•Furniture and Equipment as the Account.
Create a forecast	Create a forecast for Rock Castle Construction for FY2015, based on last year's actual amount. Increase the amount for design income by 35 percent for the year.

You may use the company file from this exercise for the Develop Your Skills exercises in the next lesson if you wish.

4.3 Use the Web as a Learning Tool

Throughout this book, you will be provided with an opportunity to use the Internet as a learning tool by completing WebQuests. According to the original creators of WebQuests, as described on their website (WebQuest.org), a WebQuest is "an inquiry-oriented activity in which most or all of the information used by learners is drawn from the web." To complete the WebQuest projects in this book, navigate to the student resource center and choose the WebQuest for the lesson on which you are currently working. The subject of each WebQuest will be relevant to the material found in the lesson.

WebQuest Subject: Learning about the depreciation of fixed assets

Correcting and Customizing in QuickBooks

LESSON OBJECTIVES

After studying this lesson, you will be able to:

- Edit and correct errors
- Issue refunds and credit memos
- Deal with bounced checks and account for bad debt
- Customize reports and graphs
- Create custom templates

It is inevitable that mistakes will be made when entering data in QuickBooks. How you deal with those errors will affect what happens behind the scenes, so this lesson will show you how to correct some common errors to maintain the integrity of your data. The not-so-pleasant topics of issuing refunds, accounting for bad debt, and dealing with bounced checks will also be covered. Finally, the artist in you gets to have some fun! It's time to learn about customizing QuickBooks forms and reports to look good and work best for your company. In this lesson, you will learn to customize your reports to include pertinent information, to jazz them up, and to make them look more attractive. Once you finish working with reports, you will create your own custom invoice template.

Chez Devereaux Salon and Spa

Chez Devereaux Salon and Spa is a small but upscale salon and spa in Rhinelander, WI. Lisa is the owner of the salon; Bill is an employee who helps out with QuickBooks. With Lisa and Bill both being new to QuickBooks, they have realized that some transactions were not entered properly. Lisa will look at the correct way to deal with these errors. She will also look at how to deal with a couple of other unfortunate tasks, such as issuing refunds, accounting for bad debt, and processing bounced checks.

Lisa, as a designer by trade, is ready to add some finesse to Chez Devereaux Salon and Spa's company reports and templates as well.

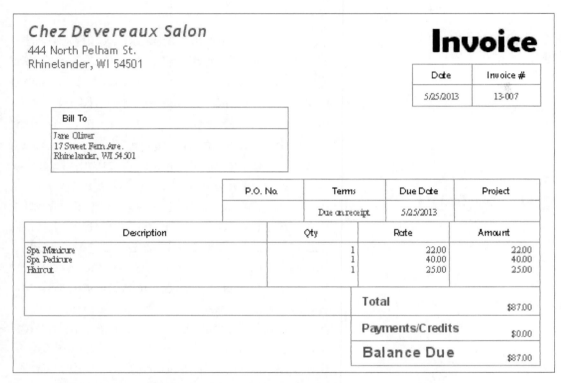

You can customize your templates to make them more appealing.

Dealing with Oops!

It is inevitable that you will need to deal with either errors or modifications to transactions in QuickBooks. It is very important that you do this properly to ensure that everything behind the scenes is correct.

Editing an Existing Transaction

To edit an existing transaction in QuickBooks, you simply open the window where the transaction is recorded and make the changes. You do need to think about the implications of any modifications that you make, though. Many transactions are tied to others, and a change to one can affect another. For instance, if a bill has been paid, both the bill and the bill payment are linked in QuickBooks.

Voiding vs. Deleting Transactions

QuickBooks allows you to either void or delete a transaction you no longer need recorded. In most cases, you will want to void a transaction so that you can keep a record of it. This will remove everything from behind the scenes and yet leave evidence that the transaction existed.

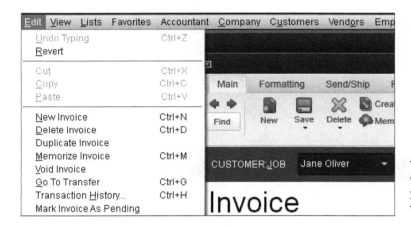

The Edit menu on the Create Invoices window provides options that allow you to work with the currently active transaction (in this case, an invoice).

Locating Transactions in QuickBooks

QuickBooks provides two methods for you to choose from in order to locate transactions in your company file.

QuickBooks Find Feature

QuickBooks provides a Find feature that helps you locate a transaction if you don't know all of the information about it. This can help save you a lot of time when you have a company file with a large number of transactions. The two options within Find are:

FROM THE KEYBOARD
Ctrl+f to open the Find window

■ **Simple** to perform basic searches

■ **Advanced** to perform more complex searches, utilizing filters to help sort through all of your data

QuickBooks Search Feature

With QuickBooks, you have the ability to perform searches based on text you enter throughout your company file and the menu commands. This feature is much more powerful than the Find feature and is similar to a search that you might perform on the Internet with any search engine. QuickBooks search allows you to find the following types of information:

- Forms/transactions (invoices, estimates, and so on)
- People and companies (customers, vendors, employees, and other names)
- List entries (items, tax items, and so on)
- Amounts and dates
- Menu commands (QuickBooks opens the menu and highlights the command for you)
- Specific text within notes, descriptions, memos, and transactions

You learned about the search feature and how to access it through the persistent search bar in *QuickBooks Pro 2013: Level 1*. You will explore it more in this lesson, and you will use it to locate a transaction to edit.

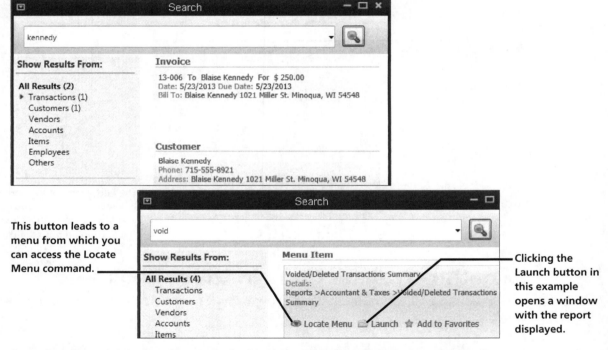

This button leads to a menu from which you can access the Locate Menu command.

Clicking the Launch button in this example opens a window with the report displayed.

A search on *kennedy* brings up the entry in the Customers & Jobs list and the customer invoice. A search on *void* brings up menu items (one displayed here). The buttons below the invoice and menu items appear when you move your mouse pointer over the entries.

Fixing Errors

The following table outlines a series of non-paycheck errors, the effects of the error behind the scenes, and how to correct the error.

Error	Effect Behind the Scenes	The Fix
An invoice is entered but the Receive Payments window is not used when the payment is deposited	Your income will be double-stated and Accounts Receivable for the customer is not "cleared out"	Delete the deposit and then enter the transaction properly using the Receive Payments window
A bill is entered but the Pay Bills window is not used when the payment is made	Your expenses will be double-stated and Accounts Payable for the vendor is not "cleared out"	Delete the check or credit card payment for the expense and then enter the transaction properly using the Pay Bills window
A "regular" check was cut to pay payroll or sales tax liabilities	The liability accounts are not cleared out; QuickBooks payroll essentially has a second set of books that are affected only when you pay the liabilities through the proper method	Void the "regular" check and then process the payment through the proper method (Pay Payroll Liabilities or Pay Sales Tax)
The wrong account type was chosen when creating a new account in the Chart of Accounts	The types of accounts involved will determine what the damage will be behind the scenes (but there will be damage!)	Edit the account through the Chart of Accounts, choosing the correct account type

FLASHBACK TO GAAP: PRUDENCE

Remember that if you need to choose between two solutions, pick the one that is less likely to overstate assets and income.

NOTE

Dealing with errors in payroll will be covered in Lesson 2, Using QuickBooks for Payroll, as they must be treated differently since QuickBooks keeps a separate set of books behind the scenes for payroll.

QUICK REFERENCE	FINDING AND SEARCHING FOR INFORMATION
Task	**Procedure**
Find a transaction in QuickBooks	■ Choose Edit→Find. ■ Choose either the Simple or the Advanced tab. ■ Enter as much information as possible about the transaction; click Find.
Search for text in the QuickBooks file and menu commands	■ Choose Edit→Search. ■ Type in the keyword on which you wish to base your search; tap Enter.

Correct Errors in a QuickBooks File

In this exercise, you will search for and edit an invoice. Then you will execute a few tasks incorrectly and then fix them. The first step is to open QuickBooks, and then either open a company file or restore a portable company file.

1. Start **QuickBooks 2013**.

Option 1: Restore a Portable Company File

2. Choose **File→Open or Restore Company**.

3. Restore the **Chez Devereaux** portable file for this lesson from your file storage location, placing your name as the first word in the filename (e.g., Lisa's Chez Devereaux Salon and Spa, Lesson 5).
   It may take a few moments for the portable company file to open. Once it does, continue with step 4.

Option 2: Open a Company File

2. Choose **File→Open or Restore Company**, ensure that **Open a regular company file** is selected, and then open the **Chez Devereaux** company file for this lesson from from your file storage location.
   The QuickBooks company file will open.

3. Click **OK** to close the QuickBooks Information window. If necessary, click **No** in the Set Up External Accountant User window.

FROM THE KEYBOARD
F3 to launch the Search feature

Use the Search Feature to Edit an Invoice

Now you will help Bill edit invoice 6 for Blaise Kennedy, who has said that he was incorrectly charged for two massages when he should have been charged for just one.

4. Choose **Edit→Search**; choose to update search information, if necessary.

5. Type **kennedy**, and then tap ⌷Enter⌷.

6. Move your mouse pointer over the invoice transaction displayed for **Blaise Kennedy** until the buttons appear, and then click **Open**.

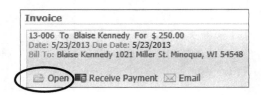

7. Change the **quantity** on the massage line item to **1**.
   Your screen should resemble the following illustration.

8. Click **Save & Close**; click **Yes** to record the transaction with the changes.

9. Close the **Search** window.

Do It the Wrong Way – Set the Account Type

The business has just received a Discover card that will be used for expenses. In this next example, you will set up the account incorrectly for the purpose of learning how to fix the error and do it correctly.

10. Choose **Lists→Chart of Accounts**.

11. Click the **Account** menu button, and then choose **New**.

12. Select **Expense** as the type of account, and then click **Continue**.

13. Type **62300** as the Number, tap ⌈Tab⌉, and then type **Discover Card** as the Account Name.

Your screen should resemble the following illustration.

14. Click **Save & Close**.

No doubt you have already realized what the error is in this example! While you will be using the card to pay for expenses, you should not set it up as an expense account. This will have huge ramifications behind the scenes, so you need to fix it pronto!

Do It the Right Way – Set the Account Type

In order to fix the error of setting up an account as the wrong type, you need to open the Edit Account window. The Chart of Accounts should still be open from the last step.

15. Right-click **62300•Discover Card** in the Chart of Accounts window, and then choose **Edit Account** from the menu.

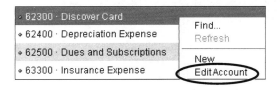

16. Follow these steps to fix the error:

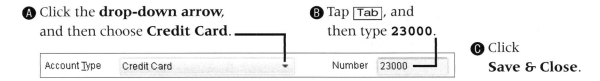

Ⓐ Click the **drop-down arrow**, and then choose **Credit Card**.

Ⓑ Tap ⌈Tab⌉, and then type **23000**.

Ⓒ Click **Save & Close**.

You must change the account number when you change the account type.

17. Close the **Chart of Accounts** window.

Do It the Wrong Way – Receive Payment for an Invoice

Bill has just received a check from Blaise Kennedy for $165. Now you will enter the payment incorrectly for the purpose of learning how to fix the error and do it correctly.

18. Choose **Banking→Make Deposits**.

19. Follow these steps to enter the check:

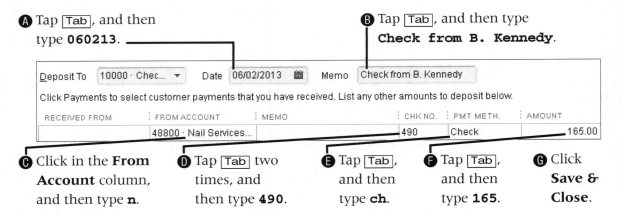

Ⓐ Tap Tab, and then type **060213**.

Ⓑ Tap Tab, and then type **Check from B. Kennedy**.

Ⓒ Click in the **From Account** column, and then type **n**.

Ⓓ Tap Tab two times, and then type **490**.

Ⓔ Tap Tab, and then type **ch**.

Ⓕ Tap Tab, and then type **165**.

Ⓖ Click **Save & Close**.

Think about this transaction. What is wrong with it? By entering the check for an invoice in the Make Deposits window, you have stated income twice and have not cleared the amount from Accounts Receivable.

BTS BRIEF

10000•Checking DR 165.00; 48800•Nail Services Income CR <165.00>

Do It the Right Way – Receive Payment for an Invoice

To fix the deposit that was handled improperly, you must delete it and reenter the payment using the Receive Payments window.

20. Choose **Banking→Make Deposits**.

21. Click the **Previous** button until the deposit you just made is displayed.
You can look for a transaction by using the Previous and Next buttons, if you believe the transaction to be easy to locate. If not, use the Find or Search feature.

FROM THE KEYBOARD

Ctrl+d to delete the selected transaction

22. Choose **Edit→Delete Deposit**; click **OK** in the Delete Transaction window.

23. Close the **Make Deposits** window.

24. Click the **Receive Payments** task icon in the Customers area of the Home page.

25. Follow these steps to enter the payment correctly:

Ⓐ Type **b** for QuickBooks to fill **Blaise Kennedy** in for you.

Ⓑ Tap Tab, and then type **165**.

Ⓒ Tap Tab, and then type **060213**, if necessary.

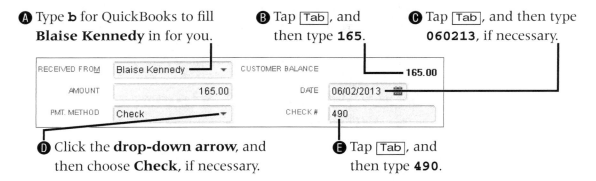

Ⓓ Click the **drop-down arrow**, and then choose **Check**, if necessary.

Ⓔ Tap Tab, and then type **490**.

BTS BRIEF

12000•Undeposited Funds DR 165.00; 12000•Accounts Receivable CR <165.00>

The Date and Pmt. Method should both be filled in for you based on information you have previously entered in QuickBooks.

26. Click **Save & Close**.

Before moving on, think about what you have just completed and make sure you understand the "why" behind it. You have deleted the overstated income by deleting the deposit and have "cleared out" Accounts Receivable for Blaise Kennedy by receiving the payment correctly.

Dealing with Bounced Checks

Unfortunately, virtually all business owners must deal with customers whose checks are returned for non-sufficient funds (NSF) at some time or another. Many people call these "bounced checks," and when Intuit briefly released a feature for certain editions of Quick-Books 2012 to deal with this issue, they also used that term. This book uses the terms *NSF* and *bounced check*, though the latter is used more often because it will likely be the term used in future versions/releases of QuickBooks.

In QuickBooks, you can deal with these NSF or "bounced" checks in either of two ways:

■ You can re-invoice the customer, although this is not the preferred method if the original transaction involved sales tax.

■ You can also generate a statement for the customer, which does not affect sales or sales tax reports.

In this lesson, we will examine how to generate a statement for a customer, which can be used for a returned check in any circumstance.

The bank may charge you a lesser amount than you choose to pass on to the customer for a bounced check. In this book, you will see that the bank charges $25. Lisa has chosen to charge $35 to the customer for the additional work of dealing with the bounced check.

Entering Statement Charges

If you wish to enter a charge for a customer without producing an invoice, you can use the Accounts Receivable register window. It is important that you choose the correct customer to whom you wish to apply the charge. Any transactions entered in a customer's accounts receivable register will show up on statements that you print for them.

Creating Statements for Customers

There are many instances when you may wish to send your customer a statement rather than an invoice. For instance, you may have one customer or job for which you do multiple projects within a billing period and you wish to bill them with an itemized statement. Another example, shown in this lesson, is to create a statement to bill a customer for a bounced check.

Statements can be produced for an individual customer or in a batch for multiple customers.

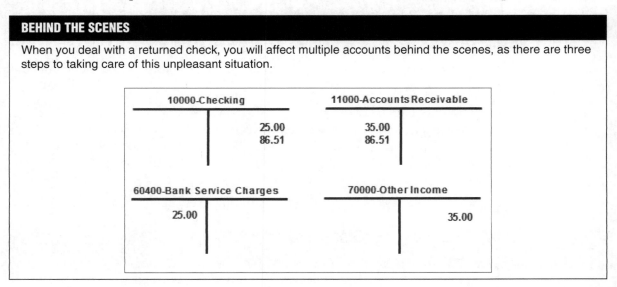

BEHIND THE SCENES

When you deal with a returned check, you will affect multiple accounts behind the scenes, as there are three steps to taking care of this unpleasant situation.

QUICK REFERENCE	DEALING WITH BOUNCED CHECKS
Task	**Procedure**
Generate a statement to account for a bounced check	■ Create an Other Charge item for the service charge, directing it to the Other Income account. ■ Record the bank's fee in your bank account register (Bank Service Charges as account). ■ Record the check in your bank account register (customer/job as payee; Accounts Receivable as account). ■ Enter a statement charge for the customer's fee. ■ Send the customer a statement that shows the bounced check and fee.
Enter statement charges	■ Choose Customers→Enter Statement Charges. ■ Choose the customer whose Accounts Receivable register you wish to view. ■ Enter the information for the statement charge; record the transaction.
Create a statement to send to a customer	■ Choose Customers→Create Statements. ■ Choose the date range for which you wish to create statements. ■ Choose the customer(s) for whom you wish to create statements. ■ Choose any additional options, as desired. ■ (Optional) Click Preview to view the statement(s). ■ Click Print or Email to deliver the statement(s) to the customer(s).

DEVELOP YOUR SKILLS 5.2
Handle a Bounced Check

In this exercise, you will account for a check that was returned to Chez Devereaux Salon and Spa for non-sufficient funds. The first step is to create an Other Charge item so you can pass the fee on to the customer. You will charge $35 to your customers for a returned check.

1. Click the **Items & Services** task icon in the Company area of the Home page.

2. Click the **Item** menu button, and then choose **New**.

Items & Services

3. Follow these steps to create the new item:

Ⓐ Click to choose **Other Charge** from the list.

Ⓑ Tap ⎡Tab⎤, and then type **Bounced Check Charge**.

Ⓒ Click in the **Description** field, and then type **Non-Sufficient Funds Service Charge**.

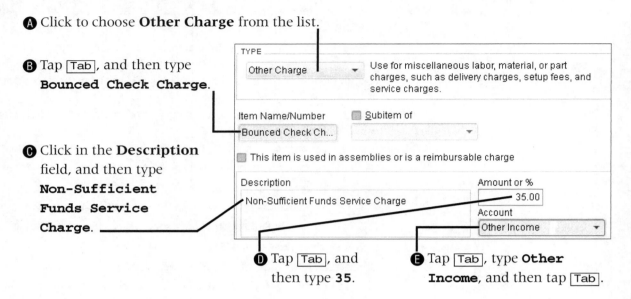

Ⓓ Tap ⎡Tab⎤, and then type **35**.

Ⓔ Tap ⎡Tab⎤, type **Other Income**, and then tap ⎡Tab⎤.

A window will appear informing you that Other Income is not in the Chart of Accounts.

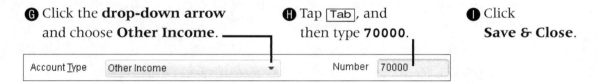

Ⓕ Click **Set Up**.

A New Account window will appear.

Ⓖ Click the **drop-down arrow** and choose **Other Income**.

Ⓗ Tap ⎡Tab⎤, and then type **70000**.

Ⓘ Click **Save & Close**.

Other Income accounts are used to track income that is not the result of your regular business operations. Since you are not running a financial institution, customer fees are not a regular source of income for you.

4. Click **OK** to save the new item; close the **Item List** window.
Notice that once you set up the new account, it will fill in to the Account field for you, account number and all.

Record the Fee and Check in the Register

In the following steps, you will record the transactions that affect your bank account balance. The bank charges you a $25 fee for handling the returned item.

5. Click the **Check Register** task icon in the Banking area of the Home page.

6. Click **OK** to choose **10000•Checking** as the account to use.

7. Follow these steps to record the NSF fee charged by the bank:

A Type **060613** as the date.

B Tap ⌑Tab⌑, and then tap ⌑Delete⌑ to remove the check number.

C Tap ⌑Tab⌑ twice, and then type **25**.

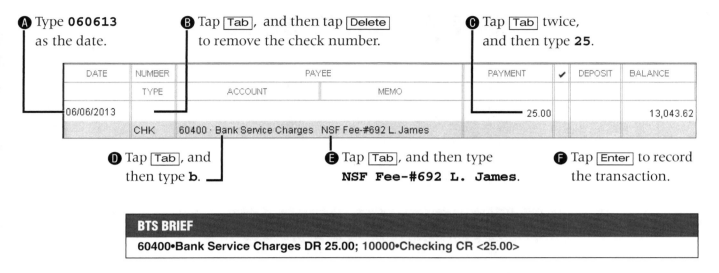

DATE	NUMBER	PAYEE		PAYMENT	✓	DEPOSIT	BALANCE
	TYPE	ACCOUNT	MEMO				
06/06/2013				25.00			13,043.62
	CHK	60400 · Bank Service Charges	NSF Fee-#692 L. James				

D Tap ⌑Tab⌑, and then type **b**.

E Tap ⌑Tab⌑, and then type **NSF Fee-#692 L. James**.

F Tap ⌑Enter⌑ to record the transaction.

BTS BRIEF

60400•Bank Service Charges DR 25.00; 10000•Checking CR <25.00>

8. Follow these steps to record the NSF check in your checking register:

A Verify **6/6/2013** as the date.

B Tap ⌑Tab⌑, and then tap ⌑Delete⌑ to remove the check number.

C Tap ⌑Tab⌑, and then type **1e**.

D Tap ⌑Tab⌑, and then type **107**.

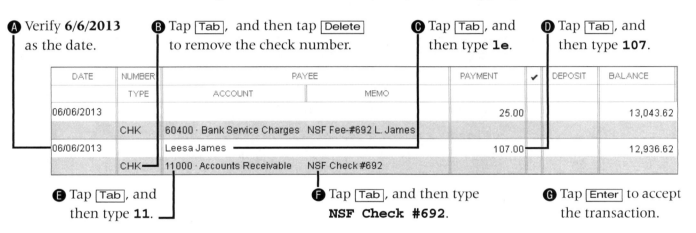

DATE	NUMBER	PAYEE		PAYMENT	✓	DEPOSIT	BALANCE
	TYPE	ACCOUNT	MEMO				
06/06/2013				25.00			13,043.62
	CHK	60400 · Bank Service Charges	NSF Fee-#692 L. James				
06/06/2013		Leesa James		107.00			12,936.62
	CHK	11000 · Accounts Receivable	NSF Check #692				

E Tap ⌑Tab⌑, and then type **11**.

F Tap ⌑Tab⌑, and then type **NSF Check #692**.

G Tap ⌑Enter⌑ to accept the transaction.

BTS BRIEF

11000•Accounts Receivable DR 107.00; 10000•Checking CR <107.00>

9. Close the **Checking** register window.
In this last step, you took the funds received from Leesa James back "out" of your Checking account.

Enter a Statement Charge for the Customer's Fee

You have recorded the NSF fee that the bank charged to your register. Now it is time to record the fee that you will charge the customer.

10. Click the **Statement Charges** task icon in the Customers area of the Home page.
When you choose to enter a statement charge, you will view the Accounts Receivable register for a customer. It is important that you choose the correct customer, as is shown in the following step.

Statement Charges

11. Click the **drop-down arrow** for the Customer:Job field and choose **Leesa James**.

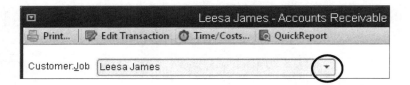

You will now be able to view the register for Leesa James.

12. Tap [Tab] to accept the date of 6/6/13 and move to the Item column.

13. Follow these steps to add the NSF charge:

Ⓐ Type **b**, and then tap [Tab].   **Ⓑ** Tap [Enter] to record the transaction.

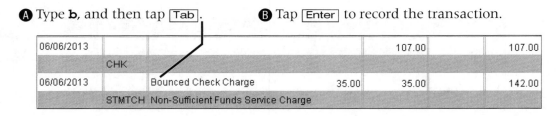

06/06/2013				107.00	107.00
	CHK				
06/06/2013		Bounced Check Charge	35.00	35.00	142.00
	STMTCH	Non-Sufficient Funds Service Charge			

BTS BRIEF

11000•Accounts Receivable DR 35.00; 70000•Other Income CR <35.00>

14. Close the **Leesa James – Accounts Receivable** window.

Create a Statement to Send to the Customer

The final step in accounting for a NSF check is to create the statement for the customer that reflects the NSF check and NSF charge.

15. Click the **Statements** task icon in the Customers area of the Home page.

16. Follow these steps to prepare the statement for Leesa James:

Statements

Ⓐ Type **060613** in the Statement Date field.

Ⓑ Click in the circle to the left of **All open transactions as of Statement Date**.

Ⓒ Click in the circle to the left of **One Customer**.

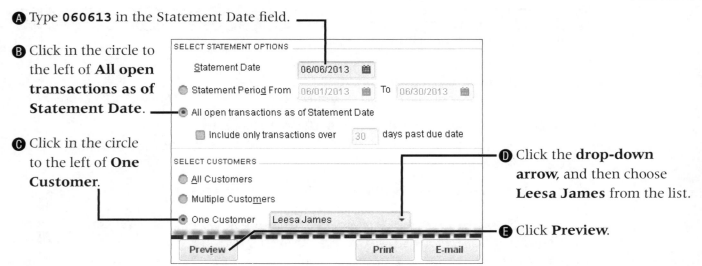

Ⓓ Click the **drop-down arrow**, and then choose **Leesa James** from the list.

Ⓔ Click **Preview**.

You will now see how the statement will look when printed.

17. Click **Zoom In** to see the information included in the statement better, if desired.

18. Close the **Print Preview** and **Create Statement** windows.

Writing Off Bad Debt

Virtually every business has to write off money owed as bad debt at some point or another. QuickBooks does allow you to do this via one of two methods: treating it as a discount or using a credit memo. Your sales tax liability will not be affected if you choose to treat bad debt as a discount, whereas it will be reduced if you use the credit memo method. It is for this reason that the credit memo is recommended when sales tax is involved. Regardless of the method selected, you will need to create an expense account in which to direct the bad debt.

Example: You learn that Leesa James has moved out of town. You believe it is unlikely that you will be able to collect for the amount of the returned check. You decide that it is time to write off the amount owed by this customer as a bad debt.

FLASHBACK TO GAAP: MATERIALITY

Remember that when an item is reported, its significance should be considered.

Treating Bad Debt as a Discount

In order to treat bad debt as a discount (not recommended for a debt that has sales tax associated with it), you would enter it as a discount in the Receive Payments window that you learned about in *QuickBooks Pro 2013: Level 1*. Make sure, though, that you use the proper expense account for the bad debt (e.g., Bad Debt Expense). If you receive a partial payment from a customer, you can also choose to "Write off the extra amount" in the Receive Payments window if you do not expect to ever receive the remaining balance.

If you were to choose to use the discount method to write off the remainder of invoice #1 for Holly Rose, you would launch the Discount and Credits window from the Receive Payments window and choose 60300•Bad Debt Expense as the account.

Using a Credit Memo to Write Off a Bad Debt

In the next exercise, you will have the opportunity to create a credit memo in order to write off a bad debt. When you choose this method, you will use an Other Charge item to "route" the bad debt to the appropriate expense account (which will be debited), and Accounts Receivable will be credited. You can include both taxable and nontaxable bad debts on a single credit memo. You will finish the procedure by applying the credit memo to the original invoice.

BEHIND THE SCENES

When you write off a bad debt, you need to credit the Accounts Receivable account and the customer sub-register (which automatically occurs when you choose the customer) and debit the expense account you created to track bad debts, in this case Bad Debt Expense.

60300-Bad Debt Expense		11000-Accounts Receivable	
121.51			121.51

QUICK REFERENCE — **WRITING OFF BAD DEBT**

Task	Procedure
Write off bad debt as a discount	■ Create a new expense account called **Bad Debt Expense**. ■ Choose Customers→Receive Payments. ■ Select the customer and set the write-off date. ■ Click the Discounts & Credits button. ■ Enter the amount of the bad debt; choose Bad Debt Expense as the Discount Account. ■ Complete the transaction.
Write off bad debt using a credit memo	■ Create a new expense account called **Bad Debt Expense**. ■ Create an Other Charge item called Bad Debt that is routed to the Bad Debt Expense account. ■ Choose Customers→Create Credit Memos/Refunds. ■ Select the customer and set the date. ■ Using the Bad Debt item, enter a line item for the total non-tax sales you are writing off; choose Non in the Tax column. ■ Using the Bad Debt item, enter a line item for the total taxable sales you are writing off; choose Tax in the Tax column. ■ Click Save & Close. ■ Choose to which invoice you wish to apply the credit (bad debt write-off).

Write Off Bad Debt

In this exercise, you will use the credit memo method to write off the amount owed by Leesa James. The first step is to create an expense account for the payment.

1. Click the **Chart of Accounts** task icon in the Company area of the Home page.

2. Click the **Account** menu button, and then choose **New**.

Chart of
Accounts

3. Choose **Expense** as the account type; click **Continue**.

4. Follow these steps to create the new account:

A Type **60300** as the **Number**.　　**B** Tap ⌨Tab⌨, and then type **Bad Debt Expense**.

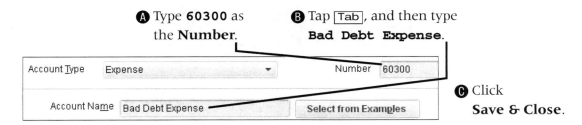

C Click **Save & Close**.

5. Close the **Chart of Accounts**.

Set Up the Bad Debt Item

The next step in writing off a bad debt using a credit memo is to create the item.

6. Click the **Items & Services** task icon in the Company area of the Home page.

7. Click the **Item** menu button, and then choose **New**.

Items &
Services

8. Follow these steps to create the new item:

A Choose **Other Charge** as the type.

B Tap ⌨Tab⌨, and then type **Bad Debt**.

C Tap ⌨Tab⌨ three times, and then type **Bad Debt Write-Off**.

D Tap ⌨Tab⌨ two times, and then type **b** to choose the Account.

E Click **OK** to create the item.

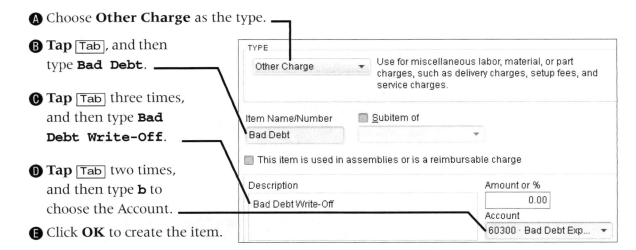

The amount is left blank here so you can fill in the correct amount for each transaction.

9. Close the **Item List** window.

Create the Credit Memo

Finally, you will create the credit memo to write off the bad debt and choose to which invoice(s) it should be applied.

10. Click the **Refunds & Credits** task icon in the Customers area of the Home page.

11. Follow these steps to complete the memo:

Ⓐ Click to remove the checkmark from this box.

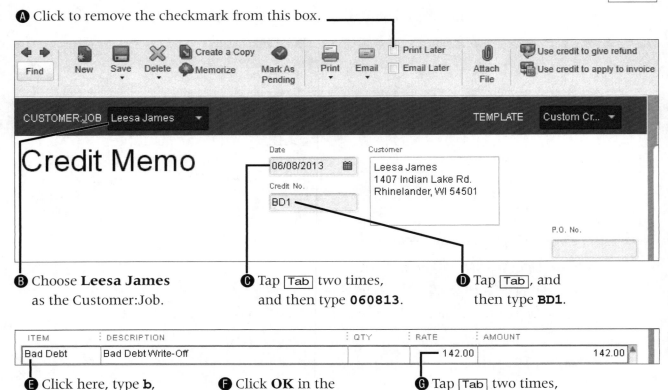

Ⓑ Choose **Leesa James** as the Customer:Job.

Ⓒ Tap [Tab] two times, and then type **060813**.

Ⓓ Tap [Tab], and then type **BD1**.

Ⓔ Click here, type **b**, and then tap [Tab].

Ⓕ Click **OK** in the Warning window.

Ⓖ Tap [Tab] two times, and then type **142**.

12. Click **Save & Close**.
An Available Credit window appears, from which you can decide what to do with the resulting credit.

13. Choose **Apply to an invoice**, and then click **OK**.
The Apply Credits to Invoice window appears, listing all open invoices for the customer. QuickBooks checked both invoices to which to apply the amount from the credit memo.

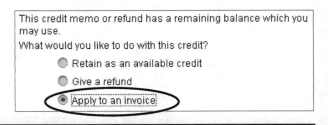

BTS BRIEF

60300•Bad Debt Expense DR 142.00; 11000•Accounts Receivable CR <142.00>

14. Click **Done**.
The total amount owed by Leesa James has now been transferred to the Bad Debt Expense account.

Working with Refunds

There are many times when you may need to issue a refund to a customer. Once a credit memo has been created, you can choose to refund a customer by returning the payment in full. Or, your policy may be to issue a credit that can be applied to another purchase or to an invoice.

Issuing a Refund

There are a variety of reasons that you may wish to issue a refund to a customer, such as:

- For merchandise that has been returned
- For an order that was canceled
- To reimburse for an overpayment

If you wish to return a customer's payment, you can choose to issue a refund check or to return the funds to a credit card.

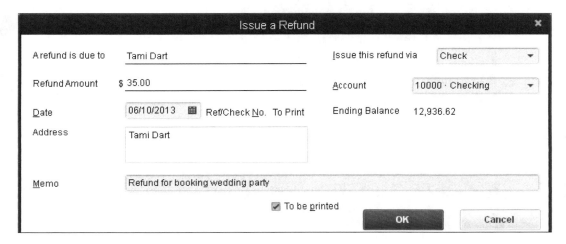

When you choose to issue a refund, the Issue a Refund window will appear. In this window, you can enter the information for the refund check.

Creating a Credit Memo

In the last section, you learned how to use a credit memo to write off bad debt. In this section, you will have the opportunity to create a credit memo as a refund for returned merchandise. Once a credit memo has been created you can choose to apply the credit to an invoice (as you did in the last exercise), or you can choose to issue a refund check to a customer.

Once you have processed a refund for a credit memo, the "Refunded" stamp will appear on the Credit Memo form.

One-Click Credit Memo

If you need to refund a customer for a purchase that was made on an invoice, you can use a feature in QuickBooks that allows you to convert an invoice to a credit memo with one click. This can save you time as you will not have to retype the information for the new transaction.

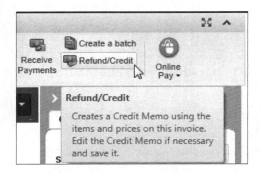

The Refund/Credit button on the Create Invoices window Ribbon allows you to easily create credit memos from invoices.

Applying a Credit as a Part of a Payment

Once a credit has been issued to a customer, you can apply it to payment(s) for future purchases. This is done through the Receive Payments window.

Entering a Credit from a Vendor

If you are on the receiving end of a credit memo, you will need to enter it in your QuickBooks company file as well. This is easily done through the Enter Bills window. Once you have recorded the credit, you can either pass it on to a customer (if you chose to do so in the Enter Bills window when you recorded it) or use it when you pay bills to this vendor in the future.

BEHIND THE SCENES

When you issue a refund, Accounts Receivable or Checking (depending on whether you have received the customer's payment or not), an income account, and Sales Tax Payable (if sales tax was charged in the original transaction) will be affected behind the scenes.

10000-Checking, or 11000-Accounts Receivable	48700-Hair Services Income	25500-Sales Tax Payable
36.93	35.00	1.93

Task	Procedure
Create a credit memo	■ Choose Customers→Create Credit Memos/Refunds. ■ Select the customer and set the date; enter the credit information.
Issue a refund check for returned merchandise	■ Choose Customers→Create Credit Memos/Refunds. ■ Choose the desired customer. ■ Enter the items being returned as separate line items. ■ Click the Use Credit button; choose Give Refund. ■ Enter a memo (optional); click OK.
Issue a refund for overpayment on an invoice	■ Choose Customers→Receive Payments. ■ Enter payment information. (The overpayment box will appear.) ■ Choose to refund the amount to the customer; save the transaction. ■ Complete the customer information in the Issue a Refund window. ■ Enter a memo as to the purpose of the refund (optional); click OK.
Issue a refund for a canceled prepaid order/deposit	■ Choose Banking→Write Checks. ■ Fill in the customer information in the top portion of the window. ■ Choose Accounts Receivable; save the check. ■ Choose Customers→Receive Payments. ■ Choose the correct customer at the top of the window; leave the amount as zero. ■ Click the Discounts & Credits button. The check you just wrote should be selected. If an invoice is selected, click to remove the checkmark. ■ Save & Close the transaction.
Enter a credit from a vendor	■ Choose Vendors→Enter Bills. ■ Choose Credit, choose the vendor, and enter the credit amount. ■ In the Account column, choose the account that you use to track vendor credits. ■ Enter the amount of the credit; indicate whether to pass the credit on to a customer. ■ Save & Close the credit.
Create a credit memo from an invoice	■ Open the invoice from which you wish to create the credit memo. ■ Click the Create button on the Create Invoices window toolbar; choose Credit Memo for this Invoice. ■ Verify the information; click Save & Close.

Issue a Refund and Apply a Credit as a Partial Payment

In this exercise, you will create a credit memo and issue a refund to a customer. The first step is to create a credit memo for the customer. In this situation, Tami Dart came in for special event styling on 5/14/13. You have told her that if she books her entire wedding party with you, you will issue a refund for this service.

1. Click the **Refunds & Credits** task icon in the Customers area of the Home page.

2. Follow these steps to record the credit memo for Tami:

A Type **t** to choose the Customer:Job.   **B** Tap ⌐Tab⌐ two times, and then type **061013**.

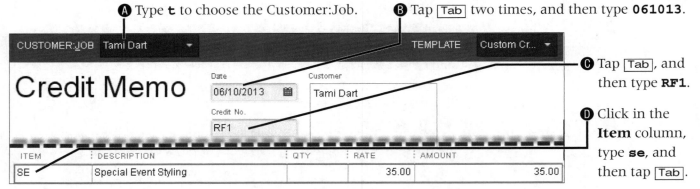

C Tap ⌐Tab⌐, and then type **RF1**.

D Click in the **Item** column, type **se**, and then tap ⌐Tab⌐.

Leave the Create Credit Memos/Refunds window open. You will issue the refund from it in the next step.

Issue a Refund Check

3. Click the **Use credit to give refund** button on the Ribbon.

4. Click in the **Memo** field and type this text.

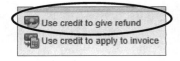

5. Review the information in the Issue a Refund window to ensure it is correct, and then click **OK**.

6. Click **Save & Close** to record the credit memo.

BTS BRIEF

60300•Hair Services Income DR 35.00; 10000•Checking CR <35.00>

Customizing Reports and Graphs

You have learned to create various reports throughout this book so far. Now you will customize the reports that you produce to make them work for you.

Customization takes place on many fronts. You may find yourself asking:

- Which accounts should I display?
- What information do I need to filter out?
- What header and footer information should I include?
- How do I want my fonts and numbers to look?

Display Properties

The Display tab of the Modify Report window allows you to change aspects of your report such as the dates it represents, your reporting basis (cash or accrual), the columns to display, and subcolumn preferences.

Report Date Range

Each preset report has a default date range displayed when the report is first created. The date can either be:

- When your reporting period ends, such as a balance sheet report created "As of June 30, 2013."
- For a range of days, such as a Profit & Loss report created for June 1-30, 2013.

  The type of date is determined by the type of report you produce.

Accrual vs. Cash Basis Reporting

If you recall from *QuickBooks Pro 2013: Level 1*, there are two methods of accounting from which you can choose for your company. You enter data into QuickBooks the same way regardless of whether you use the cash or accrual basis of accounting. When you create your reports, you can easily switch between cash and accrual basis. And when you first create a QuickBooks company, the default will be for the reports to be displayed as the accrual basis. Of course, you will want to set your company's default report basis in the report section of the Edit Preferences window. Take a look at a review of both methods.

Accrual Basis

In the accrual basis of accounting, income is recorded when a sale is made, and expenses are recorded when accrued. This method is used often by firms and businesses with large inventories; it's required for publicly traded companies.

Cash Basis

In the cash basis of accounting, income is recorded when cash is received and expenses are recorded when cash is paid. This method is commonly used by small businesses and professionals.

If you operate using the cash basis, you will not need to display Accounts Receivable and Accounts Payable on your financial statements because cash has yet to change hands.

Columns

Each preset report displays certain default columns. You can change the columns to make your report much more useful. For instance, you can choose to display multiple months on a P&L report to compare income and expenses in different reporting periods. You can also specify subcolumns you want displayed if they are available for your specific report.

Subcolumns

Some reports allow you to add subcolumns to further analyze your data. Different subcolumns are available depending on the report you run. The entire list is shown in the following illustration.

The use of columns and subcolumns to stratify data can be a very valuable way to help you analyze and scrutinize your company's financial data.

Filtering Reports

In order to have reports display only essential data, you have the ability to apply a filter in QuickBooks. A filter will let you choose what information to include in your report, thereby "filtering out" the rest of it. Filters can be applied to any report, and the specific information that can be filtered is determined by the report you run. You are also able to filter transaction reports for text that is contained in custom fields if the fields are on the forms for the transactions included in the report.

Formatting

Formatting deals with the appearance of the report; it has nothing to do with the data contained within it. You can change the report's font(s) and the way numbers are displayed.

Fonts

QuickBooks displays its preset reports in the default font. You can make many choices as to the characteristics of the font in your report, such as the font name, style, color, and size.

Negative Numbers

When you have negative numbers in your report, they can be displayed in a variety of ways, as described in the illustration to the right.

All Numbers

You can also choose how QuickBooks will display all numbers in your report. The options available are displayed in the illustration to the right.

Task	Procedure
Change the default report basis	■ Choose Edit→Preferences. ■ Choose the Reports & Graphs category, and then the Company Preferences tab. ■ Choose Accrual or Cash in the Summary Report Basis section; click OK.
Apply a filter to a report	■ Create your report, and then click the Customize Report button. ■ Click the Filters tab, apply the desired filter(s), and then click OK.
Change the font and number formatting on a report	■ Create your report; click the Customize Report button. ■ Click the Fonts & Numbers tab. ■ Select any number formatting changes. ■ Click on the report element to change; click Change Font. ■ Make your changes; click OK twice.

DEVELOP YOUR SKILLS 5.5

Customize Your Reports

In this exercise, you will help Bill create and customize a Profit & Loss report for Chez Devereaux Salon and Spa. The QuickBooks default report basis is accrual. Lisa spoke with her accountant and determined that Chez Devereaux Salon and Spa would use the cash basis for reporting. You will begin by changing the default for the company file.

1. Choose **Edit→Preferences**.

2. Click the **Reports & Graphs** category on the left side of the window.

3. Click the **Company Preferences** tab, and then click in the circle to the left of **Cash** in the Summary Reports Basis section.

4. Click **OK** to save the new preference.

Add a Filter

Bill will first run the preset Profit & Loss Standard report. Then he will apply a filter to the report to show only income accounts.

5. Choose **Reports→Company & Financial→Profit & Loss Standard**.

6. Follow these steps to set a custom date range:

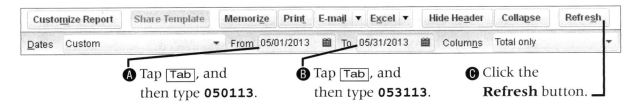

Ⓐ Tap ⌊Tab⌋, and then type **050113**.

Ⓑ Tap ⌊Tab⌋, and then type **053113**.

Ⓒ Click the **Refresh** button.

You will see the Profit & Loss by Class report displayed for May 2013.

7. Click the **Customize Report** button on the report toolbar.

8. Follow these steps to apply a filter that will include only income accounts on the report:

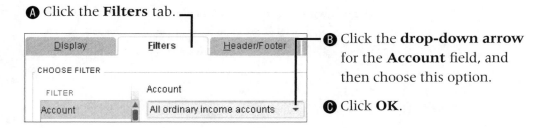

Ⓐ Click the **Filters** tab.

Ⓑ Click the **drop-down arrow** for the **Account** field, and then choose this option.

Ⓒ Click **OK**.

You will now see the report with no expense accounts shown.

Change the Font and Number Formatting

Bill wants to spruce up the report by changing the way the font and numbers appear.

9. Click the **Customize Report** button on the report toolbar.

10. Follow these steps to change the formatting:

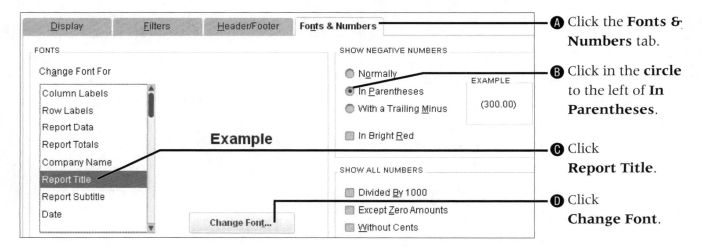

Ⓐ Click the **Fonts & Numbers** tab.

Ⓑ Click in the **circle** to the left of **In Parentheses**.

Ⓒ Click **Report Title**.

Ⓓ Click **Change Font**.

You will see a Report Title window similar to a Font dialog box that you may be familiar with from word-processing programs.

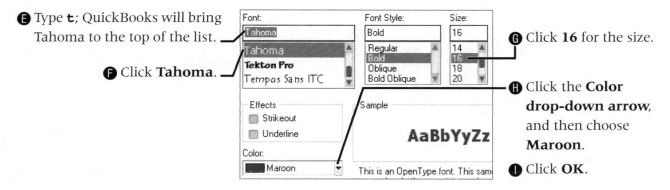

Ⓔ Type **t**; QuickBooks will bring Tahoma to the top of the list.

Ⓕ Click **Tahoma**.

Ⓖ Click **16** for the size.

Ⓗ Click the **Color drop-down arrow**, and then choose **Maroon**.

Ⓘ Click **OK**.

11. Click **Yes** to change all related fonts.

You will see the new font formatting displayed above the Change Font button.

12. Click **OK**.

You will see the font formatting changes that you just made. Leave the report open; you will continue to customize it in the next exercise.

Working with Additional Formatting Options

You have learned to choose many report customization options. Now you will learn to create a header and footer to your specifications and to memorize and recall a report.

Header and Footer Options

All preset QuickBooks reports have default headers and footers. You can change the information included and how it is formatted on the Header/Footer tab of the Modify Report window.

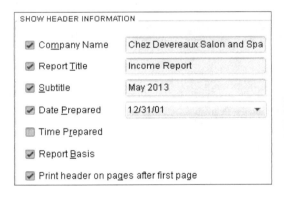

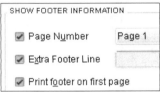

You have many options when it comes to customizing the header and footer of your report.

Page Layout

You can choose to use the default standard report layout or to use left, right, or centered alignment.

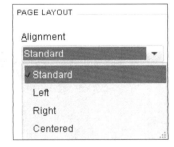

Memorizing Reports

Once you have created a report with your chosen settings, you may wish to save the report options so you can easily produce the same report again. The process of saving the settings of a report is called *memorizing* a report, and it is available for all reports. The memorizing feature memorizes the format of the report, not the data contained within it. This means that when you open a memorized report, it will contain your most recently entered data.

To recall the memorized report, you can choose it from the Memorized Report List.

Memorized Report Groups

QuickBooks allows you to organize your memorized reports into groups. There are six preset groups (accountant, banking, company, customers, employees, and vendors) for you to use, or you can choose to create your own. When you memorize a report, you can place it into a group immediately or later.

When you choose to memorize a report, you have the opportunity to save it in a memorized report group.

Batch Processing of Reports

If you have a group of reports that you run together on a regular basis, you may wish to process them as a batch to save time. You will first need to set the reports you wish to process together as a memorized report group; then you will be able to process them all at once.

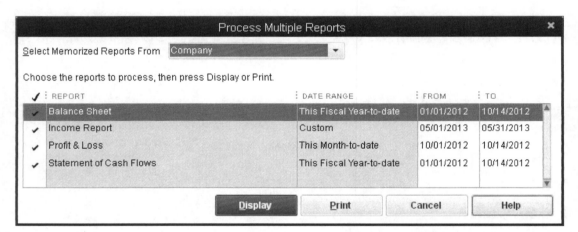

The Process Multiple Reports window allows you to choose which group of reports to process as a batch. You can set the date range in this window, too, if you need to change it from the range that was memorized.

QUICK REFERENCE	WORKING WITH AND MEMORIZING REPORTS
Task	**Procedure**
Change the report header/footer	■ Create your report; click the Customize Report button. ■ Click the Header/Footer tab and make the desired changes; click OK.
Apply the % of row feature to a report	■ Create your report; click the Customize Report button. ■ Click the Display tab and click in the box for % of row; click OK.
Create a memorized report group	■ Choose Reports→Memorized Report List. ■ Click the Memorized Report menu button; choose New Group. ■ Type the name of the group; click OK.

Task	Procedure
Place a report in the memorized report group	■ Create and modify a report to your liking; click Memorize. ■ Type the name of the report. ■ Click in the checkbox to the left of Save in Memorized Report Group. ■ Click the drop-down arrow to choose the group; click OK.
Batch process a group of reports	■ Choose Reports→Process Multiple Reports. ■ Choose the group from which you wish to process the reports. ■ Choose the reports you wish to process; click either Display or Print.

DEVELOP YOUR SKILLS 5.6

Make Additional Report Customization Changes

In this exercise, you will help Bill make additional custom changes in the report and memorize the final product. The report that you were working on in the previous exercise should still be open. If not, repeat the steps in the previous exercise to produce the report needed to begin this exercise.

1. Click the **Customize Report** button on the report toolbar.

2. Follow these steps to make the changes to the header and footer:

Ⓐ Click the **Header/Footer** tab.

Ⓑ Replace the current Report Title with **Income Report**.

Ⓒ Click to uncheck the **Time Prepared** checkbox.

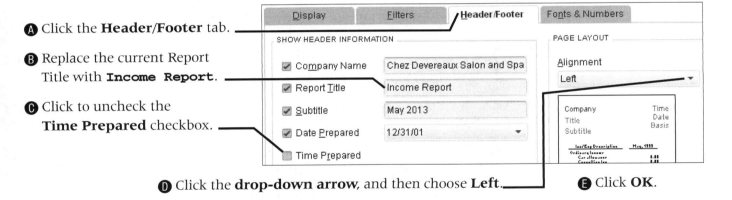

Ⓓ Click the **drop-down arrow**, and then choose **Left**. **Ⓔ** Click **OK**.

Look at the changes you have made to your report.

Change How Columns Are Displayed

Next you will help Bill modify the report so it separates the income by each two-week period.

3. Click the **Customize Report** button on the Report toolbar.

4. Click the **drop-down arrow** in the Columns section and choose **Two week**.

5. Click **OK**.

QuickBooks displays the Income Report that Bill has customized.

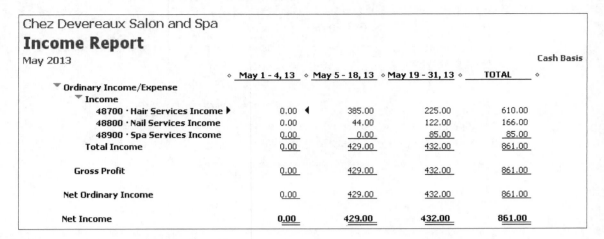

Chez Devereaux Salon and Spa

Income Report

May 2013

Cash Basis

	May 1 - 4, 13	May 5 - 18, 13	May 19 - 31, 13	TOTAL
▼ Ordinary Income/Expense				
▼ Income				
48700 · Hair Services Income ▶	0.00 ◀	385.00	225.00	610.00
48800 · Nail Services Income	0.00	44.00	122.00	166.00
48900 · Spa Services Income	0.00	0.00	85.00	85.00
Total Income	0.00	429.00	432.00	861.00
Gross Profit	0.00	429.00	432.00	861.00
Net Ordinary Income	0.00	429.00	432.00	861.00
Net Income	0.00	429.00	432.00	861.00

Memorize a Report

Now that Bill has the report just as he wants it, he will memorize it for easy recall.

6. Click the **Memorize** button on the report toolbar.

7. Follow these steps to memorize the report and place it in a group:

Ⓐ Click to place a **checkmark** in this box.

Ⓑ Click the **drop-down arrow** and choose **Company**.

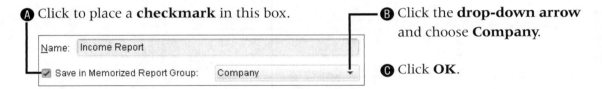

Ⓒ Click **OK**.

8. Close the **Income Report**.

Process Multiple Reports

Bill will now process a batch of reports from the Company group.

9. Choose **Reports→Memorized Reports→Memorized Report List**.

10. **Scroll down** until you see the group header **Company**.

11. Right-click **Company**, and then choose **Process Group**.

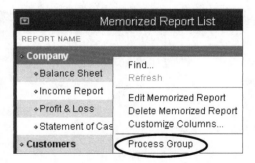

Take a look at the Process Multiple Reports window. You will see that the report that you just memorized, Income Report, is included in this group.

12. Click **Display** to process the batch of reports.

   QuickBooks will produce all of the reports in the Company group for the date ranges displayed.

13. Choose **Window→Close All**.

Creating Custom Forms

Before you customize your forms, think about what you want them to do for you:

- Do you want to include custom fields?
- Do you want to include a company logo?
- What do you want the forms you will be sending out to your stakeholders to say about your company?
- How much detail do you want to include?
- What size fields will you need?

Templates

A template is a specific form format (with no data) on which you can base future forms. QuickBooks provides several templates, but you can also create custom templates to meet the needs of your unique company, or create templates for preprinted forms. All of the templates available for a particular type of form are available from the drop-down list at the top of the form. Changing templates for a transaction that has already been entered will not change the information recorded in the transaction, even if the field is not visible on the new form.

Creating a Custom Template

When you choose to create a custom template, you begin by specifying information in the Basic Customization window. This window also provides a preview of how the template looks as you make changes to the various fields and information.

Adding a Company Logo to Templates

QuickBooks allows you to further personalize your templates by including your company logo. When you choose to add a logo to your template, the image file will be stored in the folder where your company file is located.

 To add a logo or picture on a template, the company file must be located on the computer's hard drive or on a shared server. It will not work if your company file is located on a flash drive.

The Manage Templates Window

It is in the Manage Templates window where you will assign a name for your new template. You can also access additional templates online from this window. When you click the Download Templates button, QuickBooks launches a web browser and displays the QuickBooks website from which you can choose new templates.

Using Custom Fields in Forms and Reports

You need to create your own custom form template to utilize the custom fields you set up in *QuickBooks Pro 2013: Level 1*. You can choose to add the custom field information for customers, jobs, vendors, and employees on the Header tab of the Additional Customization window. To add the custom fields for items, you must use the Columns tab. It is up to you to determine whether the various fields will be displayed on the screen, on the printed form, on both, or in neither place.

If you wish to display custom fields on reports, you can choose to display them in the Columns box on the Display tab of the Modify Report window.

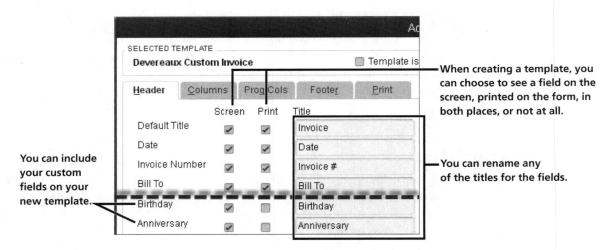

When creating a template, you can choose to see a field on the screen, printed on the form, in both places, or not at all.

You can include your custom fields on your new template.

You can rename any of the titles for the fields.

Working with the Layout Designer Window

QuickBooks allows you not only to determine what is included on a template, but also where it will be located. You can move fields and labels around your template and change the size of fields in the Layout Designer window. Each element on the template is termed an "object" in the Layout Designer window, and you can use some standard techniques to select, move, and resize all objects. The Snap to Grid feature ensures that all of your objects line up to a grid for which you can specify the spacing. In addition, you will see two shadows where the standard envelope windows are located so you can make sure to line up the addressees and return addresses properly.

QUICK REFERENCE	CREATING AND MODIFYING TEMPLATES
Task	**Procedure**
Create and name a new template	■ Choose Lists→Templates. ■ Click the Templates menu button, choose New, and then choose the desired template type. ■ Click the Manage Templates button; enter a name for the new template. ■ Click OK twice to accept the new name and save the new template.
Modify a template	■ Choose Lists→Templates; single-click on the desired template. ■ Click the Templates menu button; choose Edit. ■ Make any desired changes; click OK.
Open layout designer for a template	■ Open the template you wish to modify further. ■ Click the Layout Designer button. ■ Make any necessary changes; click OK twice.

Set Up a New Template

In this exercise, you will help Bill create a template for the company.

1. Choose **Lists→Templates**.

2. Click the **Templates** menu button, and then choose **New**.

3. Ensure Invoice is the type of template selected; click **OK**.

4. Click the **Manage Templates** button.

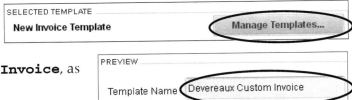

5. Replace the default Template Name with **Devereaux Custom Invoice**, as shown at right.

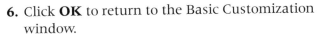

6. Click **OK** to return to the Basic Customization window.

Change the Color Scheme of the Template

You will now help Bill change the template and company name color.

7. Click the **drop-down arrow** to choose **Green** in the Select Color Scheme field.

8. Click the **Apply Color Scheme** button.
   You will now be able to view the new color in the preview area of the window to the right.

Add Customization

Now it is time to decide which customer and item fields you wish to include on the new template.

9. Click the **Additional Customization** button at the bottom of the window.

10. Click to place a checkmark in the **Due Date** checkbox in the **Print** column.
    A Layout Designer window appears to let you know how you can make changes to how the new field will be laid out on the template.

11. Click in the box to the left of **Do not display this message in the future**; tap ⌐Enter⌐.

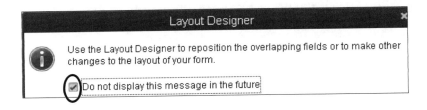

12. Follow these steps to continue to customize your template:

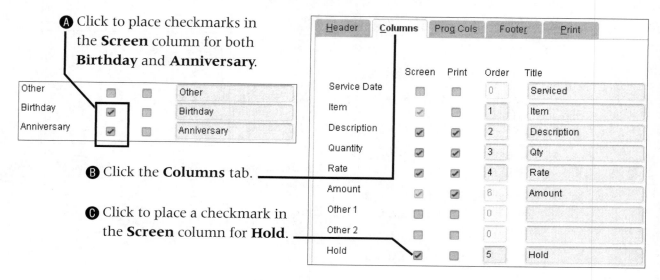

Ⓐ Click to place checkmarks in the **Screen** column for both **Birthday** and **Anniversary**.

Ⓑ Click the **Columns** tab.

Ⓒ Click to place a checkmark in the **Screen** column for **Hold**.

Notice the order column; it shows the order in which the columns will appear on the invoice from left to right.

13. Click **OK** in the Additional Customization window.

14. Feel free to play around and customize your template further, including using the Layout Designer!

15. When you are finished customizing your template, click **OK** in the Basic Customization window.

16. Close the **Templates** window.

17. Choose the appropriate option for your situation:

- If you are continuing on to the end-of-lesson exercises, leave QuickBooks open.
- If you are finished working in QuickBooks for now, choose **File→Exit**.

Concepts Review

Concepts Review http://labyrinthelab.com/qb13-level02

To check your knowledge of the key concepts introduced in this lesson, complete the Concepts Review quiz by going to the URL listed above.

Reinforce Your Skills

Before you begin the Reinforce Your Skills exercises:

■ *Restore* **Tea Shoppe at the Lake, Lesson 5 (Portable)** *from your file storage location. Make sure to place your name as the first word in the company filename (e.g., Susie's Tea Shoppe at the Lake, Lesson 5).*

You may *not* use the Tea Shoppe at the Lake file that you used in the previous lesson. Open the Lesson 5 student file provided.

REINFORCE YOUR SKILLS 5.1
Find and Edit a Transaction

Susie received an adjusted amount for the May water bill. Rather than clicking the Previous button over and over again, in this exercise, you will use the QuickBooks Find feature to locate the transaction.

1. Choose **Edit→Find**.

2. Choose **Bill** as the Transaction Type, and **City of Lake San Marcos** as the Vendor.

3. Enter the date range as **5/1/2013** to **5/31/2013**, and then click **Find**.
   The bill you are looking for will be displayed in the bottom of the window.

4. Double-click the bill dated **5/17/2013** in the bottom portion of the window.
   The Enter Bills window will open; leave it open for the next step.

Edit a Transaction

5. Change the amount of the bill to **97.37** and choose to **record the change** to the transaction.

6. **Save and close** the transaction; close the **Find** window.

Enter a Credit from a Vendor

Susie has received a credit from Vista Insurance Company to be applied to a future payment. In this exercise, you will record this credit.

1. Choose **Vendors→Enter Bills**; then, choose the **Credit** option at the top of the window.

2. Enter **6/7/2013** as the date; choose **Vista Insurance Company** as the Vendor.

3. Enter **106.94** as the Credit Amount; type **Refund on premium paid** as the Memo.

4. Ensure **Insurance Expense** is the account displayed.

5. Click **Save & Close** to enter the credit.

Apply the Credit When Paying a Bill

6. Choose **Vendors→Pay Bills**.

7. Click to the left of the **5/28/2013** bill for Vista Insurance Company to select it.

8. Click the **Set Credits** button in the middle portion of the window.
   The Discount and Credits window will appear.

9. Ensure that the credit of **$106.94 from 6/7/2013** is checked, and then click **Done**.

10. Set the date to **6/7/2013** if necessary, and then choose for the **check to be printed**.

11. Click **Pay Selected Bills**; click **Done** in the Payment Summary window.

Customize a Profit & Loss Report

In this exercise, you will help Susie create a customized P&L report for Tea Shoppe at the Lake.

1. Choose **Reports→Company & Financial→Profit & Loss Standard**.

2. Tap [Tab], type **050113**, tap [Tab] again, and then type **053113**.

3. Click the **Refresh** button on the Report toolbar.

Change the Columns Displayed

You will now display the columns by week across the top of the report.

4. Click the **Customize Report** button on the toolbar.

5. Choose the **Display** tab, if necessary.

6. Locate the **Columns** section of the window and choose to display the columns across the **top by week**; click **OK**.
   This report will allow you to compare the income and expenses from week to week.

Change the Formatting for the Header

Susie doesn't like the look of the default header, and she needs your help to get it just right.

7. Click the **Customize Report** button on the toolbar.

8. Display the **Header/Footer** tab.

9. Change the report title to **Profit & Loss by Week**.

10. Change the Alignment to **Left**.

11. Display the **Fonts & Numbers** tab.

12. Make any changes you like to the formatting of the fonts and numbers.

13. Click **OK** to save your changes.

14. Memorize the report, naming it **Profit & Loss by Week**; finally, close the report.

Modify the Custom Sales Report

In this exercise, you will create an appealing sales receipt for Tea Shoppe at the Lake. You can make changes to a template directly from an open form, and that is the approach you will use to modify the sales receipt template.

1. Choose **Customers→Enter Sales Receipts**.

2. Click the **Formatting** tab of the Ribbon, and then click **Manage Templates**. Click **OK** in the Manage Templates window.
   The Basic Customization window displays.

3. In the **Company & Transaction** area of the window, choose to **print the company phone number**.

4. Close the **Layout Designer** window, choosing to not have it appear again in the future.

5. Choose to print the **company fax number**.

6. Change the font and color scheme of the template to your liking.

7. Click the **Additional Customization** button.

8. On the **Footer** tab, add a long text that is to be printed:

   We stand behind everything we sell. Please let us know if you are not fully satisfied so that we can have a chance to make you happy.

Use Layout Designer

Finally, you will open the form in Layout Designer and make a few more changes.

9. Click the **Layout Designer** button.

10. **Scroll down**; select and move the **Phone #** and **Fax #** objects to the top of the form. (Hint: Select all four objects and move them simultaneously.)

11. Move any other objects around as you see fit.

12. When you have the template just right, click **OK** to save your changes.

13. Click **OK** in both the Additional Customization and the Basic Customization windows to save the changes to the template.

14. Close the **Enter Sales Receipt** window.

15. Choose the appropriate option for your situation:

    - If you are continuing on to the rest of the end-of-lesson exercises, leave QuickBooks open.
    - If you are finished working in QuickBooks for now, choose **File→Exit**.

Apply Your Skills

Before you begin the Apply Your Skills exercises:

■ *Restore* **Wet Noses Veterinary Clinic, Lesson 5 (Portable)** *from your file storage location. Make sure to place your name as the first word in the company filename (e.g., Sadie's Wet Noses Veterinary Clinic, Lesson 5).*

Do *not* use the Wet Noses Veterinary Clinic file that you used in the previous lesson. Open the Lesson 5 student file provided.

APPLY YOUR SKILLS 5.1

Deal with a Returned Check

In this exercise, you will help Dr. James account for check #6666 from Mary Ann Gulch for $145.65 that was returned for non-sufficient funds.

1. Create an **Other Income** account in the Chart of Accounts.
   Hint: You will find the account type in the Other Account Types drop-down list.

2. Create an **Other Charge** item for the service charge for $35, directing it to the Other Income account that you just created.

Enter the Checking Register Transactions

3. Open the **Checking** register, and record a service charge of $25 from the bank for the bounced check on 6/6/2013 using **Bank Service Charges** as the account. Leave the Payee and Number fields blank and type a message stating the customer name and check number for the NSF fee. Leave the Checking register open for the next step.

4. On 6/6/13, record the bounced check in your Checking register, filling in Mary Ann Gulch as the Payee, $145.65 as the Payment amount, and Accounts Receivable as the account. Leave the Number field blank and record a Memo of NSF Check #6666. Close the Checking register when you are finished.

Enter a Statement Charge and Create a Statement

5. Open the **Accounts Receivable** window (Hint: **Customers→Enter Statement Charges**), and then choose Mary Ann Gulch as the Customer:Job.
   Notice that the last transaction in the register is the "other side" of what you entered in the Checking register and that it increases the balance owing.

6. Enter a transaction for the Bounced Check Charge on 6/6/2013, choosing the other charge item you created.
   Once you choose the Bounced Check Charge item, all of the rest of the information will fill in from the Item List.

7. Click **Record**; close the **Accounts Receivable** register window.

8. Open the **Create Statements** window, and then choose to create a statement dated 6/6/2013 for Mary Ann Gulch with the All open transactions as of Statement Date option selected.

9. Preview the statement, printing it only if your instructor requests you to do so.

10. Close the **Print Preview** and **Create Statement** windows.

Deal with Bad Debt

Dr. James has learned that Natalie Sheehan moved out of town. You do not expect to receive payment for the two invoices (27 for $399.50 and 117 for $148.10, for a total of $547.60) she has outstanding. In this exercise, you will help Dr. James write off the amount as bad debt using a credit memo.

1. Create a new **expense** account called **Bad Debt Expense**.

2. Create a new **Other Charge** item called **Bad Debt** and route it to the Bad Debt Expense account you just created. Leave the amount as zero.

Create the Credit Memo and Apply It to the Invoices

3. Open the **Create Credit Memos/Refunds** window, and then choose **Natalie Sheehan:Dog-Sandy** as the Customer:Job.
You must choose the Customer:Job just as it appears on the invoice to which you will be applying the credit.

4. Set the date to **6/13/2013**, enter **BD1** as the Credit No., choose **Bad Debt** as the Item, and then type **547.60** as the amount.

5. Choose for the credit memo to not be printed; click to **Save & Close** the window.

6. Choose to apply the amount of the credit to an invoice, and then click **OK**.

7. Click **Done** in the Apply Credit to Invoices window, ensuring both invoices are checked first.

Issue a Credit and a Refund Check

In this exercise, you find Dr. James realizing that she overcharged the City of Seattle K-9 Unit on invoice 148, as Duke did not receive a nail trim. You will help her to issue a credit memo and a refund check to the city.

1. Open the **Create Credit Memos/Refunds** window, and then choose **City of Seattle K-9 Unit:Dog-Duke** as the Customer:Job.

2. Set the date to **6/14/2013**, enter **RF1** as the Credit No., and then choose **Nails** as the Item.

3. Click **Save & Close**; then, choose to **Give a refund** in the Available Credit window.

4. Verify that the information is correct in the Issue a Refund window, making sure that the check is set to be printed, and then click **OK**.
The refund check is now in the queue waiting to be printed.

Answer Questions with Reports

In this exercise, you will answer questions for Dr. James by running reports. You may wish to display the Report Center in List View to help you answer the questions. Ask your instructor if you should print the reports, print (save) them as PDF files, export them to Excel, or simply display them on the screen.

1. Would you create a Profit & Loss report that shows the income and expenses by week for the month of May 2013? Title it **Profit & Loss by Week** and add some color to spice it up a bit.

2. Can you show me a list of all items set up for the company, now that you have created new ones for NSF checks and bad debt?

3. Is it possible to display a report showing all transactions for each of the customers you worked with in this lesson's exercises: Mary Ann Gulch, Natalie Sheehan, and City of Seattle K-9 Unit? (Make sure to specify the correct job.)

4. Submit your reports based on the guidelines provided by your instructor.

5. Choose the appropriate option for your situation:

   ■ If you are continuing on to the Critical Thinking exercises, leave QuickBooks open.

   ■ If you are finished working in QuickBooks for now, choose **File→Exit**.

Critical Thinking

In the course of working through the following Critical Thinking exercises, you will be utilizing various skills taught in this and previous lesson(s). Take your time and think carefully about the tasks presented to you. Turn back to the lesson content if you need assistance.

5.1 Sort Through the Stack

Before You Begin: Restore the **Monkey Business, Lesson 5 (Portable)** *file from your storage location. (Remember that you are to leave the password field blank for Mary.) Do* not *use the Monkey Business file that you used in the previous lesson.*

You have been hired by Mary Minard to help her with her organization's books. She is the owner of Monkey Business, a nonprofit organization that provides low-income students with help in preparing for college placement exams and applying for scholarships. You have just sat down at her desk and found a pile of papers. It is your job to sort through the papers and make sense of what you find, entering information into QuickBooks whenever appropriate, and answering any other questions in a word processing document saved as **Critical Thinking 5.1**. Remember, you are digging through papers on a desk, so it is up to you to determine the correct order in which to complete the tasks.

- Scribbled on a piece of paper: The price on the invoice for Lakeside Christian School for the College 101 seminar was incorrect; it should have been $885. Please make this correction in QuickBooks. The customer has already been notified.

- Note: The invoice that we send out is so boring looking…Would you please fancy it up a bit, add a picture (as a logo) that relates to education, and make it a bit more colorful? Also, please include our phone number on the invoice.

- NSF notice from bank: Dated 7/18/2013, check #552 for $425 from Polk Community Center was returned for non-sufficient funds. The bank charged a $30 fee for the item. Mary wrote the following message on the notice, "Please figure out how to account for this in QuickBooks. We need to charge Polk CC a $40 NSF fee and rebill for the service!"

- Printed copy of Balance Sheet report: A note on the report reads, "Please change the font on this report and make the title align to the right. Make the color of the heading match the color on the new invoice template. Memorize it or something so it will be easy for you to run it next time with the same look."

5.2 Tackle the Tasks

Now is your chance to work a little more with Chez Devereaux Salon and Spa and apply the skills that you have learned in this lesson to accomplish additional tasks. Open or restore the **Critical Thinking 5.2** company or portable company file from your file storage location, or open the company file you used in the Develop Your Skills exercises for this lesson. Then, enter the following tasks.

Correct errors	Jane Oliver's friend joined her for a manicure on May 25. Change invoice 13-007 to reflect two manicures.
Write off bad debt	You have had no luck collecting from Curtis Balando for invoice 13-002. Write it off as bad debt as of 6/16/13. (Hint: Look at the source invoice first.)
Customize a report	Create a Balance Sheet Standard report and choose for it to display only assets. Set the date as of June 30, 2013. Customize it as you like, and then memorize it as **Assets Report**.
Create a custom form	Create a new template for sales receipts. Save it as **Devereaux Cash Sales**, and then customize it as you see fit.

5.3 Use the Web as a Learning Tool

Throughout this book, you will be provided with an opportunity to use the Internet as a learning tool by completing WebQuests. According to the original creators of WebQuests, as described on their website (WebQuest.org), a WebQuest is "an inquiry-oriented activity in which most or all of the information used by learners is drawn from the web." To complete the WebQuest projects in this book, navigate to the student resource center and choose the WebQuest for the lesson on which you are currently working. The subject of each WebQuest will be relevant to the material found in the lesson.

WebQuest Subject: Shared reporting and custom templates

Glossary

Accountant's Copy
A special copy of your QuickBooks file that can be created if your accountant needs to make adjustments to your Quick-Books file, but you do not want to lose access to it while it is being adjusted

Advanced Setup
This method of company creation takes you through a series of questions; your answer to each question determines how your company is set up

Average Cost
A method of inventory tracking where the value of the inventory is determined by dividing the total value of the inventory by the total number of inventory items

Bad Debt
Funds owed to you that are not collectable and need to be written off

Balance Sheet Accounts
The asset, liability, and equity accounts, such as bank, credit card, current liabilities (sales tax payable and payroll liabilities), accounts receivable, accounts payable, and retained earnings

Balance Sheet Report
A report that displays all assets, liabilities, and equity as of a specific date

Batch Invoicing
Feature that lets a user create invoices that are basically the same for multiple customers at one time

Batch Timesheets
Feature that allows you to create timesheets for multiple employees who work the same hours on the same jobs and using the same payroll item(s)

Behind the Scenes
The accounting that QuickBooks performs for you when you enter transactions

Bounced Check
A check returned by the bank due to non-sufficient funds in the account; also called a "NSF" check

Browser
A software application used to locate and display web pages, such as Netscape Navigator and Microsoft Internet Explorer

Budget
In QuickBooks, create a budget for your company either from scratch or based on actual values from a previous period

Closing the Books
During this process at the end of your fiscal year, QuickBooks transfers the net income or net loss to Retained Earnings, restricts access to transactions prior to the closing date (unless you know the password), and allows you to clean up your company data; you are not required to "close the books" in QuickBooks

Collections Center
Feature that helps users easily identify customers who have overdue balances; also provides contact information

Company File
The QuickBooks file you use when working with your company's day-to-day operations

Company Setup
Takes you through the steps necessary to set up a new company in QuickBooks

Company Snapshot
A window that offers a quick view of your company's bottom line in one convenient place

Contributed Reports
Feature that allows you to look for a report submitted by another user so you don't have to "reinvent the wheel"; you can also share your custom reports with this feature

Customers & Jobs List
A list in QuickBooks that stores all information related to your customers and the jobs associated with them

Customer & Vendor Profile Lists
Lists QuickBooks provides to track customer and vendor information

Depreciation
Provides a business with a way to match income to expenses; a fixed asset is used to produce income over a period of time, and depreciation allows you to record the appropriate expense for the same period; many small businesses record depreciation transactions just once a year, but they can be entered monthly or quarterly if the business produces financial statements for those periods

Doc Center
Feature that allows you to store your source documents electronically, attaching them to the transactions or list entries to which they belong

Draw
An owner's withdrawal of funds from the company

Edition
Intuit creates a multitude of editions of QuickBooks to choose from: QuickBooks Online, QuickBooks Pro, QuickBooks Premier, and QuickBooks Enterprise

Electronic Payments

Some companies receive payments from customers electronically; they can be handled by using a new payment type called Electronic Payment

Employees List

A list in QuickBooks that helps you to keep track of your employee data; can be used as a source of information to run payroll in QuickBooks; accessed through the Employee Center

Equity Accounts

Reflect the owner's investment in the company and have a credit normal balance; in a Sole Proprietorship, equity is what the owner has invested in the company and in a corporation, the equity is what the shareholders have invested in the company

Estimates

Feature that allows a user to create a proposal for a customer or job

Express Start

In this method of company creation, QuickBooks asks you for your basic company information, and it will be up to you to set up certain items such as payroll and inventory later

Field

A box into which data is entered

File Storage Location

Location where you store files for this course (USB flash drive, the My Documents folder, or a network drive at a school or company)

Filtering

Filtering allows you to include only the essential data in your report; choose to filter out many types of data such as accounts, dollar amounts, and types of customers; allows you to closely examine and report on a specific group of data

Finance Charge

A charge assessed to an overdue customer balance

Fixed Asset

An asset you don't plan to use up or turn into cash within the next year; businesses use fixed assets in a productive capacity to promote the main operations of the company; are depreciable, which means that you don't expense the assets when you purchase them, but rather over the useful life of the asset

Fixed Asset Account

Type of account that tracks the activities associated with a fixed asset

Fonts

QuickBooks displays its preset reports in a default font; you can make many changes to the characteristics of the font in your report, such as the font name, style, color, and size

Forecast

A feature that allows you to make predictions about the future; they can be created based on actual figures from the last year or from scratch

Formatting

Formatting deals with the appearance of the report; it has nothing to do with the data contained within it

Generally Accepted Accounting Principles (GAAP)

Rules used to prepare, present, and report financial statements for a wide variety of entities

Homepage

A web page that serves as an index or table of contents to other documents stored on the site; the main page for a large website; the web page that comes up by default when you open your browser

Hypertext Markup Language (HTML)

A text-based language that any computer can read; used to organize pages with devices such as headings, paragraphs, lists, etc.

Internet

A collection of computers all over the world that send, receive, and store information; access is gained through an Internet Service Provider (ISP); the web is just a portion of the Internet

Investment

Occurs when an owner deposits funds into the company

Job Costing

Allows a users to determine the profitability of each job for a customer

Lead Center

Feature that allows you to track information about potential customers

Link

Also called hyperlink; provides navigation through a website; displayed on the QuickBooks Home page to provide navigation throughout the QuickBooks program

List (Database)

Allows you to store information about customers, vendors, employees, and other data important to your business

Live Community

A place where a user can collaborate with other QuickBooks users to get advice or to provide insights

Long Term Liabilities Account

A QuickBooks account that tracks a liability (loan) you do not plan to pay off within the next year

One-Click Tasks

Feature that allows you to create credit memos, payments, letters, or memorized transactions from invoices with just one click

Online Backup

QuickBooks offers an online backup option for a monthly fee that is determined based on the amount of room you wish to have available for your backup work

On the Fly

When you type a new entry into a field that draws from a list, QuickBooks gives you the opportunity to add the record to the list "on the fly" as you create the transaction

Opening Balance Equity Account

An equity account created by QuickBooks when you start your first balance sheet account; it allows you to have an accurate balance sheet from the start

Other Current Assets Account
An account that tracks the transactions related to an asset that you plan to either use up or convert to cash within one year

Outside Payroll Service
A service that runs payroll for a company outside of QuickBooks; the company inputs the information into QuickBooks without using the payroll features

Passing an Expense On to Customers
The process of identifying an expense in a transaction for which you plan to charge a customer and invoicing the customer for the expense

Payroll Liabilities
The account in which you hold payroll taxes and other deductions until you are required to pay them

Payroll Options
Intuit provides a variety of options to run your payroll; to view and compare these options, visit the book's website at http://labyrinthelab.com/qb13-level02

PDF File
PDF stands for "portable document format;" it is a type of file that preserves formatting, data, and graphics; saves in a portable file

Petty Cash
Cash kept by businesses for small expenditures; in QuickBooks, Petty Cash is set up as a bank account in the Chart of Accounts

Portable Company File
A type of QuickBooks file that contains all company data in a compressed format; it must be restored to be utilized; it is much smaller in size than a company or backup file

Profit and Loss (P&L) Report
A financial report that can be found in the Company & Financial category of the Report Finder window; P&L reports reflect all transactions that have affected income and expense accounts within a specified time period; also called an Income Statement

Progess Invoicing
Allows you to invoice from an estimate in stages rather than for the entire estimate amount

Purchase Order
A form utilized by many companies to enter items into inventory; it does not affect anything "behind the scenes"

Quick Reference Tables
Tables that summarize the tasks you have just learned. Use them as guidelines when you begin work on your own QuickBooks company file.

Restoring
The process of decompressing a QuickBooks backup or portable company file; when you restore a file in the same location with the same name as another file, it will replace that file

Sales Orders
Allows you to manage customer orders of both products and services; available in the Premier and Enterprise editions

Time Tracking
Allows you to create weekly timesheets so you can break down the hours by customer/job or to record single activities for a customer/job

Unearned Income
Funds received from a customer as a deposit or for a gift certificate; these funds should be held in a liability account until they are "earned"

Uniform Resource Locator (URL)
A web address used to identify a unique page on the Internet

Units of Measure
Feature that allows you to convert units of measure; useful for companies that purchase and sell in different units of measure or need to indicate units on purchase or sales forms; available in the Premier and higher versions of QuickBooks

Users
You can set up an unlimited number of users for your QuickBooks company and assign a password for each person; users can only change their own personal preferences (the administrator controls the access each user has to the QuickBooks file)

Vendor
Anyone (except employees) to whom you pay money; could be the electric company, the organization to which you pay taxes, a merchandise supplier, or subcontractors you pay to do work for your customers

Vendor List
A list in QuickBooks that stores all information related to your vendors

Version
Intuit creates a new version of QuickBooks each year (such as QuickBooks 2011, 2012, or 2013) and each new version provides additional features that are new for that year

Website
Refers to a collection of related web pages and their supporting files and folders.

World Wide Web (WWW)
Also called the web; organized system of Internet servers that support HTML documents; the fun part of the Internet

Year-to-Date Amounts
If you begin to use the QuickBooks payroll feature for existing employees who have received at least one paycheck from you (and it is not the first day of January), you must enter year-to-date amounts for them to ensure that QuickBooks calculates taxes with thresholds properly and you will be able to print accurate W-2s at the end of the year

Index

S

sales discounts, 26, 30, 32–34, 205, 206
sales from inventory, 22–29
sales orders, 23–24, 25
Sales Rep List, 118, 120
sales tax, 11–15, 38–41, 199, 205
Search feature, 194, 195, 196
send method for customer
    correspondence, 22
shipping, 17, 31
Show Lowest Subaccount option, 6
Snap to Grid feature, 222
subaccounts
  display preferences, 6
  payroll accounting, 62, 64
subcontractors vs. employees, 65

T

taxes
  payroll-related, 71–75, 92–96
  sales tax, 11–15, 38–41, 199, 205
templates, 221–224
terms, payment, 18
time tracking, 128–129, 131–133,
    135–138, 143, 145
transactions
  deleting, 193
  editing, 193
  finding, 193–194
  memorized, 160–163
  recurring, 161
  voiding, 193
transferring funds, 160–163

U

unearned income, customer deposit as,
    122
units of measure, 5
unscheduled payroll checks, 87, 88,
    90–91

V

value on hand, adjustments to, 35–37
vendors
  credits from, 210, 211
  payroll tax, 74–75
  receipt of inventory items from, 17–21
  subcontractors vs. employees, 65
viewing options
  negative numbers, 214
  reports, 213–214
  subaccounts, 6

W

W-2 and W-3 forms, 92–94, 95–96
W-4 forms, 66
W-9 forms, 66
Weighted Average inventory valuation
    method, 5
Workman's Compensation, 66, 71
Write Checks window, 84, 98, 164
writing off bad debt, 205–208